STATE POLICY FORMATION AND THE ORIGINS OF THE POLL TAX

State Policy Formation and the Origins of the Poll Tax

ALLAN McCONNELL
Lecturer in Public Administration
Glasgow Caledonian University

Dartmouth

Aldershot • Brookfield USA • Singapore • Sydney

Published by
Dartmouth Publishing Company Limited
Gower House
Croft Road
Aldershot
Hants GU11 3HR
England

Dartmouth Publishing Company
Old Post Road
Brookfield
Vermont 05036
USA

A CIP catalogue record for this book is available from the British Library

Library of Congress Cataloging-in-Publication Data
McConnell, Allan, 1957-
    State policy formation and the origins of the poll tax / Allan
McConnell.
        p.   cm.
    ISBN 1-85521-488-1 : $59.95 (approx.)
    1. Poll tax–Great Britain. 2. Poll tax– Scotland. 3. Policy
sciences.
    I. Title.
HJ4935.G7M33   1994
336.2'5'0941–dc20   94-38945
                                                                CIP

ISBN 1 85521 488 1

Printed in Great Britain by
Ipswich Book Co. Ltd., Ipswich, Suffolk.

Contents

Preface

This book has its origins in a PhD. In many respects, it is the product of two long-standing themes which often sat uneasily inside my head. On the one hand, I was convinced that Parliamentary democracy in Britain was *not* a sham. I was sure that it was of *some* worth in allowing 'the people' to determine how they were governed. On the other hand, however, I was equally convinced that it *was* a sham, and that gross inequalities in society were accompanied by governments which frequently cast aside the wishes of 'the people'. The advent of the Poll Tax was the 'perfect' opportunity to study these two themes. How on earth, I had thought, can a government produce such a violently unpopular and reactionary policy, yet still do so (quite legitimately) within the confines of the British Parliamentary system?

My research set out to address this matter, although it soon became apparent that literature on the concept of 'policy formation' was extremely thin on the ground, and that what material there was, simply did not address (even in the very broadest sense) the sorts of issues that I was concerned with. Thus, this book has twin aims. Not only does it seek to address the matter of 'how the Poll Tax came about', but it also seeks to identify general principles of state policy formation. The bulk of the empirical work contained in the book is derived from the PhD, although it has been updated in the light of more recent publications - particularly the memoirs of Margaret Thatcher, Nigel Lawson, Kenneth Baker and others. The theoretical work has been substantially reworked and expanded upon from the PhD work, although needless to say it still retains the key analytical themes.

No work of this magnitude can possibly be completed without the enormous debt own to others. I am eternally grateful to John Foster, David Judge, Martin Myant for the unselfish way in which they offered me support and guidance whenever I needed it. Whilst wishing to be even-handed about the assistance which they gave to me, I must nevertheless give special mention to David Judge. Throughout my academic career, he has been there to provide constant support and guidance by example. The fact that he does everything so well is almost frustrating at times!

I am also very grateful to the numerous individuals who gave up their time in order to be interviewed. Special thanks must go to Albert Tait of the Convention of Scottish Local Authorities and Mary Whitehouse of the Federation of Scottish Ratepayers. They assisted me above and beyond the call of duty, and provided me with materials which were of immense value to the research.

The book itself was written in my present location in the Department of Law and Public Administration at Glasgow Caledonian University, and I am very grateful to a large number of people here for their help and support. Many thanks must go to Jackie Bryden and Margaret Hebenton for typing the first draft. Needless to say, their typing skills put my own to shame. I must also thank Jacki Charlton, Head of Department, who allowed me the freedom of a considerable reduction in teaching load in order to finish the book. I am also indebted to my fellow lecturing colleagues - Allan Bruce, Pete Falconer, Bobby Pyper and Kathleen Ross - for their support. If the truth be told, they did not contribute in any direct way to the finished product, but the fact that they are there is encouragement in itself.

Finally, it is difficult to put into words the thanks that must go to wife Linda, and children Paul and Kim. They have put up with me and my single-minded desire to do something that I believed in. The fact that they care nothing for 'theories of state policy formation' makes this all the more remarkable. Without them, writing this book would probably not have been possible, and certainly a lot less pleasurable.

Ultimately, however, the list of credits cannot absolve me of the fact that the book is my own work, and I alone must take responsibility for its contents.

Allan McConnell,
July 1994

Abbreviations

ACC	Association of County Councils
ADC	Association of District Councils
ALA	Association of London Authorities
AMA	Association of Metropolitan Authorities
ASI	Adam Smith Institute
BBC	British Broadcasting Corporation
BP	British Petroleum
CBI	Confederation of British Industry
CCCP	Campaign for the Communication of Conservative Policies
CIPFA	Chartered Institute of Public Finance and Accountancy
Cmnd.	Command Paper
COSLA	Convention of Scottish Local Authorities
CPAG	Child Poverty Action Group
CURB	Commerce Against the Unfair Rating Burden
DoE	Department of the Environment
EEC	European Economic Community
EIS	Educational Institute of Scotland
FSR	Federation of Scottish Ratepayers
GDP	Gross Domestic Product
GLC	Greater London Council
GREA	Grant Related Expenditure Assessment
HC	House of Commons
HL	House of Lords

HMSO	Her Majesty's Stationary Office
ICI	Imperial Chemical Industries plc
IFS	Institute of Fiscal Studies
IMF	International Monetary Fund
MORI	Market and Opinion Research International Ltd.
MP	Member of Parliament
NALGO	National and Local Government Officers Association
NFSESB	National Federation of Self-Employed and Small Businesses
NFU	National Farmers Union
NGA	National Graphical Association
NHS	National Health Service
NNDR	National Non-Domestic Rate
NUPE	National Union of Public Employees
NURA	National Union of Ratepayers Associations
NUS	National Union of Students
OECD	Organisation for Economic Cooperation and Development
PSBR	Public Sector Borrowing Requirement
R&VA	Rating and Valuation Association
RAGE	Ratepayers Action Group Executive (Lothian Region)
SCC	Scottish Consumer Council
SCUA	Scottish Conservative and Unionist Association
SCVO	Scottish Council for Voluntary Organisations
SDP	Social Democratic Party
SNP	Scottish National Party
SOLACE	Society of Local Authority Chief Executives
STUC	Scottish Trades Union Congress
TGWU	Transport and General Workers Union
TRG	Tory Reform Group
TUC	Trades Union Congress
UBR	Uniform Business Rate
UK	United Kingdom
US	United States
USA	United States of America
VAT	Value Added Tax

Introduction

This book has two interrelated aims. The first is to comprehend 'how the Poll Tax came about', and the second is to comprehend general processes of state policy formation. When we combine these together, they add up to an attempt to comprehend the Poll Tax policy formation process. It seems useful to begin by offering a brief expansion on this, in order to provide a context within which we can locate the rest of the book.

Prior to the mid-1980s and early 1990s, the 'poll tax' was a relic of the distant past. It was commonly conceived as an anachronism which belonged to the Middle Ages, and which was instrumental in sparking the 1381 Peasants' Revolt, culminating in the Chancellor (also the Archbishop of Canterbury) being beheaded. It must be recognised, however, that this and other poll taxes at the time were not the only instances of poll taxes having been applied. 'Head taxes' were introduced in some African colonies by both Britain and France at the height of their imperial power (Gann and Duignan, 1969). Furthermore, in the USA, until their abolition by the 24th Amendment to the US Constitution in 1964, 'voluntary' poll taxes were used in some southern states in the post-Civil War period. As Rose (1964, p. 157) notes, these were for 'the express purpose of restricting the vote', in the knowledge that poor blacks would be unlikely to pay. In recent years, Japan has also had something resembling a 'poll tax', although this accounts for less than a half of one per cent of Japanese local tax income (Gibson, 1989, p. 348). Despite the existence of these, however, it seems reasonable to suggest that the very idea of a 'full blown' poll tax being proposed (and then ratified by the 'Mother of Parliaments') was otherwise inconceivable in 20th century Britain.

In the mid-1980s, however, all this changed and the Government 'grasped the nettle' of a policy which it had effectively *twice* ruled out since coming to office in 1979 (Cmnd. 8449, 1981: Cmnd. 9008, 1983). The turmoil in the Conservative Party in Scotland, as a result of the 1985 property revaluation, resulted in a swift and categoric abandonment of the principles of the rating system. This then led to a search for an alternative system of local taxation - culminating in the decision to introduce a poll tax in Scotland (one year ahead of England and Wales). This proposal was contained in the Green Paper *Paying for Local Government* (Cmnd. 9714, 1986), although its 'consultative' nature was highly limited, and this was confirmed by the manner in which the *Abolition of Domestic Rates Etc. (Scotland) Bill* was rushed through Parliament, finally receiving Royal Assent on 15 May 1987.

This is important because it paved the way for subsequent legislation in England and Wales the following year. Yet it is also important as a subject of study in its own right. The property revaluation aside, there was no major public outcry at the Government's decision to opt for a poll tax, and no mass campaign by the Labour Party or the trades union movement. Other reactions at the time, however, help to convey the magnitude of what was happening. The *Financial Times* (6 February 1986) described the Poll Tax as 'an implausible scheme which involves turning the fiscal clock back several centuries...the sort of feudal levy Henry VIII might have approved.' The Tory Reform Group, hardly a fertile ground for socialist thinking, described it as '"fair" only in the sense that the Black Death was "fair"' (HC Debates, 1986-87, Vol. 105, col. 349). The Child Poverty Action Group stated that 'we find it difficult to believe that a proposal which so blatantly favours the rich over the poor can be given serious consideration' (quoted in COSLA et al. 1987). Finally, in a statement made several years later by Scots historian James D. Young (1990), the Poll Tax was described as the 'most evil and immoral piece of class legislation experienced by my generation.'

Unsurprisingly, given all this, few would argue that in the last analysis, the entire policy was anything other than thoroughly misconceived. Gibson (1989) documents in an entirely convincing piece of work, how the Government's 'presentation' of the Poll Tax to the public relied heavily on 'illogical arguments', 'misleading arguments', 'unproven assertions', 'untruths' and 'inconsistent arguments'. The Poll Tax also provoked (through a combination of necessity and intent) a massive law-breaking exercise, and legal action was taken against almost 1,250,000

Scots in the second year of its operation (*Glasgow Herald*, 19 February 1991). Its introduction in England and Wales, with the Prime Minister Mrs Thatcher, proclaiming it to be her 'flagship', saw riots in Cheltenham and London, and mass protests up and down the country, involving many Conservative supporters on a scale unprecedented from within the Party's electoral base (see Lavalette and Mooney, 1990). In the first year of its introduction South of the Border, there were roughly 4.1 million summonses for non-payment (*Public Finance and Accountancy*, 14 June 1991, p. 2), thus giving birth to what Hoggett and Burns (1991-92, p. 95) describe as 'possibly the largest mass campaign of civil disobedience in modern British history'. This also proved to be a critical factor in the effective ousting of Mrs Thatcher from her 11-year premiership. A subsequent commitment by the Government, under John Major, to the abolition of the Poll Tax less than a year after its introduction in the South, was described understandably by Shadow Environment Spokesman, Brian Gould, as the 'most complete capitulation, the most startling U-turn and the most shameless abandonment of consistency and principle in modern political history' (HC Debates, Vol. 188, 1990-91, col. 405).

Based on all of the foregoing, therefore, it does not seem unreasonable to ask a rather simple question, namely - how on earth did this happen in the first place? In order to answer this, of course, the question must be dissected further and rephrased in more tempered language in order to provide specific terms of reference which will act as a guide throughout the course of the present analysis. Thus, it must be asked - how do we understand the process of state policy formation which culminated in a poll tax for Scotland being embodied in an Act of Parliament in May 1987?

To this end, the structure of the book is as follows. Chapter One explores the way in which political science has virtually neglected the study of policy formation. It covers a range of materials from those dealing only indirectly with some aspects of policy formation (e.g. the works of Downs, Simon, Lindblom, Bachrach and Baratz, Richardson and Jordan, Miliband and Poulantzas), and those attempting to deal directly with the concept of policy formation (namely Bauer, Kingdon and Offe) but who actually fall short of providing a sufficiently comprehensive treatment of the subject. Chapter Two then attempts to fill this theoretical gap by attempting to develop broad principles of state policy formation. It does so by building on Marxist dialectical principles in an attempt tentatively to develop 'general' theoretical principles of the process of state policy formation. The next five chapters then detail both the general context and the specific development of the Poll Tax policy formation process. Chapter Three provides a wider context by outlining the origins and development of the Thatcher Government and linking this to contemporary developments in local government and local taxation. Chapter Four looks at the crucial 1985 property revaluation in Scotland and the Government's commitment to abandon the rates. Chapter Five examines the period from this to the decision to replace the rates with a poll tax. Chapter Six focuses on the medium adopted for achieving this (the Green Paper *Paying for Local Government*, Cmnd. 9714, 1986) and the public 'consultation' period which ensued. Chapter Six then completes the 'empirical' section by looking at the passage of the relevant Bill through Parliament. Finally, the Conclusion then attempts to draw together the 'theoretical' and 'empirical' strands, in order to explain the process of state policy formation which culminated in legislation to introduce a poll tax for Scotland.

In doing all this, two points require clarification from the outset. First, the four empirical chapters were derived from materials both in the 'public' and 'private' domains. Materials in the *public* domain comprised relevant journals; 'Scottish' and 'UK' newspapers; HMSO publications; political party Conference reports and press releases; and interest group publications, press releases and pamphlets. Materials in the *private* domain comprised correspondence with a number of interest groups and government offices; internal political party and interest group reports and policy documents; and finally, interviews with numerous key individuals involved in crucial areas of the policy formation process.

The second point of clarification is that, unless it is necessary for specific reasons to do otherwise, reference will be made to the 'Poll Tax' rather than the 'Community Charge'. Previous government publications had all referred to a per-capita charge as a 'poll tax' and, publicly, it was known almost exclusively as this. It was also referred to as the 'Poll Tax', quite consistently on both sides of the Commons (by Mrs Thatcher on a number of occasions) and even in a Party Political Broadcast by the Conservative Party in 1991. Indeed, as Chapter Five shows, the term 'poll tax' was dropped, essentially as a public relations exercise in order to avoid the perception that there would be a link between the Tax and eligibility to vote.

Having clarified these points, therefore, it is now possible to begin an examination of a policy formation process which led to the adoption of a Poll Tax in 20th century Britain, and Scotland in particular. It may well be that in several hundred years time, the Poll Tax of the 1980s-90s will be simply yet another footnote in history, and seen perhaps as an aberration which somehow 'happened' for one reason or another. The present work will conclude, however, that this most definitely is not the case, and that Marxist dialectical principles can be utilised both to develop *general* principles of state policy formation, and to explain the *specific* state policy formation process which led to the advent of this previously 'unthinkable' tax.

1 The Neglected Concept of Policy Formation

As already indicated, the twin concerns of this book are policy formation in general, and the Poll Tax policy formation process in particular. The common denominator in both these quests is policy formation. Logically, therefore, our first step must be to turn to existing 'theories of policy formation' in order to determine whether or not they provide a suitable foundation to assist our understanding. This is not an easy task, however, since there is paucity of literature on the concept of policy formation. Such a statement requires considerable expansion, however, because there exists a whole series of analytical perspectives dealing with such matters as policy cycles, rationality and decision-making, power and decision-making, policy networks, and the state. Initial impressions of this vast body of material might perhaps tempt us to conclude that somewhere within it there lurks a perspective on 'policy formation'. We must be wary of any such temptations, however, whilst at the same time not abandoning hope altogether. A fuller discussion of this can best be undertaken if a definition of policy formation is offered as a yardstick against which existing perspectives can be judged. The author's own definition of this will be offered in Chapter Two. In the meantime, however, and without wishing to be unnecessarily restrictive, a 'skeleton' definition can be offered which adequately encapsulates the processes which the author is seeking to address in this book. Thus, with specific reference to liberal-democratic societies, a working definition of policy formation can be described as:

the historical process leading to the demise of an existing policy (or highlighting the problems faced when there is no policy), and the way in which a multiplicity of interests gradually shape the content of a 'new' policy until it appears in legal and/or constitutionally legitimate form.

The purpose of this chapter, using this definition as a yardstick, is to (a) explore the way in which political science has to varying degrees neglected the concept of policy formation, and (b) identify those elements of existing literature which potentially are of some use to us in our attempt to develop general principles of policy formation. Discussion of these will focus on two main categories of material. First, there are a number of perspectives whose focus is on a range of matters from policy cycles to the state, and which deal with *some* aspects of policy formation as a by-product of this. Second, there are the works of Bauer (Bauer and Gergen, 1968), Claus Offe (1975, 1984) and John Kingdon (1984), which *do* attempt explicitly to deal with policy formation, but still fall short of providing an integrated view of the policy formation process as a whole.

From Policy Cycles to the State: The Neglect of Policy Formation

Policy Cycles

Our first port of call is the literature on policy analysis and in particular the writings on policy cycles. Policy analysis itself is a very broad and nebulous area, but can narrowed down immediately if we make the distinction between 'policy analysis as an academic activity concerned primarily with advancing understanding, and policy analysis as an applied activity concerned mainly with contributing to the solution of social problems' (Ham and Hill, 1984, p. 4). It is within this former category that the literature on policy cycles can be located. It has its roots in the work of Easton, Lasswell and others. As Jenkins (1978, p. 16 and p. 18) notes, 'it assumes that policy emerges via a logical path; an issue moves through the political system in a processual way from point of entry, through decision and implementation, until a final choice is made to proceed with or terminate a course of action.' A key contemporary work in this field is Hogwood and Gunn's (1984) *Policy Analysis for the Real World*, which divides the policy cycle into issue search, issue filtration, issue definition, forecasting, setting objectives and priorities, options analysis, implementation, evaluation, and policy succession and termination. Does this, we might ask, deal with matters of policy formation? The answer is that whilst it deals with stages which undoubtedly exist in policy formation processes, it does not deal with policy formation as such. There are two main reasons for this.

First, within Hogwood and Gunn's model there is no consideration of the legislative passage of Bills - without which any analysis of policy formation is incomplete, since policy cannot be enacted until it is ratified in legal and/or constitutionally legitimate form. Second, although Hogwood and Gunn do at times deal with wider political and economic matters, their focus is firmly on *stages* in the process, rather than locating these within an explicit wider view of social forces. Thus, if we wish to consider policy formation as a *historical* process (often taking several years from the problems leading to the demise of one policy until legislation for a 'new' policy becomes law), then the focus of the policy cycle perspective does not sit easily alongside matters of policy formation. For example, the origins of the reorganisation of British local government in the 1990s through the introduction of single-tier authorities could partly be explained by Hogwood and Gunn's model. It could be used to suggest that ministerial agenda-setters perceived there to be broad 'problems' with two-tier authorities in terms of waste, duplication, co-ordination, confusion, remoteness, accountability, and their general inability to fit with the continuing 'enabling' role of local government (see e.g. DoE, 1991; Scottish Office, 1991; Welsh Office, 1991). It could *not*, however (because of the emphasis of the model on a *categorisation* of stages in the policy cycle), place this within the context of wider historical processes leading to a restructuring of local Government. As Cochrane (1993, p. 20) suggests, this 'can only plausibly be explained in terms which focus on the wider break up of the British welfare settlement.' Overall, therefore, the work of Hogwood and Gunn is useful in reminding us that policy formation proceeds through stages, although it does not provide us with a theory of policy formation as such.

Rationality and Decision-Making

Another possible avenue for investigation in our quest for 'policy formation' is those writings which deal with rationality and decision-making. The term 'rationality' is often associated with Weber's 'ideal-type' bureaucracy as 'the most rational known means of carrying out imperative control over human beings' (Weber, 1971, p. 25). In reality, however, rationality is a promiscuous word. As Levine et al. note:

'for some it means achievement of goals, some associate it with individuals maximising satisfaction, others conceive of it as a decision making process without regard to how successful a person is in achieving goals, and still others consider rationality to be broadly synonymous with intelligent and purposeful behaviour' (quoted in Carley, 1980, p. 10).

For present purposes, however, two main schools of thought are relevant. The first is public choice theory, where it is rational self-interest which is seen as the driving force of policy-making. The second refers to the works of Herbert Simon and Charles Lindblom, both of whom, in substantially different ways, according to Hogwood and Gunn (1984, p. 50), 'describe reality in terms of deviations from perfect rationality.' Each of these can be considered in turn.

As Mueller (1979, p. 1) notes - 'Public choice theory can be defined as the economic study of nonmarket decisionmaking, or simply the application of economics to political science.' The path-breaking work of Downs (1957) was then complemented by Buchanan and Tullock (1962) on voters/political parties, and then subsequently Niskanen (1971) who applied similar principles to bureaucracies. Midwinter (1989, p. 9) encapsulates the central thrust of these perspectives when he suggests that

'the public choice approach has developed an economic model of politics which assumes that voters, politicians and bureaucrats engage in maximizing behaviour in the pursuit of their own self-interest. Voters seek to maximize their consumption of public goods at minimal costs, politicians to maximise votes, and bureaucrats to maximize budgets.'

In answering the matter of whether a theory of policy formation is buried within this broad perspective, the answer is 'only in part'. Taking the work of Downs as an example, it does recognise that policy can be shaped by a multiplicity of interests. This is not simply because the electoral mechanism means that policy is the product of self-interested voters and politicians, but also because policy making has specific and substantial *biases*, in that 'democratic governments tend to redistribute income from the rich to the poor' (Downs, 1957, p. 297), and that 'democratic governments tend to favour producers more than consumers in their actions' (Downs, 1957, p. 297). Once again, however, the analysis does not concern itself with the way in which such interests shape the *legislative process*. Furthermore, if one element of policy formation pertains to the historical process leading to the demise of an existing policy, then public choice theory does not deal with such specific matters. Thus, for example, whilst the advent of the 'right to buy' council houses might be explained partly by a 'Downsian' match between a body of potential purchasers and a Conservative government willing to allow council house sales with 'the implicit object to gain political advantage' (Atkinson and Durden, in Savage and Robbins, 1990, p. 120), it could not begin to explain the wider processes leading to the demise, or 'residualisation' of council housing. This is not to criticise the basic assumptions of public choice theory (although this does mean that it is free from substantial criticism e.g. see Dunleavy, 1991). Rather, it is to comprehend that despite its usefulness in indicating that policy formation may be shaped by (i) the self-interest of voters, politicians and bureaucrats, and (ii) specific biases towards particular interests, its focus is only tangential to matters of policy formation.

Another area of study within the broad field of rationality and decision-making, is with regard to *departures* from rationality through the concept of 'bounded rationality'. This originates in Simon's seminal 1945 work *Administrative Behavior* and the second edition in 1957, marking a key point in early thinking about organisational decision-making. This covers both commercial and governmental organisations, although there is an extremely sparse exposition of the latter. Simon (1957, p. 120) describes politics simply as 'changing tastes and objectives,' and that in theory, political power rests with the embodiment of these in the legislature, since 'in the governmental agency the "customer" i.e. the legislative body, is the ultimate controlling group.' In practice, however, control is seen to be relatively passive. Therefore, 'the real initiative for the formulation of objectives often - perhaps almost always - lies in the top administrative group' (Simon, 1957, p. 120). Located within this overall framework is the concept of 'bounded rationality', which contrasts with the 'ideal type' of rational decision-making, where decision-makers act 'rationally' if a choice made between competing alternatives and all possible consequences is 'conducive to the achievement of the previously selected goals' (Simon, 1957, p. 5). Bounded rationality refers to the fact that in practice, decision-making departs from this 'ideal' since 'human beings...*satisfice* because they have not the wits to *maximise*' (Simon, 1957, p. xxiv).

These ideas, whilst generating much debate (and many undergraduate examination questions!!), have severe limitations in terms of their applicability to our study of policy formation processes. The reduction of politics simply to 'changing tastes and objectives' cannot comprehend the way in which a multiplicity of interests shapes government policies. The literature on policy networks is a good example of this. Whether these networks are at the 'policy community' or the 'issue network' end of the spectrum [see pp. 15-17 for a fuller explanation], the common denominator is that policy is the product of what Hanf describes as 'a large number of public and private actors from different levels and functional areas of government and society' (Hanf and Scharpf, 1978, p. 12). To reduce the forces behind policy-making to 'changing tastes and objectives' does our understanding of policy formation little service at all. The work of Simon is also problematic because the focus is simply on the relationship between 'ideal' rational decision-making and the real world of 'satisficing', rather than the relationship between the processes leading to the demise of one policy and the gradual shaping of a replacement. Simon's work *is* useful, however, in that it highlights the role of *objectives* in policy formation, although it does not go as far as providing us with a theory of policy formation as such.

Counterposed to the work of Simon is that of Charles Lindblom. It emerges self-avowedly as a challenge to the belief that departures from 'rational' decision-making were the result largely of psychological/ organisational limitations. As Gregory (1989, p. 51) notes, Lindblom's 'enduring message is that public policy making needs to be seen as an essentially political process...It is virtually impossible to read Lindblom without seeing his intuitive understanding that political life is larger than technical and economic logic.' More specifically, this political process manifests itself in what Lindblom (1959, p. 84) portrays as 'democracies chang[ing]...their policies almost entirely through incremental adjustments. Policy does not move in leaps and bounds.' It must be recognised, however, that his work on this divides into two main phases. The thread of incrementalism runs throughout, although it is only in his later work that the 'political process' becomes truly explicit. Lindblom's earlier work (1959, 1965 and 1970 [the latter with Braybrooke]), focused on the contention that incremental policy-making exists because of (i) 'successive limited comparisons' where decision-makers limit the number of policy alternatives to be considered for reasons of simplicity and relevance, (ii) 'disjointed incrementalism' where policy-makers compare policy alternatives 'whose known or expressed social states differ from each other only incrementally (Braybrooke and Lindblom, 1970, p. 85), and (iii) 'partisan mutual adjustment' where the behaviour of independent decision-makers is co-ordinated through their adapting to decisions around them by attempting to obtain desired responses from other decision-makers.

In his later work, Lindblom appears initially to move away from the underlying 'pluralist' assumptions of these writings, because of what Ham and Hill (1984, p. 94) describe as a 'recognition that the distribution of power is less equal than he once assumed.' Thus, in *Politics and Markets*, Lindblom (1977, p. 188) argues that 'some of the most fundamental and pervasive features of industrial society are what they are because of the privileged position of business in government and politics.' Therefore, the need for profitability 'renders these political systems incapable of following many lines of policy' (Lindblom, 1979, p. 520). This is seen to be reinforced ideologically through the indoctrination of citizens via the social experience of private enterprise, the constitution, the media etc. He appears to reconcile this with incrementalism, however, by equating it broadly with pluralism and arguing that within these 'grand' parameters, policy-making is pluralistic (incremental), but is 'grossly lopsided' because of the 'disproportionate political power and influence of business in politics' (Lindblom, 1979, p. 525).

To what extent, if any, does Lindblom's perspective contain a 'theory of policy formation'? Certainly, there are embryonic elements of this. The relationship between an 'old' and a 'new' policy is considered through the notion that policy change proceeds incrementally. Furthermore, there is an understanding of the multiplicity of interests which shape policy through the contention that 'business' is dominant within a broadly pluralistic society. We cannot go as far as saying, however, that Lindblom provides us with a theory of policy formation. For example, he does not consider the passage of legislation - an important aspect of the policy formation process. Furthermore, his analytical framework could perhaps tell us that an annual public spending allocation in Britain is essentially a product of 'incremental' changes from the previous year's allocation (Heclo and Wildavsky, 1981), but it could not tell us explicitly *what* the historical processes were which led to the unsuitability of the existing policy (i.e. the pre-existing public spending programme). Similarly, whilst Lindblom would undoubtedly be able to assist us by showing the pervasive interest of 'business' in UK macro-economic policy, this is of limited utility because it does not account for divisions within 'business'. This point will be taken further in Chapter Three, however for the moment we need only illustrate through the example of the CBI, which as (Leys, 1985, p. 15) notes, may be distinguished on four dimensions of 'scale; exporters versus producers for the domestic market; degree of monopoly...[and] national versus multinational production.' Once again, therefore, we find a perspective which deals with *aspects* of policy formation. It is of some use to us - particularly in terms of recognising that policies tend to proceed incrementally and may be shaped by a multiplicity of interests with 'business' being dominant in this - yet once again it lacks a specific focus on all the key components of policy formation.

Power and Decision-Making

Another potential source for a 'theory of policy formation' is the literature on power and decision-making. For present purposes, the work of Lukes (1974) provides a useful overview of this. Lukes categorises concepts of power in terms of one, two and three-dimensional views. Each of these can be outlined before discussing them together in terms of their usefulness (or otherwise) for our concerns regarding policy formation.

The one-dimensional view is rooted in the work of 'pluralists' involved in the community power debate of the 1950s-60s, such as Polsby, Wolfinger, and notably Dahl. Dahl's (1961) classic study of 'Who Governs?' in New Haven Connecticut focuses on observable behaviour and finds that 'only a small number of persons have much *direct* influence, in that they successfully initiate or veto proposals for policies' (Dahl, 1961, p. 163). These persons are seen to be competing élites, whose powers are reinforced through most citizens operating with low levels of ideological sophistication and political information, and being 'very far indeed from exerting equal influence over the content, application and development of the political consensus' (Dahl, 1961, p. 325). Complementing this, however, politicians are constrained because of the existence of a 'democratic creed' i.e. the 'great bulk of the citizens possess[ing] a fairly stable set of democratic beliefs at a high level of abstraction' (Dahl, 1961, p. 316). Thus, because citizens hold the ultimate sanction of the vote, when the 'political stratum' and 'professionals' attempt to involve citizens in decision-making, 'no appeal is likely to succeed unless it is framed in terms consistent with the creed' (Dahl, 1961, p. 324).

The two-dimensional view of power has its clearest exposition in the work of Bachrach and Baratz. They criticise Dahl et al. for focusing simply on 'decisions' and argue that decision-making also has a second face in the form of 'non decisions'. Thus, they define non decision-making as

'A means by which demands for change in the existing direction of benefits and privileges in the community can be suffocated before they are even voiced or kept covert or killed before they gain access to the relevant decision-making arena' (Bachrach and Baratz, 1970, p. 44).

This operates through what Schattschneider termed the 'mobilization of bias.' Thus, as Bachrach and Baratz (1970, p. 105) argue:

'Political systems tend consistently to develop a mobilization of bias, a set of values, beliefs, rituals, and procedures which can be exploited by beneficiaries of the unequal value-allocation to defend and promote their preferred position.'

Importantly, however, this does not mean that policy change becomes impossible. In their model of the policy process, Bachrach and Baratz divide the community under study into groups i.e. those seeking to reallocate values (in favour of change) and those committed to existing values (in favour of the status quo). Derived from this, and echoing much of the work of Easton (1965) and his systems analysis of political life, they suggest that feedback from existing policy can either strengthen or weaken each group's sources of power (resources, alliances etc.). This can then result in new alliances, new groups, new sets of values and so on, which undermine the mobilization of bias and result in a modification of existing dominant values, procedures etc. Thus, the policy process is dynamic rather than static.

The three-dimensional view is put forward by Lukes (1974) himself, and is portrayed as a *supplement* to the two previous views, rather than as counterposed to them. In this respect, the key point which Lukes seeks to address is contained in his view of power. Thus, he suggests that '*A* may exercise power over *B* by...influencing, shaping or determining his very wants' (Lukes, 1974, p. 23). As a result, when we come to look at policy-making, it is suggested that we need to look beyond observable conflict to latent conflict, which consists of a 'contradiction between the interests of those exercising power and the real interests of those they exclude' (Lukes, 1974, pp. 24-5). There have been some attempts to test this thesis - notably John Gaventa (1980) in his study of mining in an Appalachian valley, although and explicit attempt to apply it to a process of policy-making does not seem to have been forthcoming.

Having outlined these three perspectives, we must now ask if any of them can assist us with our quest for a theory of policy formation. The answer, as far as the one-dimensional view is concerned, is to a large extent 'no'. There is no explicit theorising of the historical process leading to the demise of policies. This does not mean that the focus is simply on the stability of the political system. Dahl (1961, p. 325) is at pains to point out the fluidity of this system and the fact that it is 'always open, in some measure, to alteration through those complex processes of symbiosis and change that constitute the relations of leaders and citizens in a pluralistic democracy.' Yet the focus here is firmly on the matter of *who governs* and the values and political system surrounding this, and hence matters pertaining directly to policy (such as the demise of policies, or the processes through which they become law) are not given consideration. At best, therefore, we can take with us the importance of political values, 'democratic' constraints and competing élites, in the policy formation process.

The work of Bachrach and Baratz offers more promise, however, because it *does* deal in an embryonic manner with matters of policy formation. There is a recognition that policy may emerge as a result of feedback from an existing policy. This can create an alliance in favour of change (if the mobilization of bias has not already thwarted this). The entire policy-making process is still shaped (in part), however, by the barriers of customs, procedures and organisational devices. This seems on first impression to include the legislative stage, where as Bachrach and Baratz (1970, p. 60) note - 'Each legislative system has...barriers that serve the function of selecting in somewhat disguised fashion from among a welter of competing public demands those issues that key decision-makers are prepared or compelled to consider for decision.'

It is obvious, therefore, that here we do indeed appear to have consideration of those features deemed to be central to 'policy formation', although we must hold back and temper this slightly. In the first instance, policy formation is touched on only indirectly as a result of wider concerns in terms of power in the political process. Further to this, the brief discussion of the legislative system is concerned in actual fact with legislative agenda-setting, and it then moves on from this to consider the actual process of decision-making and then the process of policy implementation. Thus, despite first impressions, there *is* gap in terms of study of the legislative process, and hence in terms of policy formation. The ideas on both policy 'feedback' and institutional 'bias' are useful, however, and will be developed in the next chapter when an attempt is made to develop 'general' principles of state policy formation.

Finally, there is Lukes. As already indicated, he builds on the previous perspectives, and in this sense the previous comments apply to him. His own particular contribution, however, is to recognise that the 'very wants' of individuals may be a consequence of others exercising power over them through a shaping of their consciousness. Once again, therefore, we can take this general point with us in our quest for a theory of policy formation, whilst recognising that for our purposes, the work of Lukes (as with Dahl, and Bachrach and Baratz) is of limited utility because it does not focus on policy formation *per se*.

Policy Networks

Both in its historical development and contemporary usage, the concept of 'policy networks' is bound-up with other (sometimes competing/ sometimes overlapping) concepts such as 'iron triangles', 'sub-governments' and 'policy communities'. These have their modern roots in American Political Science during the post-war period, and range from the work of Truman (1951) through to (notably) Heclo and Wildavsky (1981) and their study of the public expenditure policy-making process in Whitehall. In the 1970s, the mantle was taken up in the UK by Richardson and Jordan/Jordan and Richardson (particularly 1979, 1982 and 1987), and the field has since become filled with other players such as Rod Rhodes (esp. 1981, 1986 and 1988), Maurice Wright (1988) and David Marsh (with Rhodes) (1990). The study of policy-making through this focus is currently a burgeoning field of activity, although Jordan (1990b, p. 319) recognises the danger of the debate degenerating as the reader becomes 'confused by the jargon'.

This 'confusion' has been redressed considerably by Rhodes and Marsh (1992, pp. 186-8). They use the term 'policy networks' in a generic sense, encompassing all types of interest group intermediation along a continuum. At one end point of the continuum there are policy communities. These are characterised by a limited number of participants; usually dominated by economic/professional interests; interactions are frequent; there is continuity in terms of membership, values and outcomes; there is a general consensus on basic values and the legitimacy of outcomes; negotiations are based on the exchange of resources; interest leaders can deliver the agreement/compliance of their members, and there is a generally accepted balance of power between members. At the other end point of the continuum, there are issue networks. These are characterised by a large and wide-ranging membership; contacts fluctuate in frequency and intensity; access to the network fluctuates considerably; there is some agreement on values but these are masked by ever present conflict; negotiations may be based on resource exchanges but the basic relationship is consultative; interest leaders are variable in their capacity to regulate members, and power is distributed unequally - reflecting both unequal resources and access.

To what extent, therefore, can any of the foregoing assist us in our quest for a theory of policy formation? The answer is that there are a number of problems in seeking its assistance. In the first instance there is the fact, as Rhodes and Marsh (1992, p. 198) put it, that 'in short, the concept of policy networks does not provide an explanation of policy change.' A further difficulty (in terms of present concerns) is the downgrading of the role of Parliament. At the policy community end of the spectrum, there is the now famous portrayal of a 'post-Parliamentary democracy' as contained succinctly in Richardson and Jordan's (1979, p. 74) statement that

'it is the relationships involved in committees, the policy community of departments and groups, the practice of co-option and the consensual style, that perhaps better account for policy outcomes than do examination of party stances, of manifestos or of Parliamentary influences.'

A similar, but much less explicit view is found when we move to the issue network end of the spectrum. Here, there is no single, clear exposition of the role of Parliament. Nevertheless, there are still implicit assumptions which lead us easily in this same 'post-Parliamentary' direction. For example, Richardson, Maloney and Rüdig's (1992, p. 172) study of water privatisation 'found evidence for the heuristic usefulness of two concepts - policy community, and issue network ...(and that) there appears to have been more than one characteristic policy process in this case.' The importance of this, is that the persistence of the Parliamentary system throughout, is for all intents and purposes, relegated out of existence. Whichever end of the spectrum we focus on, therefore, policy is effectively considered as formed within a *policy network*. As a further consequence of this, the legislative passage of bills is seen to be of little influence in helping form policy. As Jordan and Richardson (1987, p. 57) argue - 'whether the House [of Commons] contributes more to the policy process or to the tourist trade is a difficult question.' Overall, therefore, the policy network literature is useful in reminding us that policy may be shaped by a multiplicity of actors who vary in number and cohesion, depending on the type of network involved. In the last analysis, however, it does not go as far as providing us with a 'theory' of policy formation.

Marxism and the State

To do justice to the breadth, depth and complexity of Marxist theories of the state is all but impossible with a few pages. This is rooted in two main, interrelated factors. First, there is the existence of, and debate surrounding the numerous writings of Marx and Engels on the state - particularly in the *Manifesto of the Communist Party* where there is the now famous pronouncement that the 'executive of the modern state is but a committee for managing the common affairs of the whole bourgeoisie' (Marx and Engels, 1975d, p. 35). This is compounded by the existence of a plethora of statements on the nature of the state, and indeed Jessop (1982) suggests that there are in fact four different views on the state from within the writings of Marx and Engels. Second, and bound-up with this, there is the inter-relationship of theory and practice, as Marxist theory has developed as part of, and in response to, the development of capitalism. This has resulted in a massive revival in the role of the state in the past two decades or so.

We are concerned in this book with *state* policy formation, and it is important to try and delve into areas of this 'revival' in order to ask if it contains materials which deals with the formation of state policy. The Miliband/Poulantzas debate of the 1970s on the nature of the capitalist state - although now largely overtaken by debates which focus on the origins, development and aftermath of 'Thatcherism' - provides us with a very useful contrast between apparently competing Marxist views of the state. Each can be considered in turn.

Miliband's (1973) *The State in Capitalist Society*, published originally in 1969, is a key contemporary work which helped provide a spring-board for subsequent debate. As Held (1989, p. 68) suggests:

'Noting the growing centrality of the state in Western societies he sought on the one hand to assess the relationship Marx posited between class and state, and on the other to evaluate the pluralist model of state-society relations which was then the reigning orthodoxy.'

Thus, for Miliband (1973, pp. 132-3), the state is a capitalist state because

'business in the very nature of a capitalist system is immeasurably better placed than any other interest to do so...[i.e. oppose state policy], and to cause governments to pay much greater attention to its wishes and susceptibilities than to anybody else.'

This bears remarkable similarities to Lindblom, however Miliband in both this and his later 1982 work *Capitalist Democracy in Britain*, supplements this with a number or reasons why the state mitigates the interests of labour parties, trades unions, and the electorate in general. First, and crucially, there is the process of ideological hegemony as operating through the education system, media church etc. This helps to justify parliamentarism and the view that 'while there might be ills in the existing system, they are perfectly remediable within its framework' (Miliband, 1982, p. 77). This is typified in the attitude of social-democratic parties, trade union leaders etc. Most find attraction in party competition and therefore 'see the world through a parliamentary haze' (Miliband, 1973, p. 149), hence supporting a consensus on private ownership of the means of production. Second, political élites (decision makers) both in terms of elected representatives and civil servants, generally share common 'upper class' social origins and educational backgrounds which make them sympathetic to the interests of business. Third, the very act of parliamentary representation 'provides a buffer between government and people' (Miliband, 1982, p. 38), depopularising policy-making, leaving MPs relatively free to carry on their daily business. Finally, and carrying this a stage further, 'legislative assemblies...now tend to play a subsidiary role in the decision-making process...[as] governments seek increasingly to insulate themselves from popular pressures' (Miliband, 1973, p. 148)

Does all this, we might ask, provide us with a theory of policy formation? The answer is 'no', although it is still of considerable assistance to us. We can begin to explain this by suggesting that a problem is its generality with regard to aspects of policy-making processes. This is perhaps understandable, however, given that Miliband (1973, pp. 7-8) was self-avowedly seeking to 'remedy...[the] deficiency' of the view of the state as 'above all the coercive instrument of a ruling class.' A further problem is that it does not deal with the historical processes leading to the demise of policies and the advent of replacements, other than the implicit assumption that 'business' is liable to have been influential throughout. It does, however, recognise that policy-making is the product of political competition, and in particular 'imperfect competition' because of the influence of business. Also, it does alert us to the hegemonic ideas of parliamentarism, and the way in which grievances become institutionalised in an essentially remote, executive-dominated and conservative institution which accepts the principles of private ownership of the means of production. These points *are* useful and will be developed further in the next chapter, although we cannot look to Miliband himself to provide us with a well-developed perspective on 'policy formation' as such.

In opposition to Miliband's 'subjectivist' approach is the work of Poulantzas, which Clarke (1977, p. 1) describes as 'trying to graft the Marxist proposition that the class struggle is the motor force of history onto Althusser's structural-functionalist conception of society.' According to Poulantzas, therefore, the function of the state is doubly determined by structure and the class struggle. More specifically, the 'state is not a class instrument' (Poulantzas, 1973, p. 191). It is 'the factor of social cohesion of a social formation and the factor of reproduction of the conditions of production of a system that itself determines the domination of one class over the others' (Poulantzas, 1973, p. 246).

The way in which he locates the 'politics' of the parliamentary arena and political parties within this can be seen from his contention that 'despite the declaration of a *separation* of powers...the capitalist state functions as a *centralized* unity' (Poulantzas, 1972, p. 303). Thus, it performs the dual function of *organizing* the dominant classes and *disorganizing* the working classes. On the one hand, it *organizes* (into a power bloc) the ruling class under the leadership of the hegemonic class or fraction; representing the 'general common interest of the classes or fractions in the power bloc: this general interest consists of economic exploitation and political domination' (Poulantzas, 1973, p. 239). On the other hand, it *disorganizes* the working class by isolating then from their class position and setting them up as juridico-political subjects i.e. individual who are constituted (and 'represented' via political parties) under the sovereignty of the popular nation state, which is 'supposed to represent the general will and the political unity of the people and the nation' (Poulantzas, 1973, p. 277).

In performing this organizing/disorganizing function, the state (and hence the activity of governments and political parties) is seen to possess a 'relative autonomy' from its determination in the 'economic' class struggle in order to consolidate the relations of class domination. This 'relative autonomy' is seen to occur within limits prescribed by the power bloc and the relations within and between classes. In essence, therefore, the state is inscribed with a demarcated flexibility which enables it to concede both economic/material benefits and political rights which 'not only fail...to threaten the political relations of class domination but even constitute...and element of that relation' (Poulantzas, 1973, p. 133).

Does all this, we might ask, assist us with a theory of policy formation? The answer is rather mixed. Even more so than Miliband, there is a generality with respect to decision-making processes, and hence there is no consideration of such matters as the demise or policies or the legislative passage of bills. As Held (1989, p. 70) notes - 'How institutions operate and the manner in which the relationship among élites, government officials and parliamentarians evolves are neglected...[this] leads him to ignore the concrete social practices through which structural relations are reproduced.' Yet we need not abandon the work of Poulantzas altogether. At the very least, we can take with us the idea that the state exhibits specific characteristics of bias, and that this bias is shaped by the requirements of capital and the dominant divisions within this. Once again, therefore, existing literature provides us with themes which we can pursue in our quest for 'policy formation', but does not provide us with a fully-developed perspective on policy formation as such.

Raymond Bauer on Policy Formation

None of the works detailed previously, deal consciously with a topic which can be described as 'policy formation.' It is now time to break with this tradition and deal with three authors who *do* attempt to deal with this concept. The first of these is Raymond Bauer, who undertakes this task in a 1968 book (co-edited with Kenneth Gergen) entitled *The Study of Policy Formation*. The angle from which he approaches this is one which is 'not to supply [the practitioner with] specific solutions to specific problems. It is rather to deepen his comprehension of the range of problems with which he is accustomed to deal and thereby to help him invent better solutions of his own' (Bauer and Gergen, 1968, p. 5). In essence, therefore, it is *descriptive*, but with *prescriptive* sympathies.

His focus is on the social and intellectual processes of policy formation, whilst clearly recognising that 'it is difficult to conceive of a way in which the intellectual aspects of policy formation can ever be completely isolated from their social context' (Bauer and Gergen, 1968, p. 20). He uses a number of examples from the governmental and non-governmental worlds to illustrate that 'the bargaining process is at the heart of the policy process' (Bauer and Gergen, 1968, p. 13). A vitally important element of this process of negotiation (which may be delegated from a higher authority) is 'the presentation of policy proposals in such a form as to engage the perceived interests of members of a winning coalition' (Bauer and Gergen, 1968, p. 16). In this regard, Bauer recognises the particular importance of two main factors. The first is that study of policy formation is fraught with difficulties in trying to determine who the relevant actors are, and trying to dissect and comprehend the multitude of interests that people and organisations may have. The second is that there is a wider context to the involvement of these interests in the policy process, in that treatment of an issue will depend on such matters as its level of saliency; personal limitations of time to devote to an issue; the existence of past debts to others, and the potential for building-up future goodwill.

Turning now to an assessment of this against present concerns, it is evident that there are considerable problems. Certainly, we cannot criticise Bauer for focusing on those matters which he considers to be of relevance. This point aside, however, he leaves himself open to criticism by failing to define policy formation. In many instances, therefore, his analysis lapses at times into discussions of the 'policy process' and 'decision making'. When this lack of clarity is combined with *this* author's working definition of policy formation, a number of difficulties arise. Bauer does not consider the *process* of policy formation in terms of the forces leading to the demise one policy and the advent of another. Thus, whilst he recognises that the parties involved in policy formation 'have a past and a future' (Bauer and Gergen, 1968, p. 16), he does not replicate this with *policies*. There is also a further problem in that there is no conceptualising of legislative processes. Certainly, he does apply elements of his theorising to this e.g. when goodwill and time constraints were important influences on how Congress handled two particular bills. Nevertheless, this is still only a theorising of some aspects of legislation, rather that the legislative process as a totality. In total, therefore, Bauer can still be said to be of some use to us because of his recognition of multiple actors interacting to produce feasible coalitions, but despite his intention to study 'policy formation', he does not succeed in terms of the 'skeleton' definition set out at the beginning of this chapter.

John Kingdon on Policy Formation

Another self-avowed excursion into the area of policy formation comes from American political scientist John Kingdon, who provides us with an important yet much neglected study in his book *Alternatives, Agendas and Public Policies*. In this, he undertakes what he describes as a 'journey through the labyrinth of policy formation' (Kingdon, 1984, p. 20). In empirical terms, this is developed through a longitudinal study of health and transportation policy in the US federal government. Based on this, he attempts to address the matter of policy formation by focusing essentially on two key issues i.e. *agendas* and *alternatives*. Thus, he states that 'we seek to understand why some subjects become prominent on the political agenda and others do not, and why some alternatives for choice are seriously considered while others are neglected' (Kingdon, 1984, p. 3). In an attempt to deal with this, two categories of factors are seen to be crucial. These are (a) the *participants* (both visible and hidden) who are active in the policy formation process, and (b) the *processes* occurring in 'streams' of problems, policies and politics, through which both agendas and alternatives come to prominence. The manner in which Kingdon utilises these can be seen clearly from the way in which he deals with both agendas and the specification of alternatives.

The first of these (agenda setting) revolves around problems, politics and visible participants. Problems come to occupy the attention of government officials because of focusing events (disasters, crises etc.) or feedback from the operation of existing programmes. Politics is also crucial, and 'independently or problem recognition or the development of policy proposals, political events flow along according to their own dynamics and their own rules' (Kingdon, 1984, p. 207). Finally, visible participants also play a key role. Kingdon (1984, p. 208) notes that visible participants such as the President, high-level appointees and prominent members of Congress, can provide impetus to some issues and 'the chances of a subject rising on a governmental agenda are enhanced if that subject is pushed by participants in the visible cluster, and dampened if it is neglected by those participants.'

The second of Kingdon's primary concerns (alternative specification) revolves around hidden participants (such as academics, career bureaucrats and congressional staffers) and the policy stream. In terms of hidden participants, individuals in this category are considered dominant in the specification of alternatives because of their specialism and the fact that 'to generate alternatives, some degree of expertise and willingness to concern oneself with minute details is required' (Kingdon, 1984, p. 74). In terms of the policy stream, Kingdon (1984, p. 209) suggests that 'the generation of policy alternatives is best seen as a selection process analogous to biological natural selection.' Ideas float around in what is described as a 'primeval soup', although the selection process is not haphazard, since 'the process is evolutionary...some of the ideas survive and flourish' (Kingdon, 1984, p. 130). The criteria for selection are numerous, and include such factors as technical feasibility, budget constraints, congruence with the values of community members, public acceptability, and the receptiveness of politicians. Whichever policy alternative is chosen, Kingdon sees it as the result of a long 'softening-up' process, whereby advocates of policy push forward their ideas in a variety of forums - waiting for 'windows' to open.

This can be explained further through recognising a crucial statement by Kingdon (1984, pp. 210-11) when he suggests that 'the separate streams of problems, policies, and politics each have lives of their own...but there comes a time when the three streams are joined...this dramatically enhances the odds that a subject will become firmly fixed on the decision agenda.' This conjoining of streams occurs when circumstances (new problems, changes in public opinion, vigorous lobbying etc.) create 'open windows' which 'present opportunities for the complete linkage of problems, proposals and politics' (Kingdon, 1984, p. 213). Overall, however, whilst Kingdon stresses that there is a degree of unpredictability in this, the processes in question are not considered to be random. There are several reasons for this. First, there are the previously mentioned criteria which shape the selection process in the 'primeval soup'. Second, 'everything cannot interact with everything else' (Kingdon, 1984, p, 216) and such things as the timing of an item's arrival on the agenda (and hence the match or otherwise of the streams) limits coupling possibilities. Third, 'participants have some sense of what would constitute an appropriate solution to a problem' (Kingdon, 1984, p. 216). Fourth and finally, such things as the constitution, statutes, precedents etc., act as 'constraints on the system...[and] provide a basic structure within which the participants play the game we have described' (Kingdon, 1984, p. 217).

Taking Kingdon's theory as a whole, we are now in a position to assess the extent to which it deals with matters of 'policy formation.' We can approach this on two levels. On one level, it does not (despite Kingdon's intention) deal with 'policy formation'. He deals with formative stages of policy but does not (on his own admission) concern himself with 'authoritative choices' or the 'passage of legislation'. In this sense, the policy formation concerns of Kingdon do not match the 'policy formation' concerns of this book - as identified at the outset of this chapter. On another level, however, Kingdon *does* deal with key components of policy formation. He considers the demise of existing policies through recognising that feedback from existing programmes or focusing events may help to push an item onto the agenda, and then 'windows' may open as a result of circumstances leading to a conjoining of the streams or problems, policies and politics. He also deals with the way in which a multiplicity of interests shape policy through the interests which are implicit in the 'criteria' for selection i.e. specialists, taxpayers, the public and politicians. We must be cautious, however, of endorsing this as an unproblematic theory of policy formation. Leaving aside the fact that it does not deal with the legislative passage of bills, there are essentially three main difficulties with it.

First, it is difficult to accept Kingdon's contention that the streams of problems, policies and politics have 'lives of their own.' By viewing society in this way, randomness becomes the order of the day. Certainly, Kingdon is constantly on the verge of challenging this view, but always stops short of doing so. For example, the 'rules of the game' (the constitution, precedents etc.) are referred to as imposing order on the problem, policy and political streams. He does not address, however, the matter of whose rules these are, and who persistently wins the game.

Second, Kingdon suggests that the hidden participants in policy communities are of paramount importance because of their specialist knowledge and expertise. Yet he then contradicts this by suggesting the existence of a number of constraints, such as public acceptability and the receptiveness of politicians. In practice, the existence of both 'expertise' and 'public/political' constraints is undeniable. The problem for Kingdon, however, is that there is no theorising of the relationship between the two. Rather, we are told that the first of these dominates, and then that the second ensures it doesn't.

Third, despite Kingdon suggesting otherwise, he *does* present the criteria for selection in the 'primeval soup' as essentially random. The reason for this is that Kingdon's work (unlike that of Lindblom, Miliband and Poulantzas) contains no explicit recognition of wider power structures within society i.e. of persistent classes or categories of individuals, who can in a very general sense, be broken down into 'winners' and 'losers'. Thus, the criteria for selection (technical feasibility, budget constraints etc.) *are* haphazard in Kingdon's model, because there is no link made between these and the classes/categories of people who would tend to benefit from state policy. In the most general of senses, for example, it is difficult to deny that the Thatcher Government did more for entrepreneurs and 'business' than it did for trade unionists and the welfare state. Thus, as Douglas (1989, p. 401) suggests in his review of Thatcherism - 'the generally accepted view of what constitutes viable economic and political solutions has changed.' On even on the most general of levels, therefore, it is matters such as these which Kingdon does not address.

Overall, therefore Kingdon's model is useful in revealing to us both the complexity of the policy formation process (in terms of participants and processes, and the linkages between them), and the fact that the convergence of a number of factors may lead to the opening of 'windows' leading us towards new policies, but it stops short of providing us either with a complete or analytically coherent theory of policy formation.

Claus Offe on Policy Formation

The final body of material that we can turn to in our quest for policy formation is the work of Claus Offe. Perhaps more explicitly than any of the other materials detailed so far, this does indeed attempt to consider the subject of 'policy formation'. Offe's perspective is far from simple, however, and there is a definite lack of consistency and coherence in his numerous writings on the subject. [1] Nevertheless, it is possible to piece together a broad picture of his views on policy formation. In order to do this, however, we must first of all identify the wider context in terms of his analysis of the role of the state. For Offe, according to Held (1989, p. 70):

> 'the state is neither simply a "capitalist state" as Poulantzas contends (a state determined by class power), nor "a state in capitalist society" as Miliband argues (a state which preserves political power free from immediate class interests).'

Offe (1984) starts from the premise that 'the state seeks to implement and guarantee the *collective* interests of all members of a class society dominated by capital.' In so doing, its power is dually-determined i.e. its *form* is determined by 'democratic' government, whilst its *content* is conditioned by the imperatives of the accumulation process. This is rooted in four 'functional' conditions which the state is seen to perform.

First, the state is prohibited from directly organizing material production (labour and capital) according to its own 'political criteria'. Second, the state's political power depends on it deriving resources (via taxation) from the accumulation process, without which 'those who occupy positions of power in a capitalist state are in fact powerless' (Offe, 1984, p. 120). Third, these combine and lead to the state being linked to the accumulation process because of its 'institutional self-interest', since 'every occupant of state power is basically interested in promoting those political conditions most conducive to private accumulation' (Offe, 1984, p. 120). Fourth, as a guarantor of 'collective interests', it is a functional condition that the real content of state power is hidden by liberal representation and electoral competition - these giving predominance to the voting preferences of the electorate.

Located within this framework is Offe's view of 'policy formation'. This begins with his contention that 'the motive force of all policy formation is the problem of reconciling these...[four] elements' (quoted in Carnoy, 1984, p. 135). Yet what, might we ask, is the dynamic which causes these to be in constant need of reconciliation? This can be seen from Offe's (1984, p. 121) usage of the term 'commodification'. He argues that the 'divergent structural conditions of the capitalist state can be reconciled...as long as every owner of a unit of value can successfully exchange his/her value as a commodity.' The problem, however, is that 'the dynamics of capitalist development seem to exhibit a constant tendency to *paralyse* the commodity form of value (Offe, 1984, p. 122). The result of this is that competition in the accumulation process continually destroys the values of both labour and capital, necessitating both that the state compensate for the 'market', and engage in various social expenditures (such as the welfare state) to legitimate the very existence of capitalist accumulation. Williamson (1989, pp. 142-3) sums up Offe's position when he states that

> 'without the creation and sustenance of the commodity form there cannot be capital accumulation. To Offe, the process of commodification which is necessary for accumulation stands in contradiction to welfare and other market-compensating interventions which are necessary for legitimizing capitalist society because they take a non-commodity form, thereby reducing the scope for capital accumulation. Capitalism needs both, but they stand in contradiction...to each other, leading to crises.'

As a result of all this, the state engages in policy formation (because of institutional self-interest) in an attempt to reconcile the four functional conditions and maintain the commodity form of value. In doing so, the process of policy formation gives

> 'preferential treatment to the functional problems of the capitalist economy - a commitment guaranteed by objective, political-organizational channels and mechanisms - imply[ing] material, social and temporal "biases", i.e. privilege granting rules whose effect in turn play an essential role in "delegitimating" political conflicts' (Offe, 1984, pp. 55-6).

He argues that this formal (or *internal*) structure of policy making 'is of equal significance [i.e. compared to policy content] especially since it predetermines what can and does become the content of policy' (Offe, 1975).

Conflicting in part with this dominance given to the state's internal structure, he also sees three main factors as deciding the outcome of this political process. First, there is competition between political élites for electoral victories and scarce resources. Second, there is

> 'access to and control over the means of production, the means of organization and the means of communication [which] are highly unevenly distributed within the social structure, and each of them can be used to a different degree of effectiveness, to shape and to challenge what politicians perceive as their *environment of decision-making*...This is the level at which the agenda of politics and the relative priority of issues and solutions is determined' (Offe, 1984, p. 159).

Third and finally, there is the fact that these 'power positions are...contested and hence subject to change and redistribution' (Offe, 1984, p. 160).

Whatever the actual outcome of this, the process of policy formation is seen as doomed to failure because of the 'inability of the political system to prevent and compensate for economic crises' (Offe, 1984, p. 61). This is because the state is unable to balance the demands arising from the dynamic of the accumulation process with its own *internal* structure, and thus faces a 'crisis of crisis management'. Whichever one of the three principal processes of organization and decision-making are used, it 'tends to violate rather than to establish the balance of the state and the accumulation process' (Offe, 1975, p. 144). As Dunleavy and O'Leary (1987, p. 266) summarise:

'Bureaucratic policy-making is inflexible and incapable of forward planning or engaging external social interests in helping implement policies. Technocratic modes of policy-making conflict with democratic norms of legitimation, and create insuperable problems in gauging social preferences. Participatory modes of policy-making risk losing control of key state functions to electorally successful working-class parties and so on.'

Turning now to an assessment of Offe in terms of his treatment of 'policy formation', it is evident that it does not deal fully with matters identified in the author's own 'skeleton' definition of policy formation as set out at the beginning of this chapter. There is no consideration of the historical process leading to the demise of an existing policy. The nearest he comes to this is via the assumption that policies will emerge continually as the state attempts to reconcile the various problems created by the dynamics of the capitalist accumulation process. There is also a further problem in that Offe does not deal with the legislative stage of policy formation. Again, the nearest he comes to this is the implicit assumption that this stage is liable to give preferential treatment to the functional problems of capitalism. Despite these difficulties, however, there are still elements of Offe's analysis which we can take with us in our quest for a theory of policy formation. He *does* locate policy formation within the wider framework of capitalism, and he *does* lead us to consider the view that this can give impetus to policy formation processes. Furthermore, he *does* recognise that the state - far from playing a neutral role in policy formation - helps shape the input from a multiplicity of interests, through organisational 'privilege granting rules' which can help delegitimate political conflicts. Overall, therefore, Offe's work is useful in part, but in common with all other perspectives detailed in this chapter, it stops short of providing us with a comprehensive view of 'policy formation'.

Conclusion

This chapter has served a two-fold purpose. On one level, it has identified the way in which existing theoretical materials (ranging from those whose concerns are tangential to policy formation, to those who attempt to directly address it) fall short of dealing comprehensively with the concept of 'policy formation' as defined at the outset of the chapter. It was particularly important to do this in order to eschew any impressions that somewhere within these materials there lurked a theory of policy formation which would assist us substantially with the aims of this book. On a second level, however, the chapter has been useful in identifying a number of issues which may be of assistance to us in trying to move on and develop a more comprehensive perspective on policy formation. These range from locating the process of policy formation within the wider context of societal power structures and processes (Downs, Lindblom, Bachrach and Baratz, Miliband, Poulantzas, Offe), through to factors shaping the policy formation process itself (Simon, Bachrach and Baratz, Dahl, Kingdon, Bauer, Offe). It is towards this task of developing a more comprehensive view of policy formation that we can now turn.

Notes

1. Offe's discussion of policy formation spans several discrete works, and is indeed highly inconsistent. For example, Offe (1975, p. 132) identifies two main modes of state intervention (allocative and productive) and argues that 'the decision rules for allocative state activities can be directly derived from politics.' Also, he argues that 'rather than assuming some instance which pressures or manipulates the policy process from the "outside," the key explanatory concept which we want to suggest is the institutional self-interest of the actors in the state apparatus which determines policy outputs and outcomes' (quoted in Carnoy, 1984, p. 135). Both these 'self enclosed' views of policy-making, however, contradict his statement (quoted in the main body of the present chapter) that the politician's 'environment' can be shaped by 'outside' interests.

2 Towards a Theory of State Policy Formation

The aim of this chapter is to develop general principles through which we can comprehend processes of state policy formation, whilst also providing a basis for comprehending the Poll Tax policy formation process in particular. Such a bold task, however, requires a number of clarifications. In the first instance, it must be recognised that such a 'general theory' is simply being *explicit*, where in the work of many others it is *implicit*. As Gamble (1990, p. 406) notes, many British political scientists

'prefer to work at a less abstract level....But it is hard for...[them] to avoid general theories altogether. Even when it is not acknowledged, an organising perspective will always be implicit in the way the research is framed and the conclusions drawn.'

In addition, the paucity of writings on the subject of policy formation lends itself to establishing very broad principles which lay down some analytical 'stakes' in the ground. It is recognised, however, that further research is undoubtedly called for in other areas of policy formation in order that these general principles can be subjected to further testing on the basis of empirical evidence. Nevertheless, as the writer Aldous Huxley (1940, p. 330) commented, 'even the fragmentary outline of a synthesis is better than no synthesis at all.' If the argument presented in this chapter contributes to further discussion, then it will have served a useful purpose.

The structure of the chapter is as follows. First, it provides a brief discussion on the subject of Marxist dialectics and attempts to develop, within an *explicitly Marxist framework*, some general principles which will act as a guide to analysis. Second, it utilises these dialectical principles in order to produce a specific argument with regard to the state and its role in policy formation - thus expanding on the 'skeleton' definition of policy formation given in the previous chapter. Third and finally, it then 'fleshes out' this by discussing the role of the British Parliamentary state in the process of policy formation.

Marxism and Dialectics

The whole matter of dialectics is described in Tom Bottomore's *A Dictionary of Marxist Thought* (1983, p. 120) as 'possibly the most contentious topic in Marxist thought.' The 'materialism' of Marx's dialectic and the relationship of this to Hegel and his dialectic of 'consciousness' is a matter of intense debate (e.g. see Althusser, 1979; Howard, 1972). There is also disagreement on whether or not dialectics can be applied to nature as well as to society (e.g. see Engels, 1978; Lukács, 1971). There are, however, two general principles of dialectics upon whose existence there is substantial agreement. These two principles are *essential* to our understanding of state policy formation.

The first key principle is the concept of 'contradiction', which is described by Cornforth (1987, p. 93) as the 'unity of opposites'. There is widespread agreement within Marxism that the root of this contradiction is the antagonism between classes in post-communal societies, with these being derived from the ownership and organisation of productive capacities and their social basis, where one class exploits the other through extraction of surplus value. In terms of capitalist societies, however, this general opposition between classes is simply too broad *for the purpose of explanation* with regard to Parliament, policy formation etc. Yet if we move away from this general contradiction and adopt a narrower focus in terms of the contradiction between the forces of production (labour-power, technology, etc.,) and the social relations of production (ownership of productive forces), we find that the focus on 'production' is conversely too narrow *for the purposes of explanation* with regard to Parliament, policy formation etc. It seems useful to suggest, therefore, that wholly compatible with these, but offering us the scope to grasp the specific contradictions that will be identified in the roles of the state, policy formation, etc., it is possible to focus on and develop the contradiction between what will be called here the *leading capitalist forces* in society and the *contradictory forces* in society. These original terms have been chosen with the specific intention of constructing vehicles which, although building on core Marxist dialectical principles, focus attention firmly on policy formation, rather than becoming derailed by a series of arguments and counter-arguments from within 'Marxist' writings on the nature and dynamic of 'classes' (see Cottrell, 1984 for an overview). Bearing this in mind, the aforementioned terms can be explained in turn.

The first 'face' of the contradiction, and indicating one direction in which social life is being pulled, is the 'leading capitalist forces' in society. In essence, this is the general alliance of *all* those forces which create and perpetuate the capitalist nature of society. These revolve around the conditions which Marx (1975a, p. 142) identified as the 'fundamental conditions' for the existence of capitalism - namely the coming into contact of two very different types of commodity possessors in the form of owners of the means of production/subsistence etc., and sellers of labour power. This relationship is sustained formally through markets for commodities (including labour-power) and hence the necessity for competition. Thus, the self-expansion of capital becomes what Marx (1981, p. 358) described as 'the motive and purpose of production.' To state it rather crudely and in very general terms, therefore, the 'leading capitalist forces' are *all* those relationships buttressing the pursuit of private profit and the accumulation of the ownership and control of material resources into 'private' hands. Some important qualifying points will be made to this in a moment.

The second 'face' of the contradiction, and hence a counter direction in which social life is being pulled, is what has been called here the 'contradictory forces' in society. An explanation of this starts by recognising as Marx (1978, p. 149) did in *The German Ideology*, that 'the first premise of all human history is, of course, the existence of living human individuals.' When this is understood, we realise that the 'leading capitalist forces' in society do not have an independent existence. When viewed from another angle, we find that they continually confront and are in contradiction with their 'human' face. On one level, the seeds of these contradictory forces are comprised of the fact that people's exploitation is not limitless; they have physical limitations, and they have mental limitations. On another level, and supplementing these, individuals have feelings and the capacity and autonomy for reflective thought on their general conditions of existence, and the further ability to act upon them. In very general terms, therefore, the 'contradictory forces' in society are a range of forces continually reacting against *all* or *some* components of the 'leading capitalist forces', ensuring therefore, that the domination of these is never complete. Thus, the ruling class rules, but in a *contradictory* way.

There are a number of important qualifying points to be made to all of the foregoing. First, in talking of 'autonomy', it must be recognised that this is *not* autonomy devoid of a social setting, or the 'relative autonomy' of Poulantzas (1973) where autonomy becomes dehumanised through its being 'assigned' by the relations within and between classes and somehow being functional to class rule. It is, quite simply, the capacity for individuals to be part of, reflect, and act upon, very powerful contradictory forces in society.

Second, the conflict between the 'leading capitalist forces' and the 'contradictory forces', like all other laws of capitalism, are *not iron laws* which operate deterministically and independent of human beings utilising their capacities for reflective thought and acting 'autonomously'. Thus, the contradiction should be seen as a *law of tendency*, which can be, according to Marx (1976, p. 798) 'like all other laws modified in...[their] working by many circumstances.'

Third, it must be clearly understood that 'leading capitalist forces' are not the same thing as the 'ruling class'. The latter is certainly part of these forces, but the definition given a moment ago illustrates that 'leading' forces are essentially those of private accumulation - thus permeating 'one face' of *all* aspects of society.

Fourth and finally, it should be understood that the 'leading capitalist forces' are *not* a homogenous entity. Some 'lead' more than others and, hence the lesser elements in the alliance are also part of the 'contradictory forces' in society. This starts to overcome the problems faced by Downs, Lindblom and Miliband, who tended to treat 'producers' and 'business' as a unified block. For example, we will see in Chapter Three how the City, large industrial capital and smaller domestic-orientated capital are clearly part of the 'leading capitalist forces', because of their prominence in shaping government policy. Equally, however, there are substantive divisions within these forces. Domestic-orientated capital tends continually to suffer because of the interest/exchange rates which are necessary to protect the interests of the City (hence putting some large City-financed domestic capitals in an ambivalent position). A classic example of this is the situation in the early 1980s when a high interest/exchange rate policy led to cries of 'pain' from small businesses and the CBI Director General promising a 'bare knuckle fight' with the Government. In effect, therefore, domestic-orientated capital is *also* part of the 'contradictory forces', reacting against the 'lead' of the City and using its 'autonomy' to do so. It must always be remembered, therefore, that the first key principle of dialectics teaches us that, where there is unity, there is also contradiction.

Following on directly from this, is the second key principle of dialectics, and one which will prove pivotal to our understanding of the process of policy formation. This is, that the 'union of opposites' in society, is not static. Rather, it undergoes a continual process of development. This development is dialectical, in that there is, as Sayers (in Norman and Sayers, 1980, p. 6) notes - 'a constant process of conflict and interaction, which is at the basis of all movement and change.' To put it simply, abstractly and rather crudely, the 'leading capitalist forces' in society continually confront and create 'contradictory forces' which hold back the development of the leading forces until, through a process of struggle, there is some form of realignment (or synthesis). The contradictory nature of society, however, means that this new 'synthesis' also contains the seeds of further development and so on.

We can explore these two key dialectical principles in greater depth and turn now to apply them to the state and the formation of state policy.

The Dialectics of the State and State Policy Formation

If policy is the policy of the *state*, then it is necessary first of all to establish the dialectical role of the state. In doing so, we confront the fact, as Chapter One revealed and as Dunleavy and O'Leary (1989, p.7) indicate, that the state is subject to 'passionate disagreements about its origins, character and appropriate activities.' Once we begin thinking dialectically, however, we find that these tend to devolve into two main camps, each focusing primarily on one particular aspect of the state's contradictory role.

In terms of Marxist theory, we find on the one hand, a sharp emphasis on the state's relationship to the 'leading capitalist forces' in society, through it being conceived of as an 'instrument of the ruling class', with this generally flowing from Marx and Engels' (1975d p. 35) famous pronouncement that 'the executive of the modern State is but a committee for managing the common affairs of the whole bourgeoisie.' This view can be found to varying degrees, for example, in the works of Lenin (1965, p. 369; 1976, pp. 15-19), Kautsky (1983, p. 101 and p. 108) and Laski (1938, p. 193). On the other hand, however, we find to varying degrees an emphasis on the state's relationship to the 'contradictory forces' in society, continually pulling against the leading forces. This can be found in writings which see the state - even in some small way - as a 'factor of social cohesion', with this generally flowing from Engels'

(1972, p. 229) contention in *The Origin of the Family, Private Property and the State* that the state arises out of society to 'keep it within the bounds of order.' This tends to result in a focus on the incorporation of interests into the state apparatus, other than those simply of the ruling class. As shown in Chapter One, this can be found to varying degrees in the works of Miliband (1973, p. 242), Poulantzas (in Blackburn, 1979, p. 246) and Offe (1984, p. 120). A fairly similar emphasis can also be found in various non-Marxist writings such as Lindblom (1979, p. 525), Jordan & Richardson (1987, p. 81), Bauer (Bauer and Gergen, 1968) and Kingdon (1985), where each contains some form of 'pluralist' assumption on the state's incorporation of a multiplicity of interests into policy-making.

The argument presented here suggests that these two 'camps' are actually looking at the same thing (i.e. the state's contradictory role), but are doing so from different angles, hence contributing to, although not determining, their differing assumptions on the nature and role of the state. Thus, the role of the state is one which embodies and upholds the *contradictory rule of one class over another*.

This can be narrowed down further in order to consider both 'policy' and 'policy formation'. In considering 'policy' first of all, we can recognise, as Dillon (1976, p. 47) notes, that 'there is no one universally acclaimed definition' of policy. For example, Dror (1983, p. 14) defines it as 'general directives...on the main lines of actions to be followed.' Dye (1976, p. 1) describes it as 'whatever governments choose to do or not to do,' whilst Anderson (1976a, p. vii) defines it as 'a purposive course of action followed by an actor or set of actors in dealing with a problem or matter of concern.' Despite these varying definitions, however, each contains (implicitly or explicitly) two common denominators upon which we can build.

First, and either directly or indirectly, each contains the recognition that somehow 'policy' is a *concentration* of the state's activities. To relate this back to the suggestion a moment ago that the state upholds the contradictory rule of one class over another, it is possible to say, therefore, that:

'policy' is a concentrated activity of the state, in legal and/or constitutionally legitimate form, which contains a decision to proceed with a particular course of action (or inaction) and which will tend to uphold the contradictory rule of one class over another.

Policy may tend to benefit either all or some sections of capital and, hence, it has one 'face' in the form of the 'leading capitalist forces' in society. It cannot, however, legislate out of existence its contradictory effects or the 'human' characteristics of all living individuals. Hence, its other 'face' is that of the 'contradictory forces' in society.

An example of this which is highly relevant to the present discussion, is the modern domestic rating system. On the one hand, it was part of the 'leading capitalist forces' in society. It emerged historically to be one means - financed largely since the 1960s by the property-owning middle classes - of funding the activities of local government (see Chapter Three and Appendix). Hence, it was a means of financing the management of the uneven development of capitalism, because, as Duncan and Goodwin (1988, p. 72) suggest, 'state systems need to be developed at a local, subnational level if dominant groups are to confront fully the problems of the uneven development of societies and of nature.' Following on from this, therefore, it provided a decentralised means of financing local infrastructures, reproducing people as 'fit to work' and maintaining social stability through local electoral politics performing the role of what Cockburn (1977, p. 49) describes as 'institutionalis[ing] class contest.' In one sense, it is not possible to say that this benefited any particular section of capital more than another. For example, some capitals with an interest in the domestic transport of goods were advantaged in direct terms. Some capitals, however, also benefited indirectly. Even the City of London benefited, irrespective of whether or not it had a stake in domestic-orientated capitals, because by contributing to local social stability, domestic rates also contributed in some way to the stability of national governments which sanctioned the framework for the City's operations (and those large industrial capitals which were tied partly to its international orientations). In another sense, therefore, it *is* possible to say that some capitals benefited more than others. This is because local government and the modern domestic rating system contributed to maintaining the existing distribution of power - namely, the 'leading capitalist forces' as dominated by large internationally-orientated financial and industrial capital. A further exploration of this will be conducted in the next chapter.

Correspondingly, however, when the rating system is viewed from another angle, we realise that it was not simply a one-sided vehicle for the 'leading capitalist forces' in society. It was also part of the 'contradictory forces' in society because it contained the seeds for a reaction against the 'leading' forces. The setting (or non-setting) of rates levels allowed 'left-wing' councils and others the opportunity to react against central government's general strategy and specific policies. This was evident in the campaign against rate-capping in the mid-1980s (see Chapter Three), with this being generally indicative of the potential for the resources of domestic and non-domestic ratepayers to be spent on services not only inimical to the philosophy of central government, but favourable to what Gyford (1985, p. 21) describes as 'bodies of ideas...which create a climate of opinion favourable to a more decentralised form of socialist politics.' Furthermore, the nature of rates as a tax which Richards (1988, p. 25), describes in pre-Poll Tax days as 'the most unpopular of all taxes', resulted in a number of middle-class revolts which to varying degrees (as in the revolt which led eventually in 1967-68 to the introduction of 100 per cent rebates), inflicted 'damage' on the centre's overall strategy (see Appendix). For all of these reasons, therefore, the rating system, as a state policy, should also be seen as embodying the 'contradictory forces' in society, and hence upholding the *contradictory rule of one class over another.*

Second, in terms of the main components of 'policy', each of the definitions assumes the necessity of future activity, and in effect that 'something has to be done'. Why, it might be asked, is this the case? The answer, in many respects, lies in 'policy feedback' as outlined by Bachrach and Baratz, but needs to be extended and viewed from the standpoint of the present discussion on dialectics and dialectical movement. Thus, it can be suggested that the necessity of future activity - namely the impetus for policy formation - arises because:

'leading capitalist forces' in society continually confront and create 'contradictory forces'. Policies are part of these leading forces, which can develop to such an extent that the 'contradictory forces' in society (which policies are also part of because the contain the seeds for a reaction against the leading forces) may hold back the development of these same 'leading capitalist forces'.

In terms of local taxation, we can see, for example, that this is precisely the situation that existed from the 1830s-40s to the 1920s (see Appendix). A key component of the 'leading capitalist forces' was the rise of industrial capital, with this helping to create 'contradictory forces' in the form of the ravages of industrialisation and its effect on the revolutionary potential of the working class. Thus, the leading forces were creating pressures for a mechanism which would help to finance local infrastructures for the transport of goods, and at the same time ameliorate working class social deprivation in order to reproduce people as 'fit to work' and dampen their revolutionary potential. As a result, the existing policy (i.e. an essentially fragmented system of financing local government through a multiplicity of rates), simply held this back because it could not cope with the problems of co-ordinating and collecting a growing volume and magnitude of local rates.

Returning to a general level, the key characteristics of this can be extrapolated and applied to the process of policy formation. In essence, these are 'dialectical' developments of themes outlined in Chapter One in term of the role of decision-making objectives (Simon), policy formation proceeding through stages (Hogwood and Gunn), and biases within the policy formation process (Downs, Bachrach and Baratz, Lindblom, Richardson and Jordan et al., Miliband, Poulantzas and Offe). Thus, policy formation can be described, at some length, as:

> the historical process arising as a result of 'leading capitalist forces' continually confronting and creating 'contradictory forces'. Policies are part of these leading forces, which can develop to such an extent that the 'contradictory forces' in society (which policies are also apart of because they contain the seeds for a reaction against the leading forces) may hold back the development of these same 'leading capitalist forces'. This results in the state concentrating its activities in order to formulate a decision to proceed with a particular course of action (or inaction). This then gives rise to a struggle between an array of interest, with the state being part of and mediating between these as it attempts to *take the lead and take control* gradually of the process of policy formation and uphold the contradictory rule of one class over another. All things being equal, this culminates in a new 'policy' and a further development in the *contradictory rule of one class over another class*.

It should be clearly understood that a new policy does not *automatically* result from the initial impetus, and the remainder of the chapter must be read with this in mind. Hogwood and Gunn (1984, p. 21) note, for example, that 'policy behaviour includes failures to act and deliberate decisions not to act.' Governments may also set up enquiries which are essentially 'palliatives', in the hope that the issue will pass quickly through the 'alarmed discovery' stage of Downs' (1972) 'issue-attention cycle' and public interest will gradually subside. Similarly, governments may produce what Stringer and Richardson (1980, p. 29) term 'placebo policies' which introduce highly minimal measures to do little else than remove an item from the political agenda. Correspondingly, however, seemingly well-intentioned attempts to produce a new policy may never be realised. To varying degrees the 1971 Green Paper (Cmnd. 4741, 1971), the setting up of the Layfield Enquiry and the 1981 Green Paper (Cmnd. 8449, 1981) all fall into this category (see Chapter Three). In their various ways, each resulted in the conclusion that a workable replacement for domestic rates was not possible. More generally, policy-makers may fail to produce what Bauer termed a 'minimum winning coalition', sufficient to allow the policy formation process to proceed with a workable degree of legitimacy.

These points, and also the definition given of policy formation, immediately beg two important questions. First, it must be asked - when do contradictions become so problematic for key decision-making actors within the state that they embark on a process of policy formation? The answer to this is that there is no scientific 'point' which is reached. It is simply a matter of key decision-making actors within the state, perceiving that an existing policy, or the absence of one, is incompatible with their general strategy. To put it in the language used by Kingdon, the convergence of problems, politics and policies may result in policy makers perceiving that there is an 'open window', allowing them to look out (by desire or necessity) at the prospect of a 'new' policy. The aforementioned (failed) attempts to reform the rating system seem to indicate an initial perception of 'incompatibility' (i.e. the 'window' seemed to be open), but then a subsequent resigned acceptance of the prevailing situation(s) as more compatible with their general strategies than any replacement for domestic rates would have been (i.e. there was little option but to close the 'window'!).

Second, what is meant in terms of the state attempting to 'take the lead and take control' of the process of policy formation? This can be answered through an attempt now to 'flesh out' the process of policy formation by looking 'dialectically' and in detail at key features of the liberal-democratic Parliamentary state. The focus here will be on the British Parliamentary state, although there is certainly the potential to consider the broad principles as applicable to states in other liberal-democratic polities. [1]

The Parliamentary State: Taking Control of Policy Formation

Parliament in 20th century Britain is not a 'sham'. It embodies legal rights of citizenship which, as Anderson (1976b. p. 28) observes, are 'not a mere mirage...[but] a tangible reality.' The starting point for consideration of these is Britain's largely unwritten constitution (see Norton, 1984, pp. 1-32) where the quintessential feature is that Parliament is sovereign. Dicey (1965, p. 40) in his classic 1885 work on the constitution, described this as 'the right to make or unmake any law whatever', and as de Smith (1974, p. 65) notes 'every other law-making body within the realm either derives its authority from Parliament or exercises it at the sufferance of Parliament.' If Parliament is sovereign, however, most writings on the constitution recognise ultimately in their own way, as Tony Benn (1982, p. 55) puts it, that 'the people are sovereign and Parliament is their voice.' This is crucial, because, if through Parliament the 'people' are sovereign and they are imbued with certain rights (the right to vote, free speech, political activity, etc., which underpin the writings of Dahl, Lindblom, Richardson and Jordan et al.), then how can this possibly be reconciled with the dominance of one class over another? An attempt can be made to answer this by looking in turn at the *nature*, *structure* and *operation* of the parliamentary state, and the way in which each of these plays a key role in controlling the process of policy formation and upholding the role of 'leading capitalist forces' in this process and so upholding the *contradictory rule of one class over another*.

The Nature of Parliamentary Democracy

There are two key components of this which are central to the present discussion, and these link-in to themes outlined in Chapter One in terms of electoral mechanisms (Downs), democratic constraints (Dahl), and the shaping of consciousness (Lukes). These key components are the ideology of liberalism and the related matter of the sovereignty of Parliament.

The first of these refers to Parliament's permeation and dominance by liberal theory ever since the 1688 settlement which secured its dominance over the Crown within the state. As Eccleshall (1984, p. 40) notes 'liberalism is the ideology most intimately connected with the birth and evolution of the modern, capitalist world.' The key point to be made here is that the works of individuals such as Locke (1990), Bentham (1970), J.S. Mill (1984) and others have helped to provide the ideological justification for the establishment and continuing development of Parliamentary government. A central tenet of these and all liberal theories is that, in their various ways, they uphold the key principles which are necessary for capital accumulation, since, within each, there is the recognition of the right to private property. Thus, as MacPherson (1978, p. 4) argues 'democratic government...exists to uphold and enforce a certain kind of society, a certain set of relations between individuals, a certain set of rights and claims that people have on each other both directly and indirectly through their rights to property.' Thus, the liberal ethos helps to control the process of policy formation by setting 'capitalist' parameters, but with the embodiment therein of liberal freedoms resulting in it upholding the *contradictory rule of one class over another*.

The second factor to be considered is the sovereignty of Parliament. This is rooted in the hegemony within the tradition of modern Parliamentary government of a particular variant of liberal democracy which, as Lukes (1974, p. 34) puts it highly rarefied terms 'takes men as they are and applies want regarding principles to them, relating their interests to what they actually want or prefer, to their policy preferences as manifested by their political participation,' these being expressed through 'representatives' in interest groups and competing political parties'. In practice, of course, people are not as 'rational' as this and there is unequal access to information and inequalities of knowledge (Bealey, 1988, pp. 8-13). Nevertheless, Parliamentary sovereignty is seen constitutionally, and however nebulously, as embodying the 'will of the people'. Thus, in very broad terms it seems reasonable to concur with Anderson (1976b, p.31) when he suggests that there exists 'a belief by the masses that *they exercise an ultimate self-determination* within the existing order.' Parliamentary sovereignty, therefore, should be seen as a 'leading capitalist force', and as an expression of Marx's 'ruling ideas' of the ruling class, and also of Gramsci's (1978, pp. 181-2) 'intellectual and moral unity, posing all the questions around which the struggle rages...thus creating the hegemony of a fundamental social group over a series of social groups.' As a result, it is possible to talk of a general consent (genuine, false or resigned) on the part of working class people that their rights to free expression, autonomous action, political participation in the process of policy formation etc., are subject ultimately to channelling through and governance by Parliament. Dialectically speaking, however, there is also a contradiction in this. Namely, that by performing a pivotal role in co-ordinating and controlling the process of policy formation and allowing working class people (and capital) access to Parliamentary state power for what Miliband (1982, p. 54) describes as 'the smooth functioning of capitalist democracy', then Parliamentary sovereignty simultaneously upholds the contradictory class nature of society and hence the *contradictory rule* of one class over another in the process of policy formation.

A brief additional point must be made with regard to this, in that whilst Parliament itself is sovereign, the state is fragmented. With specific regard to present concerns, the state has its 'local' arm in terms of local government. Dialectically speaking, however, the local state embodies a contradictory role. On the one hand, it is part of the 'leading capitalist forces' in society, through its being tied inexorably to central government's general strategy via centrally-determined legislation, reinforced by the doctrine of *ultra vires*, and relying heavily on central funding and persistent changes in its volume and character. On the other hand, however, it is also part of the 'contradictory forces' in society. Elcock's (1982, p. 45) statement that there exists 'two contradictory constitutional traditions' is useful here, because it indicates that there exists, even in the vaguest constitutional sense, a 'right' of local authorities to pursue policies/activities which react in some way against the centre's leading strategy. The campaign against rate-capping in the mid-1980s is a case in point (see Chapter Three). Overall, therefore, Miliband (1982, p. 49) makes a useful point when he suggests that local states are 'instruments of central control and obstacles to it.' Thus, the local state should be seen as embodying and upholding the *contradictory rule of one class over another*. This point will be returned to briefly in the Conclusion, when it is related directly to the Poll Tax policy formation process.

The Structure of the Parliamentary State

The position of the Executive (the Cabinet) is also crucial, as recognised by Miliband, to our understanding of the way in which the parliamentary state takes the lead and takes control of the process of policy formation.

In the first instance, there are the authoritative decision-making powers of the Parliamentary state. These are invested constitutionally in the Executive because it is drawn from the ranks of the majority party in the Commons. Thus, imbued with these executive powers, it is the focal point for wider contradictions in society and has the authority to 'act' on them by proposing legislation. As a consequence, it is a crucial component of the 'leading capitalist forces' in society. Dialectically speaking, however, the Cabinet is not simply a one-sided vehicle for initiating policies in the interests of 'leading capitalist forces'. It also embodies the 'contradictory forces' in society because it is not isolated from the external world and the range of 'contradictory forces' which are constantly manifesting themselves. The Cabinet also contains individuals who have the autonomy for recalcitrance and/or to propound alternative policies/strategies.

In performing this leading decision-taking role (imbued with contradictions), it is important to recognise the point made by Peter Hennessy (1988, p. 4) when he suggests that 'Cabinet Government remains a putty-like concept. A prime minster can make of it very largely what he or she will, provided colleagues do not baulk at their treatment.' This is indeed a profound statement. It indicates that Cabinet government, depending on the precise historical circumstances, is sufficiently *flexible*, in that it can accommodate a variety of types of decision-making (with the results backed by the doctrine of collective responsibility) which arise to promote policies that are intended to become part of the 'leading capitalist forces' in society. In Margaret Thatcher, for example, we find what Kavanagh (1986, p. 3) describes as a 'mobilising style' of leadership, in a period when a general restructuring of class relations in favour of capital, required something like an 'extraordinarily assertive' personality (King, 1988, p. 118) to ensure that Cabinet and Backbench 'wets' and 'shirkers' did not lose their nerve (if they didn't lose their posts) in following through a radical strategy. Thus, Cabinet government is sufficiently flexible to ensure that in a variety of historical circumstances, it is able to embody and uphold the *contradictory rule of one class over another* in the process of policy formation.

The position of the Executive is also crucial in the passage of Bills through Parliament - thus raising questions over the importance given to the social/educational backgrounds of MPs by Miliband (see Chapter One). The position of the Executive can be viewed as one where the Executive dominates, but in a contradictory way. Let us consider each of these elements in turn.

On the one hand, Lord Hailsham's (1978) famous charge of an 'elective dictatorship' is well supported by a host of evidence and arguments. John Garrett (1992, p. 16) sums up this view when he suggests that 'in every function of Parliament, government throws its weight, not only against any opposition to its will, but against enquiry, scrutiny and discussion.' There are a number of factors which have facilitated this. In the first instance, gradual extensions of the franchise have 'served as a powerful incentive for the parties to attune and expand their embryonic organisations to the requirements of the developing "mass democracy"' (Judge, 1993, p. 77). Thus, bolstered by the vagaries of the first-past-the post electoral system, the Commons has tended to devolve along party lines and be dominated by the two main parties. Furthermore, once a government is installed within the Parliamentary structure, as Judge (1983, p. 190) suggests - 'the normative system of the House...reflects the predilections of the most powerful actors and so supports the existing distribution of power.' This occurs because the Executive is at the apex of the hierarchies of both the Civil Service and the House. Consequently, it has access to the specialist knowledge of the Civil Service, and it can buttress this through the Prime Minister's powers of patronage which help promote generalist norms in the House. Given, therefore, that 'the norms of the House and the career aspirations of most backbenchers are...focused upon, the executive itself' (Judge, 1983, p. 189), and allowing for the conjunction of this with the whip system and the broad intra-party ideology which tends to make partisan allegiance a desirable activity anyway, then as Brand (1992, p. 20) suggests, 'the party will normally stand behind its chosen leader and his or her team to reject virtually any criticisms from the other side.'

When viewed from one angle, therefore, there is indeed a case for perceiving that Parliament is dominated by the Executive, and this is borne out by empirical evidence. For example, Norton (1993, p. 80) reveals that on only three occasions this century, has a bill been lost at the crucial Second Reading stage, and it is only on the most recent of these (the 1986 *Shops Bill*) that the Government commanded an overall majority in the House. Thus, 'the hegemony of government in achieving the passage of its bills is clear' and Parliament's ability to substantially alter a Bill exists 'only at the margins' (Norton, 1993, pp. 80-1).

The principle of dialectics, however, tells us that there is also a contradictory tendency towards independence from executive domination. As Adonis (1990, p. 18) suggests - 'The power of Parliament may be difficult to weigh and measure; but it is a reality nonetheless.' A number of factors are important in facilitating this. The relationships with the governing party (indeed within any party) are not a one-way flow of information and influence from the government to backbenchers, and Executive dominance does not preclude the widespread articulation of dissatisfaction. The potential for this increases because parties are 'broad churches' which contain formal/informal factions within them. More specifically, Rose (1982) makes the distinction between inner circle and outer circle MPs. The behaviour of the former is very much influenced by government, whilst the behaviour of the latter is very distant from this because some MPs may adopt roles as expressive enthusiasts for causes and interests, publicity-seekers, extra-parliamentary careerists and constituency representatives.

When viewed from this other angle, therefore, there *is* a case for perceiving that Executive domination is not absolute. This is also supported by empirical evidence. For example in 1969, the Labour Government abandoned proposals to introduce an Industrial Relations Bill partly as a result of the combination of (i) a Cabinet split and (ii) 55 cross-votes against the White Paper *In Place of Strife* and the Chief Whip being unable to guarantee the Bill's legislative passage (Norton, 1975, pp. 611-13). In 1981, the Government abandoned plans to introduce referendums on local rates levels, after substantial resistance from Conservative backbenchers, including 30 who signed and Early Day Motion in protest (*Local Government Chronicle*, 20 November 1981). Also, in 1984, Education Secretary Sir Keith Joseph's attempt to increase parental contributions for students in higher education, was withdrawn after a motion of protest was signed by 93 Conservative backbenchers (Derbyshire and Derbyshire, 1990, p. 130).

Overall, therefore, in terms of the structure of Parliament and in particular the House of Commons (the House of Lords will be dealt with briefly in Chapter Seven), it can be suggested that the Executive dominates, but in a contradictory way. Thus, Parliament is largely a vehicle for 'getting things done' in terms of policy formation in a capitalist society. It is part of the 'leading capitalist forces' whilst containing a multiplicity of partly countervailing views and thus also embodying the 'contradictory forces' in society. As a result, it takes the lead and takes control of the process of policy formation and so embodies and upholds the *contradictory rule of one class over another*.

The 'Discretion' of Key Actors in the Parliamentary State

State actors, as already suggested, have 'autonomy' in the sense of being part of and able to reflect and act upon very powerful contradictory forces in society. This autonomy is crucial, since it illustrates that key decision-makers within the Parliamentary state have substantial freedom to determine the precise way that a policy formation process will be led. This can be expanded by recognising, as Hogwood (1987, Ch. 3) does, that there are a whole host of ways (although still rooted in particular historical circumstances) in which issues can be 'processed' once on the political agenda. He categorises these as (i) imposition, (ii) internalised within Government, (iii) processable through consultation, (iv) policy emerges from practice, and (v) non-internalisable.

It seems useful to focus briefly on *one* of these (consultation) because of its relevance to the Poll Tax policy formation process (see Chapter Seven for details). It is recognised, of course, that consultation may take place in 'policy communities', but it seems useful to narrow this down even further and focus *specifically* on the 'consultative' nature of Green papers. In the first instance, therefore, as Englefield (1985, p. 62) notes, there is 'no inter-departmental policy, indeed sometimes no clear policy within a single department, as to the status and form of publication of these papers.' This is important, because it shows that in the same manner as Cabinet Government (and indeed, the bulk of the British 'constitution'), they can be 'moulded' with relative ease. This malleability gives them the potential to play a leading role in the policy formation process - depending on the prevailing circumstances. Given the sovereignty of Parliament and the existence of a widespread 'consent' that political grievances should be channelled through it (directly or indirectly), then Green Papers should be seen as one component of the 'leading capitalist forces' in society. They 'suck in' a variety of opposition to policies, yet it is constitutionally legitimate for governments to then interpret the results of a consultation exercise in any way that they want (provided that they stay within the unwritten convention of doing so in the 'national interest') in order to decide whether or not to proceed with a particular policy.

In a sense, then, Hogwood's (1987, p. 49) adaptation of Wildavsky in the statement 'If consultation is everything, maybe it's nothing' is partly correct. The malleability of consultation does mean that it is not 'everything', although it is certainly far from 'nothing'. In providing the opportunity for a 'trial' opposition to a policy, it also embodies 'contradictory forces' because it allows a range of interests to react against a policy proposal. Thus, Green Papers 'lead' but incorporate discontent in doing so, and hence as one component of a process of policy formation, they embody and uphold the *contradictory rule of one class over another*.

Conclusion

This chapter has attempted to go some way towards filling the 'gap' in our understanding of state policy formation. It began by arguing the usefulness of Marxist dialectical principles as a foundation for analysis. It then used these in order to produce a general definition of state policy formation and its dynamic nature. Finally, it 'fleshed out' this definition by discussing the contradictions of the British Parliamentary state - focusing particularly on its 'leading and controlling' roles in the policy formation process. It seems useful here to recap and summarize the main principles identified as central to our understanding of state policy formation in liberal democracies.

1. 'Leading capitalist forces' in society are continually confronting and creating 'contradictory forces'.

2. Policies are part of these leading forces, although these forces can develop to such an extent that the 'contradictory forces' (with policies also being part of these) may hold back the development of the leading forces to the extent that key decision-making actors within the state perceive a particular policy to be incompatible with their strategy.

3. A commitment may then be made to begin a process with a view to producing a replacement policy.

4. This gives rise to a struggle between an array of interests, with the state being part of and mediating between these as it attempts to take the lead and take control gradually of the policy formation process.

5. In terms of the British Parliamentary state, it does so through (i) the capitalist parameters set by liberalism, (ii) the sovereignty of Parliament which acts as a focus for expressed interests, (iii) the dominance of the Executive in terms of decision-taking and the legislative passage of Bills - acting as a vehicle for 'getting things done' in the policy formation process, and (iv) the autonomy of key state actors in deciding the particular type of strategy used to 'lead' the policy formation process i.e. consultation, imposition etc.

6. The end result is a 'new' policy, containing within it the seeds for further development as it operates in the context of the pressures of a contradictory class society.

As identified at the beginning of this chapter, further research is undoubtedly called for in order to subject these principles to more comprehensive analysis. Furthermore, any attempt to identify 'general' principles is liable to be criticised on the grounds that it is not rooted in historical or empirical research. Nevertheless, an initial attempt can be made to address such criticisms through a case study of one particular policy formation process i.e. the Poll Tax. It is to this task that we can now turn.

Notes

1. Much of the discussion hereafter on the contradictions of Parliament is contained and explored further in McConnell and Pyper (1994). This is a case study of the Select Committee on Scottish Affairs and the 'contradictions' within it.

3 Origins and Development of the Thatcher Government

David McCrone (1987, p. 7) describes the Poll Tax as a 'creature of its time.' This is an important statement, because it begs us to ask two vital and interrelated questions. First, what actually is the 'time', or the 'political' and 'economic' context within which the Poll Tax policy formation process took place? Second, given that historical relationships are not continually created anew, but are what Dobb (1947, p. 11) describes as 'contained within the womb of the old', then what aspects of the 'time' preceding it are relevant to our understanding of this? In order to address these questions, the structure of the present chapter is a follows.

First, it outlines briefly the 'political' and 'economic' legacies of the 1970-74 Heath Government, and locates within these a failed attempt to abolish the domestic rating system. This seems a useful period to commence with, given both its impact on the Wilson/Callaghan/Thatcher Governments, and the fact that the period contains the first apparently serious attempt in the post-war period to *abolish* the rating system. Second, it builds on this and identifies the development of key relationships under the 1974-79 Wilson/Callaghan Governments, and also identifies in the context of these, a 'crisis' in local finance and yet another failure to find a suitable alternative to the rates. Third, it takes all this a stage further in terms of the 1979 to 1984-85 Thatcher Government (until the 1985 property revaluation in Scotland), and identifies its immediate origins in the 'failures' of the previous Heath and Wilson/Callaghan administrations. It also locates within this the substantial developments in local government and local taxation - including a further failed attempt to find an alternative to the rating system. Finally, the Conclusion will briefly place the chapter in its policy formation context. It will focus particularly on the 'leading capitalist forces' under the directorship of the Thatcher Government, and the way in which they helped create a series of 'contradictory forces' - thus allowing us to identify the general forces which will feed-in to our study of the Poll Tax policy formation process in the next four chapters.

There are two points of note which need to be added to all this. In the first instance, the prime focus of the chapter (in each of the periods mentioned above) is on the dynamic relationship between the electorate and the labour movement on the one hand, and key sections of internationally oriented and domestic capital on the other. These *dynamic* relationships are explored throughout the chapter in terms of (a) the relationships and alliances that formed the basis of each government coming to power, (b) the main thrust of the policies that were pursued, (c) the contradictions that emerged as a result of these, thus paving the way for subsequent development, and (d) the overall impact of these on the development of local taxation. The organisation of material in this way will assist our focus on policy formation as a dialectical process.

A second and final point of note is that given the importance of Scotland within the Poll Tax policy formation process, the comparative 'uneven development' of key Scottish 'political' and 'economic' relations will be located within the discussion, where appropriate. In doing so, it is obvious that coverage of a vast array of historical relationships within the space of one chapter requires a considerable degree of selectivity. It is also obvious that any outline of historical relationships is open to criticism from the predilections of others. It is hoped that such matters will not be problematic, however, and that the approach taken here will be justified through its laying of a clear and coherent *general* foundation for detailed discussion in the next four chapters, of the Poll Tax as a *specific* process of policy formation.

The Legacy of the 1970-74 Heath Government

The nature of key relationships under the Wilson/Callaghan Governments can best be understood by considering first of all their relationships to the 'failures' of the preceding Conservative Government under the leadership of Ted Heath. Two main factors are important in this respect.

In the first instance, Heath had failed in his attempt to introduce free-market 'Selsdon Man' policies, in the form of such measures as free collective bargaining (within the restrictions of the 1971 *Industrial Relations Act*), a 'hands-off' approach to industrial subsidies, and the phasing out of the Regional Employment Premium. This strategy was effectively destroyed because world commodity prices increased; inflation almost doubled to 8 per cent by 1972 (Donaldson and Farquhar, 1988, p. 9); unemployment reached 950,000 by 1972 (Pollard, 1983, p. 328), and there was substantial trade union opposition to the *Industrial Relations Act* and Heath's 'hands off' approach - exemplified by a reversal of the decision to let Upper Clyde Shipbuilders slip into liquidation (see Foster and Woolfson, 1986). Acting in conjunction with the collapse of the post-war fixing of exchange rates against the Dollar (which seemed to remove the balance of payments constraint on domestic expansion), Heath then performed a U-turn and the economy was expanded via the so-called 'Barber Boom', with a prices and incomes policy being introduced to suppress inflationary pressures. In the event, however, of OPEC's four-fold increase in oil prices in November 1973 and the subsequent rise in inflation to 20.5 per cent in the month before Heath departed office (Central Statistical Office, June 1974), the trades unions fought to defend the real value of wages - epitomised in the miners' strike and a direct challenge to Heath's pay policy. The result of this at a time when coal stocks were diminishing and the price of oil was rising dramatically, was a State of Emergency; a three-day week, and finally the calling of a General Election - effectively on the matter of 'Who Governs Britain?'

In the second instance, and building upon the foregoing in order to provide us with an overall picture of the historical circumstances prevailing when Labour came into office, there is the crucial position of three main sections of capital. It is necessary to provide a brief overview of each of these, since they permeate and are central to the discussion of the Poll Tax policy formation process in subsequent chapters.

First, there is large internationally oriented finance capital, which can be equated here with the 'City of London'. It is principally through the levers of interest rates and exchange rates that the City, as Costello et al., (1989, p. 122) suggest, 'has shaped state policies throughout the century and effectively writes the rules of the game for British governments.' By the end of 1973, however, the position of sterling was being threatened. This was because of the domestic and international surge in inflation, leading to a decline in the attractiveness of sterling (hence devaluing it) because UK inflation was higher than elsewhere (Gardner, 1987, pp. 84-5).

Second, there is large industrial capital (as represented principally through the CBI and the Institute of Directors), which has both domestic *and* international links - often through the City. Certainly, there is considerable debate as to the extent of this linkage and to whether or not there is real coherence between the City and large industrial capital (see Thompson, 1977; and Fine and Harris, 1985 for competing views). It is undeniable, however, that they are not isolated from one another and that there *is* some form of integration. As Overbeek (1980, p. 102) notes, this has been 'informal', through informal and familial ties. It has also been 'formal', however, through advising on mergers and takeovers, managing investment portfolios, share ownership, long-term credits and bonds, short-term credits and interlocking directorships. This link reveals to us the contradictory position of many big industrial capitals. On the one hand, their fortunes depend on the promotion of the international interests of the City, through, for example, the trading in shares, and the benefits of cheap imports of materials through a high exchange rate. On the other hand, their fortunes are contingent on the promotion of the interests of their domestic activities, through for example a maintenance of domestic demand which is not impinged upon by deflationary measures, or in a low exchange rate which results in more competitive exports. It must be stressed that these are general examples, but nevertheless they illustrate the ambivalence of many large industrial capitals in having essentially conflicting international and domestic orientations.

In terms of the position of large industrial capital when Wilson came to office, it was obvious that its domestic 'face' had been suffering in the post-war period from 'de-industrialisation' because of competition (particularly from Japan and West Germany), the decline of colonial markets, and periods of domestic deflation to maintain the value of sterling. This was then exacerbated by Heath's 'hand off' approach and the surge in inflation, with manufacturing employment falling by just over 12 per cent between 1969 and 1973 (Buxton in Saville, 1985, p. 58). [1]

Third, there is medium and small capital which is essentially domestic in its operations, and which is represented by the various Chambers of Commerce and trade associations. These tended continually to bear the brunt of domestic deflationary measures, especially since they were unlikely to have access to funds in the City. Figures given by the *Bolton Report* (Cmnd. 4811, 1971, p. 58) show that the contribution of small businesses towards UK manufacturing employment declined from 37 per cent in 1948 to 29 per cent in 1968. Between 1970 and 1973 under Heath, it declined further to an average of 27 per cent in this period (Barber, 1989, p. 142).

The Legacy in Scotland

It is important to realise that the economic characteristics detailed above were spread unevenly throughout the country - particularly in Scotland. It is necessary that we consider why this is so, given that it is in Scotland that the impetus for the Poll Tax would finally emerge in 1985. Thus, just as Scotland was uneven 'politically' (i.e. compared to the UK as a whole) in that there was a Labour electoral majority and had been since 1964, it was also uneven 'economically' in that the process of domestic contraction was felt particularly in the regions. Why, might we ask, was this so? Certainly, large Scottish capital had undergone integrating processes similar to British capital as a whole. Scott and Hughes (in Brown, 1975, p. 179) found a growing link (as a consequence of 60 individuals holding a series of interlocking directorships) between (i) major industrial capitals such as Burmah Oil and Scottish & Newcastle Breweries (represented by an independent Scottish CBI and again to a lesser extent a Scottish Institute of Directors), and (ii) Scottish financial capital - particularly investment trusts and particularly in Edinburgh. Nevertheless, the key factors in differentiating this and the Scottish economy from the South were three-fold.

First, there was its physical distance from the vast bulk of Britain's financial institutions in the South-East, and hence from the benefits accruing from this in terms of growth, employment and incomes. Second, there was the higher incidence of manufacturing and traditional heavier industries in Scotland (principally coal, iron and steel, mechanical engineering and shipbuilding), compared to the UK as a whole. Finally, and even before the Heath Government, the process of contraction was *not* matched by a strong regional policy, despite such measures as the Regional Employment Premium and financial incentives associated with Special Development Areas. Certainly, in comparative terms to the cutbacks of the 1980s, the 1960s and early 70s were what Parsons (1988, p. 179) calls 'almost like a golden age' in regional policy. The period was dogged, nevertheless, by a lack of sufficient funding, with the UK lagging behind its main competitors in terms of industrial assistance (Martin, in Mohan, 1989, p. 97). As a result, according to Firn (1975, p. 1):

'such regions [i.e. Scotland, Wales, Northern Ireland and the north of England] continue to display above average levels of unemployment and net migration together with employee activity rates, per capita incomes and infrastructural developments that are all below the national average.'

Outcomes such as this, compounded by a relatively weak regional policy, indicate a preparedness on the part of governments, to see the decline of Scottish owned and controlled capital, which less than a hundred years previously, had dominated the Scottish economy (Boyle et al. 1989, p. 8). In its place, essentially as a partial substitute for regional policy, there was the willingness to let the Scottish Economy become increasingly reliant on, and thus tied-in to the fortunes of, external capital. This took two main forms.

First, it allowed the integration of Scottish financial capital with the City of London - thus leaving very few sectoral barriers (Gaskin in Saville, 1985). Given its integration with much large industry, then control of this was also transferred South of the Border, and indeed by 1968, 38.3 per cent of employees in Scottish manufacturing plants were subject to control from the South (Boyle et al. 1989, p. 10). This enabled these sectors to gain access to state power at a British level, although it was also accompanied by the vagaries (again due to a variety of circumstances) of profitability relying on both domestic and international factors.

Second, and again as a partial substitute for regional policy, there was a preparedness to let the Scottish economy become particularly open to the fluctuations of the world economy, by allowing the Scottish economy to become a site for inward investment - especially from US multinational capital. Thus, externally owned manufacturing plants accounted for only 4.3 per cent of employment in Scotland in 1950, but this had increased almost four-fold to 16.6 per cent in 1970, with the move being towards such sectors as light engineering and electronics, and the tendency being towards branch-plants (Industry Department Scotland, 1990). In such industries, there was a move towards the payment of higher wage rates, thus partly eroding Scottish/UK wage differentials and hence Scotland's traditional competitiveness.

The Legacy in Local Government Finance

In turning now to Heath's 'legacy' in local government finance, reference must be made first of all to the Appendix (i.e. of the present work), which summarises the main developments in local taxation from feudal times through to 1970. This indicates that by the time the Heath Government came to office, local taxation displayed a number of key characteristics. First, the 'rates' were calculated on the basis of the notional annual rental value of properties in both the domestic and non-domestic sectors (with these being subject to five-yearly revaluations in Scotland). These were then multiplied by separate domestic/non-domestic rates poundages (set by the local authority) in order to determine the sum due. Second, and particularly since the introduction of 100 per cent income-related rebates in the wake of the Allen Report (Cmnd. 2582, 1965), the burden of locally-raised tax revenues fell largely on the propertied middle classes. Third, the autonomy of local authorities in being able to set rate poundages was a constant source of conflict in a number of respects. Local government was seen by many on the 'left' (particularly the Fabians), as a means of providing the finances and the autonomy to build some form of 'municipal socialism'. This unleashed a counter-force, however, (heightened by the visibility of an annual rates bill) in the form of vociferous ratepayers' groups - exemplified by the view of the Secretary of the Sunderland Property Owners Association that 'there exists between Socialism and our Association an open warfare' (quoted in Englander, 1983, p. 65). A final and crucial countervailing force against local autonomy in tax matters, was the reaction of central Government at Westminster - rooted in what Elcock (1982, p. 45) calls 'two contradictory constitutional traditions' whereby there exist two democratically elected governments, each claiming a mandate from the electorate. Thus, in 1928, for example, Churchill could talk of protecting industrial ratepayers from excessive rates burdens, and that 'the working class electorate and its representatives cannot be trusted to perceive where their real interests lie in the matter' (quoted in Mair, 1986, pp. 164-5).

From the point of view of all concerned, therefore, rates were probably what Richards (1988, p. 25) describes in pre-Poll Tax times as 'the most unpopular of all taxes.' Earlier attempts to find a suitable alternative had all failed (see Appendix), and as the Heath Government came to power, local taxation was proving increasingly problematic (also illustrating to us the way in which the rating system is linked inexorably to wider 'economic' and 'political' factors). In 1971, therefore, Heath made an attempt to reform local government finance. This was rooted in proposals to reform the structure of local government - based on the recommendations of the Wheatley Report for Scotland and the Redcliffe-Maud Report for England and Wales. These were intended to tackle the mismatch between the burgeoning responsibilities of local government in the post-war period, and its anachronistic and highly fragmented structure. Thus, as one component of structural reorganisation, it was intended to reform local government finance and to investigate the possibility of an alternative to the rates. Proposals were contained in the Green Paper *The Future of Local Government Finance* (Cmnd. 4741, 1971). The basic 'problem', suggested the Green Paper (Cmnd. 4741, 1971, p. 9) was that local government was 'steadily absorbing an increasing share of real national resources.' The result of this was a gap which had to be filled from either rating yield *or* central government. Both of these solutions, however, were considered to be problematic. On the one hand, rating yield was becoming insufficient because real growth in property values had been slower than the growth in services, and hence large increases in rate poundages would create political problems in the form of hostility from ratepayers. On the other hand, and fitting in clearly with Heath's initial macro-economic policy of fiscal restraint, there was the requirement that the 'Government must remain responsible for controlling the level and distribution of public expenditure in the proportion of national policies' (Cmnd. 4741, 1971, p. 1).

In order to find a suitable alternative, the Green Paper discussed a number of possibilities such as introducing charges, improving the existing rating system, transferring services to the centre and replacing/supplementing the rates with other sources of local revenue. [2] The Green Paper expressed a desire for reform at the 'earliest opportunity', although in the last analysis, this was to fall by the wayside. By the time the Government had gathered the responses to the consultation exercise in the summer of 1973, it was clear that the macro-economic 'U-turn' had effectively blocked any major reform in local government finance. As the Government stated in July 1973, 'the public would not welcome at the present time of price and pay restrictions, the introduction of additional new taxes locally' (quoted in *Municipal Review*, July 1973, p. 194). It is this overall legacy in terms of general 'economic' and 'political' relations, Scotland and local taxation, that now provides us with the basis for comprehending the nature of the incoming Labour Government, and its paving the way subsequently for the Thatcher Government in 1979 and its assault on local government and its autonomy in tax matters.

The Legacy of the Wilson/Callaghan Governments 1974-79

The Labour Party governed from March to September 1974 on the basis of a 'hung' Parliament, until its electoral support increased by 2.1 per cent in the October 1974 General Election. This was sufficient to give it a small working Parliamentary majority of three (Butler, 1989, p. 31). In 1970, Labour had lost a significant number of working class voters to the Conservatives (Franklin, 1985), but it had now managed to recoup some of these votes in the light of Heath's 'failures' - particularly in terms of his trade union legislation and then latterly the massive rise in inflation. In Scotland, Labour remained the dominant party, with 36.3 per cent of the vote and 41 seats, although the Scottish experience of Heath's policies and the question of who would benefit from North Sea Oil (which was due to reach British shores the following year), resulted in a rise in electoral support for the SNP to 30.4 per cent (Kellas, 1989, p. 106). Kellas (1989, p. 134) describes this as 'easily the biggest nationalist advance in recent British electoral history.'

In general terms, therefore, we find that Labour had come to power faced essentially with two main 'problems'. On the one hand, it had entered Parliament on the back of increased working class electoral support, but faced a confident trade union movement that had effectively managed to bring down the Heath Government and was not prepared to see inflation erode incomes. On the other, it faced the power of a fusion of the City and large industrial capital, where a high UK rate of inflation was threatening its profitability both at home and abroad. We can now see how the strategy and policies of the Labour Government were borne out of these relationships.

Strategy and Policies

Founded on its electoral promises, both for its supporters in the labour movement and in the regions, there was the promise of elected Scottish and Welsh assemblies; social security reforms; a transfer of 'wealth and power' back to working people; increased employment protection and a repeal of Heath's *Industrial Relations Act*. In return for these, there was the 'social contract' - an agreement between the TUC and the Labour Government on voluntary wage restraint.

This was also an integral part of Labour's overall strategy for the revival of industrial capital, and in particular its larger sections that had now gained access to EEC markets since joining the European Community on 1st January 1973. In essence, it involved an increased role for the state, and the availability of financial assistance in the form of the National Enterprise Board; planning agreements, and further nationalisation (particularly British Aerospace, British Shipbuilders and the creation of the British National Oil Corporation). Small businesses were also given some consideration after the findings of the *Bolton Report* (Cmnd. 4811, 1971), and the main impact was a small firms employment subsidy in manufacturing and the setting up of the Small Firms Counselling Service. Furthermore, for Scotland and the regions (the promise of devolution aside), there was a strengthening of regional policy through the Scottish Secretary being given the power to grant Selective Financial Assistance; a doubling of the Regional Employment Premium and a further welcoming of external multinational capital via the creation of the Scottish Development Agency.

The City's link with large industry meant that it would also benefit from the 'social contract', through both keeping costs down for industries that it was helping to finance, and through helping to lower inflation and so promote confidence in sterling and the British economy. As a potential obstruction to this, however, there was the problem for the Government of what to do about a massive balance of payments deficit. It could not be tackled by devaluation (because exchange rates were no longer fixed) and the weakness of the pound ensured that a further slide was not a feasible option. Thus, in deference to this and with an unwillingness to deflate the domestic economy because of its 'reformist' promises, it was decided to finance the deficit via external borrowing, on the assumption that future revenues from North Sea Oil would enable repayments to be met.

Local Government and the Rates

Heath's failure to produce an alternative form of local government finance had left the rating system exposed to the massive increase in inflation. Acting in conjunction with costs associated with local government reorganisation and the budget decisions of local authorities attempting to minimise the impact of rising costs, this led to average increases in non-domestic rates bills by 40 per cent in April 1974, and average increases in domestic rates bills of 29 per cent, with some increases being as high as in excess of 160 per cent (Cmnd. 6453, 1976, p. 5; Cmnd. 6813, 1977, p. 16). The result was a backlash from ratepayers. In the October General Election, therefore, the Conservatives' response in their manifesto (with Margaret Thatcher now Shadow Environment Secretary) was to state that 'within the normal lifetime of a Parliament we shall abolish the domestic rating system and replace it by taxes more broadly based and related to people's ability to pay' (Craig, 1975, p. 436). The Labour Government's response, however, was more cautious. In the short-term, it increased Rate Support Grant (as a percentage of Relevant Expenditure) from 60.5 per cent in 1974-75 to 66.5 per cent in 1975-76 (Travers, 1986b, p. 41). In Scotland, the rise was from 71 per cent to 75.4 per cent over the same period (Heald et al. 1981, p. 31). In the long term, however, Labour set up the Layfield Committee. Its remit was to review the system of local government finance and to make recommendations - the entire area being treated as a matter of urgency by the Government

The Contradictions of the Government's Policies

The policies of the Labour Government reacted back on the general 'political' and 'economic' environments in two main stages. These were also to provide the basis for a crucial watershed in local government finance.

First, there was the combined impact of the international economy and the labour movement's experience of the 'social contract', resulting in a sterling crisis and policy change. In considering these in greater detail, inflation for 1976 had come down to an average of 17 per cent from the 24 per cent figure for the previous year (Artis, 1989, p. 48), yet this was far higher than most other developed economies (Gardner, 1987, p. 68). As a result, currency holders began speculating, not just because of this, but also because of what Burden and Campbell (1985, p. 29) describe as 'some concern that the government might stick to its radical manifesto.' The impact of all this was a gradual weakening of sterling to a low of $1.50 in October 1976, and the Government's currency reserves becoming virtually depleted. Thus, with borrowing repayments in excess of £1 billion due in December, the Government applied to the International Monetary Fund for a loan of £3.9 billion (Gardner, 1987, p. 64). The loan was provided, subject to the conditions that the UK discipline its economy by cutting the PSBR; selling £500 million BP shares and reducing the money supply. As a result, the Labour Government began to deflate the economy and reverse much of its earlier 'radical' programme. Monetary targets were adopted and public expenditure (as a percentage of GDP) fell from 45.4 per cent in 1975-76 to 40.4 per cent in 1978-79 (Jones, 1987, p. 116). This resulted in cuts in spending on the NHS, education, regional policy (with the abandonment of the Regional Premium), housing, roads and local government (Bosanquet, 1983).

The cuts in local government funding were to prove critical for its future. Local authorities were told by Environment Secretary, Anthony Crosland, in a now famous statement, that the 'party's over'. Rate Support Grant (as a percentage of local authority Relevant Expenditure in England) was cut progressively from 65.5 per cent in 1976-77 to 61 per cent in 1979-80 (Travers, 1986, p. 48). The figures for Scotland over the same period were 70.8 per cent and 64.5 per cent (Heald et al. 1981, p. 31), and this marked a turning point in local finances as the impact of the sterling crisis fed through to local government.

In addition to all this, the Layfield Committee produced its report (Cmnd. 6453, 1976) on local government finance in May 1976, providing what Richards (1988, p. 36) describes as 'the most comprehensive review of the subject ever.' The Report saw the 1974 rates outcry as simply one manifestation of the underlying weakness of a system which was riddled with 'confusion' regarding the relationship between central government and local authorities, in terms of each others responsibilities, needs and difficulties. This was epitomised in financial matters, where Layfield concluded that 'there is at present no coherent system' and it does 'not make clear where the real responsibility lies' (Cmnd. 6453, 1976, p. 35 and p. 41). The Report stated that a choice would have to be made as to whether responsibilities should lie largely with central government or with local authorities. It left the Government to make this choice, although it was clear that a majority on the Committee favoured supplementing rates with a local income tax. This, the Report suggested, would 'sustain a vital local democracy...enlarge the share of local taxation in local revenue and thereby make councillors more directly accountable to local electorates' (Cmnd. 6453, 1976, p. 301).

The Labour Government responded to this via the Green Paper *Local Government Finance* (Cmnd. 6813, 1977). As Travers (1986, p. 77) notes, however, 'little or nothing came of Layfield or the 1977 Green Paper.' The reason for the Government's unwillingness to accept an alternative to the rates fitted clearly with the post-IMF period. As Stewart (1977, p. 12) notes, the Green Paper was underpinned by 'the search for effective control of expenditure.' Central-local relations, therefore, were deemed to require 'flexibility and rapidity of response to new circumstances' (Cmnd. 6813, 1977, p. 4). This could best be achieved through modifying the existing system (see Foster, 1977), rather than abolishing rates, which 'could prove to be equally or more unpopular' (Cmnd. 6813, 1977, p. 16). Once again, therefore, prevailing economic and political circumstances ensured that the abolition of domestic rates would proceed no further.

Returning now to a general level in terms of both 'economics' and 'politics', the contradictions of the Labour Government's new-found strategy produced the conditions that would lead eventually to a second 'crisis', and would provide the conditions for its downfall and a springboard for the Conservative Party, and its subsequent thoroughgoing changes in local government and its financing. By 1978, therefore, inflation had come down to an average of 8 per cent (Artis, 1989, p. 48), although this was still greater than the UK's main competitors. Thus, as Coates (1980, p. 51) notes, 'wage restraint was vital to strengthen the pound.' In 1978, Prime Minister, Jim Callaghan, attempted to impose a 'voluntary' 5 per cent limit on pay increases under the next phase. In the event, however, this was rejected by both the TUC and the Labour Party conferences, thus paving the way for individual settlements. The end result was the 'Winter of Discontent'; a record 29 million days lost through industrial action in 1979 (Jones, 1987, p. 113); a growth in Conservative and anti-union support, and then finally, a General Election (in the aftermath of the arguments surrounding the Scottish 'no' vote in the referendum on devolution), the outcome of which would mark, as Douglas (1989, p. 400) notes - 'something more than the usual post-war alternation between the parties competing for office.'

The Legacy of the Thatcher Governments 1979 to 1984-85

Victory for the Conservatives in May 1979 came on the basis of obtaining 43.9 per cent of the vote and a Parliamentary majority of forty three (Penniman, 1981, p. 335), with the Party gaining a vital 44 per cent of the skilled-manual vote (only 1 per cent behind Labour) - almost double what they had achieved in the October 1974 Election. In Scotland, Labour's vote stood at 41.6 per cent (forty four seats) (Kellas, 1989, p. 107) and managed to hold up reasonably well. The Conservatives still made significant advances, however, increasing their share of the vote to 31.4 per cent (twenty two seats) (Kellas, 1989, p. 107).

This increase in Tory support, again must be considered in conjunction with a recognition of how the ranks of capital had fared under Labour, and the position which it found itself in as the Thatcher Government came to office. It is only by doing this that we can begin to comprehend the basis of its leading strategy and the way that this fed through to local government.

Under Labour, the City had initially recovered after the trauma of the sterling crisis in 1976. At the end of 1978, however, the Iranian revolution and the ensuing oil shortage increased oil prices. This pushed up inflation to just over 10 per cent (with Britain still a net importer of oil), worsening the balance of payments to £1,000 million in the first four months of 1979 (Bruce-Gardyne, 1984, p. 23), and thus putting pressure on sterling. The City of London was also still perturbed by its experience under the Labour Government - particularly the threat from the inflationary wage demands which followed the break-up of the 'social contract'.

In terms of big industrial capital, the resurgence of sterling damaged export competitiveness and, when we take manufacturing as a whole, employment in UK manufacturing fell from 7.994 million in 1974 to 7.378 million in 1978 (Lythe and Majmudar, 1982, p. 164). This was compounded just before the Thatcher Government came to office, because of the threat to profits from the further rise in oil prices and the rise in inflation.

Turning to the position of small business capital under Wilson and Callaghan, in general terms it had actually managed to flourish with the help of Labour's targeted policies. Employment in small manufacturing enterprises (often 'feeding' the larger companies), increased slightly as a percentage of all manufacturing employment, from 21.5 per cent in 1974 to 22.8 per cent in 1978 (Stanworth, 1982, p. 8). Again, however, just before the Thatcher Government came to office, small business, like every other section of capital, was being threatened by the rise in inflation.

Moving finally to Scottish capital and the Scottish economy, it was clear that it had been let down badly by the cuts in regional policy after 1976. Industrial policy expenditure in Scotland fell in real terms from £512.6 million in 1975-76 to £209.2 million in 1978-79 (Swales, in Ingham and Love, 1983, p. 193). Scottish-owned large and small businesses had also been particularly affected after the world-wide recession of the mid-1970s, because of the heavier reliance on supplying to or sub-contracting for, inward investors. The impact of this was a process of rationalisation and disinvestment (mostly US companies), resulting in 26 plant closures between 1976 and 1978 (Hood and Young, 1982, p. 30) and a further decline in Scottish manufacturing unemployment from 676,000 in the quarterly period when Labour took office, to 598,000 in the period when it departed office (Scottish Office, 1982). There was also a further integration of Scottish capital (ultimately) with the City, through the takeover of William Teacher's by Allied-Lyons, and Barr & Stroud by Pilkington.

To summarise, then, in 'political' terms we have the Thatcher Government coming to power on the back of increased electoral support from skilled manual workers and a general increased concern about the 'union' issue. We also have the main 'economic' problem of inflation (fuelled by the unions, it was argued), which was threatening all sections of capital - with the City and large industrial capital having most to lose from its effects. The Scottish economy was also looking particularly vulnerable because of this, and because of cuts in regional policy and multinational disinvestment. We can see now, therefore, how these 'problems' and relationships interacted with Conservative ideology and practices, and how local government and the rates were situated within them.

Strategy and Policies

The Conservatives' strategy which emerged from the foregoing relationships was intended as a radical departure from the latter period of the Heath Government - effectively pouring scorn on the 1972 U-turn. The Tories had moved to the right in 1975, after the election of Margaret Thatcher as new Party Leader. Thus, the Party was now led by a woman determined to abandon 'consensus' politics and to destroy what she described as 'the socialist fallacies - indeed the whole fallacy of socialism' (Thatcher, 1977, p. 52); a woman compared by Anthony King (in Skidelsky, 1988) to Machiavelli's 'The Prince', and a woman convinced, as Marquand (in Skidelsky, 1988, p. 165) puts it, that 'she embodies the real will of the people.'

Drawing inspiration from Monetarist thinking and free-market solutions as developed particularly in right-wing bodies such as Keith Joseph's Centre for Policy Studies and the Institute for Economic Affairs (headed by Ralph Harris), the main thrust of the Government's new ideological frame was a combination of two main factors.

First, there was perceived to be the need for an assault on the Labour movement (apparently confirmed by the 'winter of discontent'), whose inflationary wage demands and propensity for industrial action was damaging competitiveness. Second, and linked to this, there was perceived to be the need to adopt monetary targets in order to control inflation (a move inspired particularly by the American economist Milton Friedman), and cut public expenditure and state intervention - replacing them with the free-market, private enterprise and self-reliance. This would discipline the labour movement (it was argued) and would also reduce private sector tax burdens - thus shifting the balance of power in favour of private enterprise. We can see now, therefore, how this general ideological frame was transformed into specific policies within the first few years.

The Government's overall strategy (assisted gradually by massive oil revenues) was effectively 'sold' to the electorate by a variety of policies, attempting to appeal to 'self-interest' and encourage individual incentive. Particularly important was a reduction in the basic rate of income tax from 33 per cent to 30 per cent and the top rate from 83 per cent to 60 per cent, and the introduction of the 'right to buy' for council tenants. Such apparently 'generous' measures were double-edged, however, in that they were combined with deflationary policies and an attempt to cut state welfare provision. This was based partly on the Monetarist assumption that inflation is the result of an increase in the money supply, in excess of economic growth. Thus, VAT was increased from 8 per cent to 15 per cent; Public Sector Borrowing was reduced from 4.8 per cent of GDP in 1979-80 to 3.5 per cent in 1981-82 (Riddell, 1989, p. 31), and cash limits were made within some budgets. These were mostly in the area of 'welfare' - particularly in housing, education, NHS and social security. In conjunction with these, it was intended that potential opposition from the labour movement would be emasculated by curbing trade union power. This was enacted via the 1980 and 1982 Employment Acts. These made sympathy strikes and secondary picketing illegal, and imposed conditions on the establishing of 'closed shops'.

All this was an integral part of the Conservatives' strategy for increasing the competitiveness of British capital. This envisaged that the City would benefit from the short-term domestic deflation and union legislation. It would do so because, in the long term, this would promote its various interests in domestic capital by forcing the unions along the 'Americanised' path of flexibility in practices and manning levels, and accepting single-union, no strike agreements. Also, in the long-term, the City's international interests and its role as a leading European banker would be promoted by allowing the British economy to become integrated even further with the world economy. Thus, exchange controls were abolished in October 1979, encouraging outward capital flows, whilst sterling was allowed to rise steadily to $2.44 in October 1980 (Central Statistical Office, November 1981). Interest rates were also raised to a record 17 per cent in November 1979 (Riddell, 1983, p. 64), and were still as high as 14 per cent in January 1982 (Central Statistical Office, June 1982).

The City also benefited from the disposal (both whole and partial) of state assets. By the end of the financial year 1981-82, 13 major privatisations had been carried out (notably BP, Ferranti, North Sea Oil licenses, British Aerospace, Cable & Wireless and the National Freight Corporation), valued in total at some £1,270 million (Labour Research, 1985, p. 101). The City benefited not just in terms of ownership of some two-thirds of the shares (Labour Research, 1985, p. 101), but also from the 'knockdown' prices, with shares increasing in value by an average of 26 per cent in the period immediately after the issues (Mayer and Meadowcroft in Kay et al. 1986, p. 325).

In terms of big industrial capital, whilst it could benefit to a certain extent from the revival of its backers in the City, the domestic economy was squeezed by high interest rates and the rise in sterling. In effect, this and the ensuing 'great shakeout' was the price that domestic manufacturing had to pay for long-term trade union remodelling and increased efficiency (in order to revitalise its domestic and international roles), with the conditions for City financing of domestic investment being more favourable after this had been completed. Small businesses without access to the City were especially vulnerable to the market and its deflationary thrust, although this was tempered slightly by the 1981 Loan Guarantee Scheme. The 'market' was also the tendency that was being reflected in policy for Scotland and the regions, which Balchin and Bull (1987, pp. 52-3) describe as 'the spatial manifestation of...monetarism and free-market economics.' Planned regional expenditure was cut from £609 million in 1979-80 to £376 million in 1982-83 (Balchin and Bull, 1987, p. 53). It was clear, therefore, that despite a further reliance on attracting inward investment, the Government was prepared to see Scotland and the regions contract at an even greater rate than the UK as a whole.

We will see in a moment how the contradictions of this and all the foregoing policies had an immediate effect on general 'political' and 'economic' relationships. Before this, however, we can see clearly how the Government's attitude to local government and the rating system fitted in with the main thrust of its general strategy.

Local Government and the Rates

The 1979 Conservative manifesto placed rates reform on one side, stating that 'cutting income tax must take priority for the time being over abolition of the domestic rating system' (Conservative Party, 1979, p. 14). Local government itself, however, was far from neglected, and the message was clear. As Jones and Stewart (1985, p. 3) suggest, the 'message of central government was that it needed to control disobedient local authorities.' In trying to comprehend the reasons for this, there were no recent dramatic developments in terms of the rates, which would have increased concern within the Conservative Party or its supporters that major control of local government and rates levels was necessary. In addition, local spending in England and Wales, in each of the three previous financial years, had actually fallen *below* Rate Support Grant targets by 1.8 per cent, 1.5 per cent and 1 per cent (Duncan and Goodwin, 1988, p. 105). This suggests that, if we want to comprehend the Thatcher Government's attitude to local government and the rates, we must locate these within its general strategy. In essence, this can be broken down into two main elements.

First, and 'economically', there was cutting public expenditure as part of its anti-inflationary strategy - designed to revive the fortunes of British capital. A statement on public expenditure by Environment Secretary, Michael Heseltine, only two months after the General Election, specified that he would allow local authorities 'to decide on the allocation of funds in accordance with their own spending priorities' but that this could *only* take place 'within the overall need for spending reductions' (quoted in Travers, 1986b, p. 82).

Second, and 'politically', there was an attack on the labour movement, with this being another crucial component of the Government's strategy for reviving British capital. Local Government Minister, Tom King, stated that the 'Government faces a challenge to the traditional voluntary relationship between central and local government' (HC Debates, 1981-82, Vol, 16, col. 113). Jones and Stewart (1985, p. 53) have argued convincingly, however, that the Government invented this 'implicit consensus' view of the past to provide a rationale for curbing the expenditure and activities of local government. The focus of this was not on local government in general, but was clearly on Labour-controlled authorities. Local Government Minister, Tom King, for example, talked of the political opposition as being 'not prepared to recognise the national interest', whilst Michael Heseltine talked of 'Labour authorities using their position in local government to challenge the electoral mandate of the national Government' (HC Debates, 1981-82, Vol. 16, cols. 49 and 114).

In the first few years of the Thatcher Government, the policies which emerged from this generally two-fold strategy were underpinned by attempts to enforce economies on local authorities via cuts in Rate Support Grant. In Scotland, Rate Support Grant as a percentage of Relevant Expenditure was cut from 64.5 per cent in 1979-80 to 62.5 per cent in 1982-83 (Heald et al. 1981, p. 31: COSLA, 1984). In England and Wales over the same period, the cuts were even larger, falling from 59.6 per cent to 52.7 per cent (Travers, 1986b, p. 213). These cuts were complemented by successive pieces of centralising legislation in both England and Wales and Scotland. Each of these can be considered in turn.

In England and Wales, the 1980 *Local Government, Planning and Land Act* placed restrictions on capital expenditure; opened up Direct Labour Organisations to compulsory competitive tendering, and introduced the Block Grant, which was distributed according to Grant Related Expenditure Assessments (GREAs). As a result, according to Newton and Karran (1985, pp. 116-7), 'the basis for deciding the distribution of grant was shifted from spending patterns set by local government to calculations determined by central government.' In addition, any authorities deemed by the centre to be 'overspending' would have their grant reduced progressively as spending was increased.

After an initial period, it was clear that local authorities were not going to stay within targets and that the burden was going to fall on ratepayers.

As a result, the Government introduced a new system of targets for individual authorities; replaced grant tapering with a new 'hold back' system, and published 'hit lists' of local authorities that were incurring its wrath. As Duncan and Goodwin (1988, p. 113) note:

> 'the objections to these particular councils was both financial (they spent more than most on service provision) and political (they were Labour-held authorities which supported policies that central government particularly disliked, polices like cheap public transport which would actually *extend* service provision or demonstrate *alternative* policies).'

After further tinkerings with the system and a 'hold back' of £124 million grant in 1981-82 (Travers, 1986b, p. 132) the government finally produced the 1982 *Local Government (Finance) Act*. In addition to setting up the Audit Commission to oversee the auditing of local expenditure, it legalised retrospectively the interim system of targets and penalties, and abolished the right of councils to raise supplementary rates - thus cutting off one potential source of recouping grant loss.

In Scotland, the legislation was different from that in England and Wales. This was not just because of the separate Scots legal system, but also because of the uneven development of Scotland in comparison to England and Wales, and the response to this by the state through partially devolving political and administrative power to the Scottish Office. Duncan and Goodwin (1988, p. 173) note that because of both this and the existence of (post-reorganisation) Regional Councils with wider powers than authorities South of the Border - 'Local government...was left to represent this potentially explosive mixture of nationalism, political opposition and local feeling.' This was reflected, as Midwinter (1984, p. 32) describes, in the 'decision of Lothian Region to budget for growth of 2 per cent...at a time of rising interest rates, cuts in grant and high inflation,' resulting in a 41 per cent rise in rates. Reacting to this, Scottish Secretary, George Younger, (although managing to negotiate retention of the Rate Support Grant, as opposed to the Block Grant) adopted an even tougher line than his southern counterparts.

The net result was the 1981 *Local Government (Miscellaneous Provisions (Scotland) Act*, which gave powers to the Scottish Secretary to intervene selectively in local spending decisions by reducing grant during any particular financial year, if he considered that spending was 'excessive and unreasonable'. The Act also blocked off the recouping of grant loss via borrowing, stating that the local authority 'shall neither wholly nor partially offset the reduction (or anticipated reduction) with sums advanced from their loan fund' (quoted in Jones and Stewart, 1985, p. 41). In practice, however, the contradictions of the Act soon became apparent. There was resistance from seven Labour-controlled authorities (Lothian, Cumnock and Doon Valley, Dundee, Dumbarton, East Lothian, Renfrew and Stirling) with announcements of rates rises as high as 122 per cent in Stirling and 150 per cent in Dundee (Midwinter, 1984, p. 35). The short-term reaction by the Scottish Secretary was selective action, and after a combination of resistance and negotiation on the part of the authorities, cuts of £33.7 million were made in local budgets for 1981-82 (Rhodes, 1988, p. 279). In the medium-term, along with continual cuts in Rate Support Grant levels, there was the 1982 *Local Government and Planning (Scotland) Act*. This allowed the Secretary of State, entirely at his discretion, to 'cap' local authority rate levels - a move which would set the pace for future controls in England and Wales.

In the longer term, and more generally, the Government also sought to 'do something' about domestic rates. This was in the knowledge that the existing system was proving incompatible with its general strategy. The setting of rate poundages gave local authorities the ability to increase public spending, and to raise resources which gave them the power base to promote policies antithetical to the ideology of 'prudency' which was emanating from the centre. The result of the Government's deliberations was a consultative document, the Green Paper *Alternatives to Domestic Rates* (Cmnd. 8449, 1981) which was published in December 1981. On the one hand, it sought to protect the Government's monetary strategy by restating the scale of local spending and that 'the levels of revenue raised and expenditure incurred...[should] not prejudice the Government's objectives for the national economy' (Cmnd. 8449, 1981, p. 3). On the other hand, it sought to ensure that local services were provided 'to acceptable standards' (Cmnd. 8449, 1981, p. 3). Although put in muted terms because of the 'consultative' nature of the document, the 'acceptable standards' were clear. It meant producing budgets which would hold down rates levels and protect both the Government's electoral base of support (domestic ratepayers) and local businesses, whilst at the same time attempting to head off what Stoker (1988, p. 251) describes as 'the challenge of local socialism', by 'bypass[ing] opposition and overcom[ing] resistance to their policies.'

In order to achieve these objectives, the Green Paper discussed a number of options - notably reforming the existing system, local sales tax, local income tax, assigned revenues and a poll tax. [3] It expressed no particular preference for any of these, although it stated that 'the country views this matter with a sense of urgency and the government therefore wishes to move ahead as quickly as possible' (Cmnd. 8449, 1981, p. 63).

Precisely what happened to this opportunity for the Conservatives to fulfil their earlier pledge to abolish the rates, can be seen now as we move on to explore the contradictions of the Government's general strategy, and the location within this of local government and the rates.

The Contradictions of the Government's Policies

Capital flowed out of the country because of high interest rates and the abolition of exchange controls, and these acted in conjunction with the increase in VAT to produce an inflation rate which peaked at 21.9 per cent in August 1980 (Riddell, 1989, p. 27). This high interest and exchange rate policy had a devastating effect on the domestic economy and especially the manufacturing base, in what Martin (in Mohan, 1989, pp. 101-2) describes as 'the most intense phase of contraction and restructuring in its history.' Investment in manufacturing fell by 4.8 per cent in 1980, 13 per cent in 1981 and 9.9 per cent in 1982 (OECD, 1983, p. 43). Also, UK unemployment (as a percentage of the total labour force) more than doubled from an average of 4 per cent in 1979 to 9.5 per cent in 1982 (Artis, 1989, p. 364). Large industry was certainly not exempt from this squeeze, with the CBI Director General promising a 'bare knuckle fight' with the Government. The largely self-sufficient and/or bank-loaned small business sector, however, was by far the worst hit. One study revealed that, whereas the typical larger company actually improved its profits by twenty per cent, the medium-sized saw a fall of roughly twenty per cent, and the smaller company a fall of over 47 per cent (Harcourt, 1982, p. 23).

Scotland was also on the receiving end of the worst excesses of these processes. This was due to four main factors. First, there were the cuts in regional policy and its more market-oriented thrust. Second, there were the general cuts in public expenditure, which were felt particularly in Scotland, which commanded a higher per capita public expenditure than the UK as a whole (see Kellas, 1989, p. 214). Third, there was the countervailing promotion of financial services in and around London and the South-East. Finally, and again as a countervailing factor, there was a 24.8 per cent rise in defence spending between 1978-79 and 1982-83 (Coxall and Robbins, 1989, p. 538) [4], with the bulk of state contracts being awarded to companies in the South-East. Thus, the unemployment rate in Scotland rose from 4.7 per cent in 1979 to 11.3 per cent in 1982 (Artis, 1989, p. 364), with manufacturing employment declining from 604,000 in 1979 to 477,000 in 1982, and the smaller indigenous firms being the worst hit (Scottish Office, 1989).

The contradictions of the attempts to control local government spending were also proving to be problematic throughout late 1982 and early 1983. There were essentially three main 'problems' and these were common to both Scotland and England & Wales. First, the challenge of 'local socialism' was not being thwarted. Through what might be termed 'juggling' with rates levels and penalties, the Labour-controlled GLC, Metropolitan County Councils, Sheffield City Council and others, were still able to provide 'alternative services' such as cheap transport (as in the case of Sheffield) and make strong attempts to protect local services and jobs in the face of cuts in Rate Support Grant. Second, and linked to this, there was the fact that the rates had borne the burden of this, and that the Government was coming under pressure from industrial and commercial ratepayers, and from its electoral base of support in the form of domestic ratepayers. Between 1979-80 and 1982-83, domestic rates bills in Scotland increased by an average of 27.9 per cent per annum, whilst bills in England and Wales increased by an average of 20.6 per cent between 1980-81 and 1982-83 (Keating, 1985b, p. 842; Stoker, 1988, p. 159). [5] Third and finally, the Conservative Party was coming under fire from within its own ranks. MPs from the shire counties continually abstained or voted against the Government as Rate Support Grant settlements came before Parliament, whilst various Conservative local authority associations and groupings were unhappy at the cuts in Rate Support Grant and the vagaries of the financial controls which often penalised low-spending councils.

The outcome of the consultations and deliberations on the 1981 Green Paper (Cmnd. 8449, 1981) was one possible source of reforming/abolishing the rating system and attempting to overcome such problems. By 1982, however, no decision had been taken by the Government, although the difficulties of producing an adequate system were evident in the findings of a report by the House of Commons Select Committee on the Environment, on the Government's 1981 Green Paper (HC217-I-II-III, 1981-82). It expressed some sympathy for a Local Income Tax, but concluded nevertheless that 'abolition of the domestic rating system would not command widespread support and would not be justified' (HC217-I, 1981-82, p. xi).

The Second Wave of Policies

Faced with the contradictions of its original policies and the attendant problems in local finance, the Government embarked on a strategy for recovery from 1982-83 onwards. This strategy was reinforced by the re-election of the Conservatives in June 1983, obtaining 42.4 per cent of the vote and a 144 seat majority (Derbyshire and Derbyshire, 1990.p. 112), on the back of a 12 per cent lead over Labour among skilled workers (Butler and Kavanagh, 1985, p. 291). Correspondingly, Labour dropped to 27.6 per cent of the vote - its lowest showing since 1918, and substantial votes were lost to the right-wing breakaway from the Party (the SDP). Thus, in conjunction with the vagaries of the first-past-the-post voting system, this enabled the Conservatives to obtain their massive Parliamentary majority with only just over 42 per cent of the vote. In terms of Scotland, there was a slight swing to the Conservatives, mostly among owner-occupiers (Bochel and Denver, 1984, pp. 8 and 13), although Scotland's experience of the worst effects of the recession resulted in an increase in the electoral divide between Scotland and England & Wales. In 1979, Scotland diverged by 19 points, but this had increased to 24 points in 1983 (Bochel and Denver, 1983, p. 8). The results were Labour 35.1 per cent (41 seats), Conservative 28.4 per cent (21 seats), Alliance 24.5 per cent (8 seats) and SNP 11.8 per cent (2 seats) (Kellas, 1989, p. 107).

With this support, the Government embarked on a second wave of policies in 1983 and 1984, leading us gradually towards the conditions prevailing at the time of the 1985 property revaluation in Scotland. It continued its attempt to 'bear down' generally on public expenditure and the PSBR, and from March 1984 onwards, was in full-blown conflict with the miners, who had come on strike against pit closures. The Government also attributed the cause of high unemployment to high wage levels, and introduced further constraints on trades unions via the 1984 *Trade Union Act*. The City would benefit from this through its interest in large industry, as would large industry itself, which had the added benefit of lower interest rates and a lower exchange rate. The City would also benefit from continued support for outward capital flows and from a stepping up of the privatisation programme - notably Britoil (£627 million) and seven per cent of BP (£564 million) (Labour Research, 1985, pp. 101-2). Small businesses were also given an increasingly high priority. The 1983 Business Expansion Scheme was central to this and aimed to encourage equity investment in small firms, although there was a distinct regional bias, with 42 per cent of funds being channelled into the south-east (Barber, 1989, p. 51) and investment was again often contingent on forging links with larger concerns.

Policy for Scotland and the regions was essentially 'more of the same'. Following a White Paper on regional policy, the Government introduced more market-orientated measures, designed to cut the UK budget by £300 million to £690 million (Begg and McDowall, 1986, p. 217). It would do this by increasing the relative importance of selective financial assistance in terms of the perceived 'worth' of claims - often in terms of what they could do for 'big' industry in the regions, or what they could do to attract inward investors.

In terms of policies for local government, the possibility of radical reform of the domestic rating system effectively came to nothing. A Cabinet committee (Misc. 79) charged with producing concrete proposals, was dogged by divisions, and as the *Economist* (1985, p. 40) noted - 'Ministers could only agree to disagree.' Even after Mrs Thatcher herself took charge of another committee, the end product was a White Paper entitled *Rates* (Cmnd. 9008, 1983), which was resigned in its acceptance that reform was not feasible. On the one hand, it was evident that the Government could not command the political support to proceed with any particular alternative, since it found that 'there was no consensus in the substantial response received...[and that] none was a clear favourite and all had opponents' (Cmnd. 9008, 1983, p. 12). On the other hand, all other local taxes were fraught with practical difficulties (compared to domestic rates) and there was not a single alternative that seemed capable of fitting in practically with its general strategy of restricting public spending, reducing the autonomy of Labour-controlled local authorities, protecting the profits and confidence of business ratepayers, and consolidating its electoral base of support in the form of domestic ratepayers. Indeed, in a statement that would come back to haunt the Government in a few years time, a Poll Tax was deemed 'hard to enforce...[and] its costs would be very high in relation to yield...this option should be rejected' (Cmnd. 9008, 1983, p. 12). Conversely, it suggested that domestic rates were 'highly perceptible to ratepayers and they promote local accountability...[they] should remain for the foreseeable future the main source of local revenue for local government' (Cmnd. 9008, 1983, p. 14).

This did not mean, however, that the entire system was to remain unchanged. In England and Wales, in conjunction with further cuts in Rate Support Grant, further reform was enacted via the 1984 *Rates Act*, which was supported by among others the CBI, Association of British Chambers of Commerce and the Institute of Directors (See HC Debates, 1983-84, Vol. 52, col. 244). This gave the Environment Secretary the power to 'cap' the rates of either selected authorities, or all authorities if this was deemed to be necessary - thus ending the right of local authorities since 1601 to set their own rate levels. This fitted-in clearly with the Government's developing strategy as it sought to keep down local spending and taxation levels, and prevent a local 'labourist' challenge. Thus, on the one hand, according to Environment Secretary Patrick Jenkin, the legislation was underpinned by 'a duty to protect ratepayers from blatant exploitation...a duty to ensure that all parts of the public sector work within national economic policies.' On the other hand, according to Environment Under-Secretary, William Waldegrave, 'modern populism is the most acute problem that we face and any government committed to responsibility in public finance will have to deal with it' (HC Debates, 1983-84, Vol. 52, col. 252).

The Contradictions of the Government's Policies

It is these contradictions which are now crucial to the present study because they lead directly to the processes which form the 'political' and 'economic' backgrounds to the late 1984-early 1985 period, and hence to the immediate beginnings of the Poll Tax policy formation process in the statutory property revaluation in Scotland. There are six key interrelated processes in total, and these can be outlined in turn.

First, sterling depreciated slowly to reach an average of $1.34 in 1984 (Johnson, 1988a, p. 156), because of the appreciation of the dollar as portfolio investment increased in the US, and because of the post-1982 slump in world oil prices. Nevertheless, the absence of exchange controls ensured that overseas investment continued unabated, and portfolio investment in particular, increased from £7,563 million in 1982 to £9,866 million in 1984 (Toporowski, in Green, 1989, p. 252). Thus, by late 1984 and early 1985, re-investment in the domestic economy (which was now lagging behind in technology compared to Japan and West Germany) held only a limited attraction for the City.

Second, and linked to this, there was the impact on the domestic economy. Manufacturing (as a whole) recovered partly from the 1981-82 trough and gross profits increased to 5.9 per cent by 1984 (Mohan in Anderson and Cochrane, 1989, p. 92). Large industry was the main beneficiary of this, however, and the aftermath of the 1981-82 recession saw a wave of 1,478 mergers between 1981 and 1984, financed considerably through the City (Hughes, in Fairburn and Kay, 1990. pp. 38-9).

Third, and again located within the partial revival of the domestic economy, the Tories' particular predilection for policies geared to encourage small businesses, ensured that small businesses (defined as employing less than nineteen people) actually increased employment by 3.2 per cent between 1982 and 1984 (Hughes in Barber et al. 1989, p. 142). Again, however, as we move towards the period of the property revaluation in Scotland, partly because of the nature of markets and partly because of the conditions of government assistance, there was an increasing propensity for small firms to become dependent on larger concerns - linked through technical assistance, trade credit, sub-contracting and long-term contracts (McGee in Barber et al. 1989, pp. 182-3).

Fourth, and again located within the domestic economy, there was the position of the Scottish economy. In essence, its increasing 'political' divergence from the UK as a whole, was also becoming an increasingly 'economic' one by late 1984-early 1985. The cuts in regional policy ensured that the effects of increased unemployment at a UK level were far worse North of the Border. Unemployment increased from 302,000 in 1982 to 329,000 in 1984 (Scottish Office, 1989), and by 1984, average per capita income for full time male workers was £189.70 in Scotland, £192.40 in Great Britain and £213.80 in the South-East (Government Statistical Service, 1986). Thus, Scotland was not benefiting from the beginnings of a consumer boom in the South; it was removed to a large degree from the increased promotion of the City and its activities; it was more dependent on public spending (and hence more susceptible to spending cuts, including those in regional policy), and it did not benefit to the same degree from increased defence spending. Scottish capital was also undergoing a further period of change. Scottish owned and controlled capital declined further from 1982 to 1984, including takeovers of major companies such as Anderson Strathclyde, Amalgamated Distilled Products, and Stenhouse (Boyle et al. 1989, p. 12).

Fifth, there was the reaction to the foregoing processes by the Labour Party and the trades union movement. The Labour Party's defeat in 1983 led to a move to the right (under new leader Neil Kinnock), and setting out on a pathway leading to such destinations as support for council house sales; refusing a straightforward repeal of the Tories' trade union legislation and rejecting the 'traditional' call for blanket re-nationalisation. The trades union movement came along partly with this, largely in terms of some sections of the union leadership, imbued with the 'new realism' of moderation and employer/union co-operation. In general, however, for those in employment, living standards had been defended and earnings outstripped inflation by an average of 2.5 per cent in the years 1979-84 (Derbyshire and Derbyshire, 1990, p. 177), although 'inflation' had now replaced 'full employment' as the main priority of government. [6]

Sixth and last, there were the developing contradictions of the Government's policies towards local government, reinforcing the earlier trends. There were several main processes at work, and each can be considered in turn.

In the first instance, despite cuts in Rate Support Grant and successive pieces of centralising legislation, the challenge from Labour-controlled local authorities was not being suppressed. In 1984, 18 local authorities in England (16 of them Labour-controlled) were targeted for rate-capping the following year, and by the end of 1984, legislation was going through Parliament, which would abolish the Labour-controlled GLC and the six Metropolitan County Councils.

Another process at work as we approach the 'beginnings' of the poll tax policy formation process, was the continual squeezing of ratepayers. Certainly, increases in rates bills had diminished as a result of progressively restrictive legislation and grant cuts, yet they were still at a level that brought forth attacks from ratepayers. For the financial year 1984-85, domestic rates bills increased from the previous year by 6 per cent in Scotland and 6.8 per cent in England and Wales (Keating, 1985b, p. 842; CIPFA, 1988, p. 46). Also, pressure was still being put on the Government by numerous domestic and business ratepayers, particularly the CBI which was waging a campaign against rates levels, stating that its members paid £6,000 million per annum - the largest single tax paid by trade and industry (*Municipal Journal*, 19 October 1984).

The final main process at work in this period was criticism of the system of local finance from within the ranks of the Conservative party itself. For example, MPs from the Shire counties continued to 'revolt' every year as the Rate Support Grant settlement came before Parliament. The Tory Reform Group believed that rate-capping was inferior to full rating reform (*Times*, 14 January 1984). Conservative MPs and some Ministers were also becoming increasingly concerned at the inability of the system of local government finance to achieve the objectives of controlling council spending and keeping down rates bills. Giving further impetus to this view, the system of local finance also came under attack from the Audit Commission - a body created by the Government only a few years previously to oversee the whole system of local government finance. In a report published in August 1984, it criticised the block grant arrangements for producing higher rates bills than were necessary, whilst local authorities' current spending was in fact roughly in line with central targets. Furthermore, it criticised the system of shifting targets and penalties, as unfair, ineffective and producing no positive incentives for spending economies. As Pilgrim (1984, p. 1355) notes - 'the clear message struggling to escape from the Audit Commission verbiage...[is that] local government finance is a mess.'

The Government was faced on the one hand, therefore, with a system of local finance which was proving unable to support its 'political' aims of suppressing labour-controlled local authorities, consolidating its traditional base of support among domestic and business ratepayers and satisfying its own party ranks. Correspondingly, on the other hand, it was faced with a system of local finance which was proving unable to satisfy its interrelated 'economic' aims of controlling local spending in order to revitalise the position of British capital - through both reducing the bills for those sections who paid rates, and by reducing tax burdens through a reduction in public expenditure. At the Conservative Party Conference in October 1984, therefore, Environment Secretary Patrick Jenkin announced the setting-up of an internal Department of the Environment enquiry into the rating system, this being, as Clayton (1984, p. 12) suggests, 'a tacit acknowledgement that years of efforts had produced few results.' Most commentators felt, however, that this enquiry was simply 'yet another' investigation which would confront the same problems as previous enquiries, and inevitably no major reform of the rating system would result. It is this rather 'tepid' enquiry and the forces behind it which provide the general background for the Poll Tax policy formation process.

Conclusion

Given the breadth of material covered in this chapter, it seems useful to summarise the main strands that have been evident throughout, and to indicate briefly how they fit-in to the process of policy formation as detailed in the previous chapter (a more detailed discussion of the 'match' between theory and practice will be conducted in the Conclusion to this book).

First, we saw the Heath, Wilson/Callaghan and Thatcher Governments each coming to power within a particular 'political' and 'economic' context. They derived their power in Parliament through electoral support and were faced on the one hand by the trade unions and the labour movement displaying strengths or otherwise in particular historical circumstances, and on the other by the ranks of capital, again exhibiting particular strengths or weaknesses depending on the particular historical context. Then, derived from an overall strategy, these Governments pursued policies and held the directorship of the 'leading capitalist forces', with these tending to be dominated by the City of London and large industrial capital, which was generally linked to the interests of the City and its international interests in some form or another. The Thatcher Government exhibited the most determined effort yet - as a key component of the 'leading capitalist forces' - to shift the balance of power in favour of capital as a whole. In particular, it used interest and exchange rates to unashamedly promote the interest of the City and those sections of capital connected to it - thus provoking a 'great shakeout' of domestic-oriented capital whilst linking the British economy further to the fluctuations of the world economy and particularly the USA. In the longer term, when combined with an assault on the labour movement and state provision and spending, it was assumed by the Government that domestic-oriented capital would benefit because trades unions would be forced along the path of 'flexibility'.

We then saw how these 'leading capitalist forces' produced a series of 'contradictory forces', thus paving the way for further development. The domestic economy was usually subservient to this aforementioned dominance (particularly in the early 1980s), suffering at various times because of high interest rates, a high exchange rate, and cuts in public expenditure. This tended to reinforce a loss of international competitiveness, leading to a process of deindustrialization and so compounding the situation even further. Much of large industry was in an ambivalent position, in that its profits were dependent on both domestic and international factors. The tendency, however, was for small business to suffer the most, although this was ameliorated somewhat by a positive policy towards small businesses under the Thatcher Government, but often at the expense of becoming dependent on large business.

Located within these processes was the position of Scotland. It was 'led' by the forementioned leading forces, coupled with the encouragement of inward investment and cuts in regional policy. The effect of these (in part) was that Scotland displayed uneven development from the UK as a whole in terms of both 'economics' and 'politics'. Essentially, it had most to lose economically form the foregoing processes, and hence the 'contradictory forces' were more intense than elsewhere. It was physically distant from the City of London; it had a higher incidence of manufacturing industries; it did not benefit to the same extent as the South from defence contracts, and it was dependent on regional policy and a higher share of public expenditure - thus being particularly susceptible to spending cuts. This manifested itself in the continual decline of Scottish-owned and controlled capital, and the Scottish economy becoming increasingly dominated by links with (or ownership by) industrial and financial sectors in the south, or through ownership by external multinational capital. Scotland, therefore, had tended to perform poorly on most 'economic' indicators and, therefore, it is unsurprising that it was uneven 'politically' in that the Labour Party was dominant in electoral terms - and was becoming increasingly so in the early 1980s.

Finally, and again located within the foregoing processes, there was local government and the rates. In the period covered by this chapter, all governments sought to ensure that local government and the rating system played their part in the 'leading capitalist forces', and showed concern with the overall level of local spending because of the impact that it had on 'economic' management and so on policies which were dominated by the City and large industry. Under the Thatcher Government, as part of the 'leading capitalist forces', legislative controls and cuts in funding to local authorities were designed to curb public spending and inflationary pressures, hence assisting the general revival of British capital. Alongside this, there was the intention of suppressing the challenge from 'local socialism' and buttressing the Conservative's electoral base of support among domestic ratepayers.

The 'contradictory forces' created by all this were never far away, however. No government can afford to have a deeply unpopular local tax which allows local authorities the freedom to impede macro-economic management, this being a problem particularly in the wake of the IMF's stringent deflationary conditions. Hence, throughout the entire period since the early 1970s, the incompatibility of the rating system with the foregoing concerns resulted in a number of attempts to find an alternative system, although these were persistently found to be wanting.

In terms of the Thatcher Government, the main 'contradictory forces' of local government and local taxation (impeding its leading strategy) were resistance from the 'left' in local government; the squeezing of domestic and non-domestic ratepayers because of high rates bills, and the system of local finance coming under attack from within the Tory Party itself. Once again, therefore, as we approach the period in which the Poll Tax policy formation process begins, we find that yet another enquiry was under way as the Government sought to suppress the challenge from 'local socialism', to buttress its support from domestic and business ratepayers, and to satisfy its own party members.

It is against this background of the 'leading' Thatcherite strategy and its resultant contradictions, that we can begin a detailed examination of a policy formation process which would culminate in the rates being swept away and replaced with a poll tax - thus adopting a system of local finance which as the *Financial Times* (6 February 1986) suggested, 'would turn the fiscal clock back several centuries.'

Notes

1. This figure has been calculated from the work cited.

2. As a matter of interest, and as Travers (1986b, p. 38) notes, it was the first contemporary government document to mention a poll tax. Its tone was unenthusiastic about this, however, because of (i)

administrative difficulties and costs, and (ii) the implications for the invasion of privacy that would result, with local authorities being required to investigate personal household circumstances. In addition, and in direct contrast to the Green Paper which introduced the Community Charge/Poll Tax (Cmnd. 9714, 1986), it suggested that non rate-paying wage earners *did* contribute to local authority income through payment of national taxes, and therefore it 'would be wrong...to think that the earning non-householder escapes altogether from paying for the local services that he receives' (Cmnd. 4741, 1971, p. 25).

3. Again, as a matter of interest, it thought that a poll tax was unlikely to be suitable unless it was supplemented by another tax. It also suggested that it would lead to a disincentive to vote and evasion and mobility would present difficulties, whilst administrative costs would be high. As another point of note, the Green Paper (Cmnd. 8449, 1981, p. 39) gave a likely poll tax figure of £25-30 per head, and provided a detailed breakdown (regional and household) of gainers and losers. This is in complete contrast to the subsequent Green Paper (Cmnd. 9714, 1986) which paved the way for the Poll Tax, and which gave *no* indicative figure, and was extremely vague in identifying gainers and losers (see Chapter Six).

4. This figure has been calculated from the work cited.

5. Figures calculated from both works cited.

6. This figure has been calculated from the work cited.

4 1985 Property Revaluation in Scotland

This is the first of four 'empirical' chapters. It focuses on the 1985 property revaluation in Scotland and the Government's commitment to abolish domestic rates. The remaining chapters deal with the emergence of a poll tax as the Government's favoured option; the public consultation exercise which followed on from this, and the passage of the relevant Bill through Parliament. This current chapter, therefore, outlines the key issues, events and arguments surrounding the 1985 property revaluation in Scotland and focuses on a period from early December 1984 until the end of March 1985. During this period, the Conservative Government announced two separate relief schemes on 7 December 1984 and 7 March 1985 in an initial attempt to mitigate the impact of revaluation on domestic ratepayers and to alleviate a 'crisis' in its political support. Then, latterly, it took a decision that no other government had ever taken. It committed itself unequivocally to abandoning the existing rating system, thus reversing its earlier acceptance only two years previously in 1983 that rates were 'here to stay' (see Chapter Three).

The structure of the chapter is as follows. First, it outlines the principles of property revaluation and the initial impact of the 1985 revaluation. Second, it details the reaction to this by domestic ratepayers and non-domestic ratepayers, opposition parties and Scottish local authorities. Third, it examines the impact of this at all levels within the Conservative Party. Finally, it integrates these in a summary and conclusion, and relates them briefly to matters of 'policy formation'.

Revaluation

Principles of Property Revaluation

Under the rating system, the basis for a tax on property was known as a 'rateable value'. In Scotland, this was calculated by the Assessor (as opposed to England and Wales where it was a Valuation Officer of the Inland Revenue). In the case of domestic properties, for example, a property was attributed a Gross Annual Value, with this being an estimate of the expected rental income if it were 'let' for a one-year period. After deductions for repairs and maintenance, these being assumed to be the responsibility of the tenant, this gave a figure known as the Net Annual Value. This corresponded with what was known commonly as the 'rateable value'. Each local authority within which the property was situated (Regional, District and Island as the case may be) applied to this figure a 'rate poundage' (including a 'rate' for water provision in Scotland). This was calculated in pence per pound. The combined rate, which was a multiplication of 'rateable value' and 'rate poundage(s)', was the sum which the occupier was obliged legally to pay the appropriate local authority/authorities (although in practice, it was normally the owner who was responsible for payment). It should be noted that in November 1984, just prior to the announcement of the revaluation figures, the domestic and industrial sectors were subject to various forms of exemption from full rates bill liability. Domestic ratepayers were subsidised by the Exchequer at a rate of 3 pence in the £, thus effectively reducing the rate poundage by that amount. Depending on income, it was also possible for domestic ratepayers to obtain up to 100 per cent rates relief through the Housing Benefit system. In addition, industrial ratepayers were subject to 50 per cent derating, thus exempting them from 50 per cent of their rates liability. [1]

As is evident, revaluations needed to take place at regular intervals if rateable values were to take account of the changing property market, rental evidence and a number of other general factors. These are listed by Thomson as being (in terms of property) age, degree of attachment, construction, amenities and quality (quoted in Fairley, 1988, p. 50). In recent years, property revaluations in Scotland had taken place in 1961, 1966, 1971 and 1978. The 1975 *Local Government (Scotland) Act* prescribed a revaluation every five years and a revaluation should have taken place in 1983. With the agreement of the opposition parties and the Convention of Scottish Local Authorities (COSLA), however, the Secretary of State used the powers granted to him under Section 1 of the

1981 *Local Government (Miscellaneous Provisions) (Scotland) Act*, in order to delay the next revaluation until April 1985. [2]

Initial Impact of Revaluation on Rateable Values

Given that there was a seven-year gap between the impending revaluation and that of 1978, the revaluation of property would have to take account of what Midwinter et al. (1987b, p. 35) describe as 'seven years of fairly traumatic changes in the British economy.' Thus, following on from processes identified in the previous chapter, two main factors can be identified.

First, there was the decline in manufacturing industry and the growth of both the service sector and new technology. In manufacturing, employment fell by 24.8 per cent between 1978 and 1985 (Scottish Office, 1986b). Correspondingly, in the service sector, for example, employment increased by 9.2 per cent over the same period (Scottish Office, 1986b). Second, there was an increase in home ownership and a relative decline in public sector housing stock as a result of both the Government's 'right-to-buy', and restrictions on local authority capital spending. Thus, between 1978 and 1985, 86,106 public sector houses were sold, with the proportion of private sector housing increasing from 45.7 per cent to 49.6 per cent of the total housing stock in Scotland (Scottish Development Department, 1988). This tended to push up domestic rateable values, the reason being, as Bailey (1986, p. 22) notes, that 'despite increasing unemployment, average earnings for those remaining in work grew faster than inflation so that demand for housing...[was] maintained.'

The foregoing processes were reflected in rental values, these being underpinned by the demand for properties and the ability of each sector to pay. Thus, the overall change in rental values (compared to the previous year's valuations as derived from the 1978 revaluation) was a factor increase of 2.33. Within this, however, the multipliers (CIPFA, 1984 & 1985A) [3] in the main rating sectors [4] were Domestic Sector (2.66), Industrial Sector (2.16), and Commercial Sector (2.20). This meant that the initial impact of revaluation was:

- an *increase* in the share of the rateable value borne by the domestic sector

- a *decrease* in the share of the rateable value borne by the industrial and commercial sectors.

Prior to the announcement of these figures, the Secretary of State, George Younger, pressed the Cabinet to have a revaluation south of the border in order to ensure that Scotland was not isolated. This was turned down by the Cabinet, although Younger did not seem unduly perturbed, since he was initially of the view (advised by his civil servants) that there was no reason to assume that the impending revaluation would have a substantially different impact than previous revaluations. When the precise figures were available and released, however, the magnitude of the shift between the sectors (see Table 4.1) prompted Younger into swift action in order to avoid a major political crisis. On 7 December 1984, against the expressed interest of the Scottish CBI and heeding the advice of the Labour Party and COSLA, he acted to temper the impact of the impending revaluation by reducing industrial derating to 40 per cent and increasing domestic relief from 3 pence in the £ (before revaluation) to 5 pence in the £ (after revaluation). Paradoxically, this £50 million relief package was funded by all ratepayers. The overall impact of the revaluation itself and of the relief (purely in terms of rateable values and with rate poundages still to be applied), can be shown as follows:

Table 4.1
Average Increased Share of Rate Burden

Sector	Before Adjustments (%)	After Adjustments (%)
Domestic	+ 17.0	+ 8.0
Industrial	- 25.0	- 10.7
Commercial	- 1.0	- 1.3
Others	- 11.0	- 10.5

Source: Paterson, 1984, p. 2002.

It is important to understand that these are *average* figures. This means that they mask 'inter' and 'intra' regional, district and sectoral variations. In the domestic sector, for example, (as can be seen from Table 4.2), the average valuations for private housing increased by a greater amount than those in the public sector. [5] Furthermore, the range of regional variations is illustrated via Table 4.3 (see p. 85). As can be seen from a comparison of average national multipliers and their regional equivalents, the areas which tended to experience the highest rateable value increases were Dumfries & Galloway and Grampian. In these regions, *all* of the main sectoral increases were in excess of the national average. In contrast, the regions with all average valuations below the national average were Strathclyde and Orkney.

Table 4.2

Changes in Rateable Value (RV) Within the Domestic Sector

Sector	Average RV 1984-85	Average RV 1985-86	Multiplier
Public	£219	2.58	2.58
Private	£265	2.71	2.71

Source: Calculated from CIPFA 1984; CIPFA 1985a.

In attempting to build up a picture of key variations in the revaluation of rateable values, it seems useful to break down the figures even further and to consider the impact which revaluation had on rateable values in the constituencies of Scotland's 21 sitting Conservative MPs. This is particularly important since many ratepayers simply (and erroneously) translated increases in rateable values into equivalent increases in rates bills. Thus, Table 4.4 (pp. 86-7) calculates this on the basis of the rateable values for the district councils which lay within each constituency boundary. The figures reveal that in all the main rating sectors, a majority of Conservative MPs experienced multipliers in excess of the average for Scotland as a whole, and thus were more likely (all things being equal) to experience the wrath of ratepayers. Bearing in mind that there were 21 such MPs, the figures are:

Table 4.5

No. of Tory MPs Experiencing Multipliers Above the National Average

Rating Sector	No. of MPs	As a Percentage of All Scots Tory MPs
Domestic	14	67%
Industrial	15	71%
Commercial	12	57%

The hardest hit in terms of rateable value increases were Gerry Malone (Aberdeen South), Peter Fraser (Angus East), Hector Munro (Annandale & Eskdale), Ian Lang (Galloway & Upper Nithsdale), Alick Buchanan-Smith (Kincardine & Deeside), Nicholas Fairbairn (Perth & Kinross), Michael Forsyth (Stirling) and Bill Walker (Tayside North). In each of these constituencies, *all* average rateable values increased in excess of the national average. This seems to illustrate that the seven years of 'fairly traumatic changes' in the British economy *tended* to benefit areas represented by the Conservative Party at a Parliamentary level. This suggests that, in comparative terms, therefore, these areas *tended* to prosper. In other words, the *tendency* compared to nationwide averages, was for manufacturing to decline less; commerce and the service sectors to grow, and for more council houses to be sold.

Up to the present point, therefore, a picture has been built up which shows rateable values increasing in the domestic sector (in average terms), with these manifesting themselves particularly in the private housing sector, and particularly in the constituencies of sitting Conservative MPs. In order to have a complete picture, however, it must be noted that there were substantial variations *within* each rating sector. Thus, the range of sectoral variations was:

Table 4.6
Sectoral Variations in Multipliers as a Result of Revaluation

Sector	Range of Multipliers
Domestic	2.4 to 2.9
Industrial	0.6 to 2.8
Commercial	1.3 to 3.4
Others	1.5 to 3.6

Source: Midwinter et al. 1987b, p. 43.

What this indicates it that, in addition to the overall shift in the burden of revaluation, *all* sectors contained ratepayers who 'suffered' because their rental values increased by a factor greater than the 2.33 average. The media continually reported 'horror' stories of increased assessments: a New Town five apartment terraced flat in Edinburgh - £478 to £1,572 (*Scotsman*, 21 February 1985); a retail warehouse in Aberdeen - just over £100,000 to more than £330,000 (*Scotsman*, 18 March 1985); Scotland's largest department store, Lewis's in Argyll Street, Glasgow - £626,663 to £1,644,000 (*Scotsman*, 18 March 1985). Throughout Scotland, roughly 130,000 domestic ratepayers faced multipliers which increased their rateable values by more than three-fold (Cmnd. 9714, 1986, p. 61). In the House of Commons, the stories were similar. For example, Labour MP Jim Lambie claimed that garages throughout Scotland were going bankrupt. He cited the case of the rateable value of a garage in Dalry, increasing from £10,247 to £19,150 (HC Debates, 1984-85, Vol. 76. col.

Table 4.3

Regional Impact of Revaluation on Average Rateable Values (RV) (£s)

Local Authority	Domestic Sector			Industrial Sector			Commercial Sector		
	RV 1984-85	RV 1985-86	Multiplier	RV 1984-85	RV 1985-86	Multiplier	RV 1984-85	RV 1985-86	Multiplier
Borders	207	564	2.72*	4,530	8,542	1.89	469	1,270	2.71*
Central	241	629	2.61	34,777	85,066	2.45*	2,611	5,807	2.22*
D. & Galloway	225	614	2.73*	8,197	20,336	2.48*	1,012	2,970	2.93*
Fife	252	627	2.49	14,691	51,375	3.50*	2,716	6,220	2.29*
Grampian	223	620	2.78*	11,843	27,577	2.33*	2,405	6,601	2.74*
Highland	200	520	2.60	12,743	27,855	2.19*	1,510	3,089	2.05
Lothian	274	731	2.67*	13,305	28,101	2.11	1,779	3,814	2.14
Strathclyde	248	657	2.65	11,260	20,732	1.84	3,315	7,046	2.13
Tayside	225	612	2.72*	9,102	19,545	2.14	2,171	4,845	2.23*
Orkney	119	312	2.62	14,352	14,019	0.98	10,066	17,116	1.70
Shetland	129	344	2.67*	286,683	550,465	1.92	3,696	5,740	1.55
Western Isles	101	254	2.51	2,239	4,531	2.02	761	1,768	2.32*

* Denotes multiplier in excess of the national average i.e. Domestic (2.66), Industrial (2.16) and Commercial (2.20).

Source: Calculated from CIPFA, 1984; CIPFA 1985a.

Table 4.4

Average Rateable Values (RV) (£s) in the Constituencies of Sitting Conservative MPs

Conservative MP (Constituency)	Domestic Sector			Industrial Sector			Commercial Sector		
	RV 1984-85	RV 1985-86	Multiplier	RV 1984-85	RV 1985-86	Multiplier	RV 1984-85	RV 1985-86	Multiplier
G. Malone (Aberdeen South)	231	668	2.89*	9,081	23,260	2.56*	4,938	12,368	2.51*
P. Fraser (Angus East)	214	589	2.75*	9,565	22,021	2.30*	1,202	3,189	2.65*
J. MacKay (Argyll & Bute)	217	549	2.53	2,937	6,887	2.35*	1,265	2,737	2.16
G. Younger (Ayr)	299	741	2.48	7,403	14,495	1.96	3,000	5,665	1.89
A. McQuarrie (Banff & Buchan)	203	537	2.65	23,183	34,384	1.48	1,055	2,423	2.30*
J. Corrie (Cunninghame North)	255	626	2.46	13,262	30,583	2.31*	3,000	4,568	1.52
H. Munro (Annandale & Eskdale)	220	600	2.73*	10,587	27,136	2.56*	756	2,073	2.74*
A. Stewart (Eastwood)	405	1,123	2.77*	3,314	6,281	1.90	2,427	5,630	2.32*
A. Fletcher (Edinburgh Central)	276	756	2.74*	14,099	32,264	2.29*	2,560	5,463	2.13
M. Rifkind (Edinburgh Pentlands)	276	756	2.74*	14,099	32,264	2.29*	2,560	5,463	2.13
M. Ancram (Edinburgh South)	276	756	2.74*	14,099	32,264	2.29*	2,560	5,463	2.13

Name									
J. Douglas-Hamilton (Edinburgh West)	276	756	2.74*	14,099	32,264	2.29*	2,560	5,463	2.13
B. Henderson (Fife North-East)	273	689	2.52	5,781	10,435	1.81	1,576	3,924	2.49*
I. Lang (Galloway & Upper Nithsdale)	227	619	2.72*	7,049	16,956	2.41*	1,093	3,262	2.99*
A. Buchanan-Smith (Kincardine & Deeside)	240	661	2.75*	4,303	21,072	4.90*	926	2,325	2.51*
A. Pollock (Moray)	210	546	2.60	13,421	35,087	2.61*	1,036	2,682	2.59*
N. Fairbairn (Perth & Kinross)	229	638	2.78*	6,364	18,118	2.85*	1,601	4,075	2.55*
A. McCurley (Renfrew West & Inverclyde)	256	676	2.64	12,900	24,550	1.90	3,846	7,455	1.93
M. Forsyth (Stirling)	267	748	2.80*	6,453	17,675	2.74*	2,581	5,944	2.30*
M. Hirst (Strathkelvin & Bearsden)	338	916	2.71*	16,189	31,729	1.96	2,637	5,672	2.15
W. Walker (Tayside North)	229	638	2.78*	6,364	18,118	2.85*	1,601	4,075	2.55*

* Denotes Multipliers in excess of the national average i.e. Domestic (2.66), Industrial (2.16) and Commercial (2.20).

Source: Calculated from CIPFA, 1984; CIPFA 1985.

338). Furthermore, Conservative MP Hector Munro said that he had 'heard of increases from £5,000 to £25,000 for shops in Dumfries and of three-fold and even five-fold increases for other properties' (ibid. col. 328).

On one level, therefore, the numbers 'suffering' because of increases in rateable values was substantial. It must be clearly understood, however, that such increases in rateable values did not translate directly into equivalent increases in actual rates bills, even although many ratepayers and MPs tended to assume that this was so. Thus, we must consider the interaction of valuations with rate poundages, as derived from local authority spending decisions and the framework within which they were taken.

Interaction with Local Authority Spending

Since 1979, local government had been under attack from the centre, both in terms of its expenditure and its activities (see Chapter Three). In terms of expenditure and the experience of Scottish local authorities in the specific period until the property revaluation, this took two main forms. First, there was the level of central funding. The percentage of Relevant Expenditure, funded by Exchequer grant, fell from 68.5 per cent in 1980-81 to 57.7 per cent in 1985-86 (Scottish Office, 1986a). The change from the financial year prior to revaluation to the one succeeding it (i.e. the financial year within which local authority budgets interacted with revaluation figures), was a reduction from 60.2 per cent in 1984-85 to 57.7 per cent in 1985-86 (COSLA, 1985a). Second, there were grant-loss penalties for 'overspending', with 1 per cent overspend resulting in a grant-loss equal to 90 per cent of this figure. In terms of 1984-85 figures, local authorities were 2.8 per cent above Government expenditure guidelines (CIPFA, 1985b, p. 29).

The combined impact of these was a 'gap' between central funding and local authority spending commitments of some £249 million (COSLA, 1985a). Given the structural framework of local government finance, and Exchequer grant, by its nature being set by the centre, then the only way of compensating for this in order to maintain revenue was through an increase in rating income. Table 4.7 (over) was produced by COSLA at the end of March 1985, subsequent to a second domestic relief package announced by the Secretary of State (see p. 102) and reveals what it envisaged to be the combined impact of revaluation and intended local authority budgets.

Table 4.7
Potential Changes in Rating Liabilities (RL) of Different Sectors
Based on Local Authority Spending

Sector	%of RL 1984-85	£m	% of RL 1985-86	£m	% Change
Domestic	36.9	£533*	42.2	£652*	+ 18
Industrial	11.8	£181	10.4	£186	+ 3
Commercial	28.2	£434	27.2	£486	+ 12
Others	23.1	£356	20.2	£361	+ 1
Totals	100.0	£1,524	100.0	£1,685	+ 10

* Figures include Domestic rates relief of £14 million (1984-85) and £102 million (1985-86).

Source: Adapted from COSLA, 1985a.

These figures illustrate that whilst only domestic ratepayers lost (on average) as a result of revalued rateable values (i.e. revaluation itself), *all* ratepayers stood to lose (on average) in terms of actual rates bills. In addition to *actual* increases, however, it is also of importance if ratepayers merely *think* that their rates liability will increase. In this regard, it seems evident that, for a period of four months from December 1984 until the end of March 1985, ratepayers were bombarded by a variety of 'signals' which helped to promote this view.

First, there was an increase in rateable values. All things being equal, an *increase* in rateable value and a stable level of local authority rating income, should result in a compensating *decrease* in the rate poundage. Revaluation simply redistributes the burden between the different rateable sectors, it *does not* mean an increase in rating income for local authorities. A generally poor understanding of the workings of the rating system, however, meant that many ratepayers - particularly in the domestic and commercial sectors - simply translated increased assessments into equivalent increases in rates bills. Second, there were the 'signals' which emanated from the Scottish Office, especially in the case of domestic rates. Generally, the Scottish Office attempted to play down the impact that revaluation would have. Nevertheless, figures released at various times, suggested average domestic increases of about 13 per cent (Paterson, 1984, p. 2003) through to 21 per cent (*Scotsman*, 26 March 1985). [6] Third, there were the 'signals' which were sent from COSLA and also from the individual authorities themselves. At the beginning of March, COSLA indicated that domestic rates bill increases would average 27 per cent for Scotland as a whole. Within this, Edinburgh and Stirling District Councils were intent on defying Government spending limits by proposing increases of 43.1 per cent and 34.1 per cent respectively. Even in authorities which had set legal budgets, however, bills were going to increase, for example, by 23.8 per cent in Independent-controlled Tweedale; 21.5 per cent in Labour-controlled Clydebank, and 38.5 per cent in Conservative-controlled Eastwood (Scott, 1985a, p. 11).

It is evident from all this, therefore, that the typical signal to the ratepayer was one of 'increase'. Certainly an increase which was well in excess of inflation which was running a just under 7 per cent (Central Statistical Office, May 1985). When this is combined with the complexities of local government finance and the variation within and between Regions, Districts and rating sectors, it seems obvious that we have a recipe for confusion, panic and anger from ratepayers on a massive scale.

Reaction to Revaluation

From the initial release of the revaluation figures, through to the arrival of rates bills on 1 April 1985, there was what Fairley (1988, p. 50) describes as an 'outraged response from a range of domestic and non-domestic ratepayers.' It culminated with George Younger, the Secretary of State, stating that 'no-one is prepared to put up with the system as it stands and I agree with them' (*Scotsman*, 27 March 1985). The immediate reasons behind this can best be understood through a detailed discussion of the reaction to revaluation.

Domestic Ratepayers

The organisation in Scotland which represented the various individual ratepayers and Ratepayers' Associations was the Federation of Scottish Ratepayers (FSR). It was formed in the wake of the 1975 local government reorganisation, with its stated objective being 'to obtain a fundamental and far-reaching reform of the rating system; if possible its abolition and replacement by a fairer system of raising finance for local government' (FSR, 1984). Its rationale for this, as stated in its campaign literature (FSR, 1984) was that:

- Rates bear no relation to the ability of the ratepayer to pay them

- Rates have little or no effect upon the accountability of local politicians. This is especially true since many ratepayers have some or all of their rates bill paid by rate rebates or by Social Security payments.

- Rates levels can be arbitrarily affected by revaluations which are very badly understood by the general public.

- Most people benefit from the services provided by local government; however, the amount that is paid to support these services is solely decided by a notional value of property that the individual owns.

The Federation viewed local government essentially as something of a 'spending-machine', particularly, although not exclusively, Labour authorities. Thus, as Mary Whitehouse (1990), the FSR Chairwoman argued 'Councils always cash in on revaluations. They know they can get away with it.' This acted in conjunction with the fact that there had been no revaluation in England and Wales since 1973. This was because there was no statutory duty to hold periodic revaluations south of the border, and logistical difficulties coupled with the continuing hope that an alternative to the rates would be found, ensured that no government would give the go-ahead for revaluation. When the 1985 revaluation in Scotland came along, therefore, it provided the catalyst for all of the FSR's views to be expressed and for it it be at the forefront of a campaign to abolish the rates. In this regard, three main tactics were pursued. The first was to encourage individual ratepayers to write to the Prime Minister, the Secretary of State, Scottish Office Ministers, the Scottish Party Chairman Sir James Goold, or any Conservative MP. The result was a barrage of complaints, demanding that 'something be done' about the rates. Scottish Secretary George Younger, was reported to have received over 15,000 letters (*Scotsman*, 6 August 1986); the Party Chairman, Sir James Goold received 7,500 letters from domestic ratepayers alone (Goold, 1991), whilst the Prime Minister herself received about 760 representations (*Times*, 19 April 1985). In addition to this, the letters columns of the *Glasgow Herald* and the *Scotsman* were bombarded with letters from disgruntled ratepayers. For a period of four months, revaluation was one of *the* main subjects of discussion.

The second tactic employed was for the Federation itself to lobby the Conservative Party at all levels. A series of letters was sent to Conservative MPs, Scottish Office Ministers and, latterly, to the Prime Minister. A letter to the Scottish Secretary of State from Richard Adlington (Chairman of the Lothian Ratepayers' Group - RAGE) was typical in its plea that 'revaluation has shown up the rating system for the nonsensical thing that it is and we urge that it is abolished now' (RAGE, 1985). The third tactic was the personal lobbying of Conservative MPs and Scottish Office Ministers. In their local 'surgeries', MPs were inundated with complaints about revaluation and about the rating system. As the *Glasgow Herald* (27 March 1985) noted - 'Backbenchers are saying privately that they have never known such a hostile reception from their natural supporters.'

In addition to all this, the FSR found two particularly sympathetic 'ears' in the form of Conservative Junior Minister, Malcolm Rifkind (later to become Scottish Secretary, with the responsibility for introducing the Green Paper which advocated the Community Charge/Poll Tax), and Conservative MP, Michael Forsyth, who had links with the Adam Smith Institute and who was about to publish a pamphlet advocating the introduction of a Poll Tax (and who was later to become Scottish Party Chairman at the time of the introduction of the Poll Tax). Malcolm Rifkind was the constituency MP for two key figures in the FSR, Chairwoman, Mary Whitehouse, and RAGE Chairman, Richard Adlington, whilst Michael Forsyth had strong links with the FSR and also the prominent Stirling Ratepayers' Association.

The FSR's primary aim was to abolish the rating system, although there was also the matter of what to replace it with. According to Chairwoman Mary Whitehouse (1990), the FSR was informed at an early stage by Michael Forsyth that a Poll Tax 'was very much on the cards'. However, Local Government Minister, Michael Ancram (1991) (a member of the internal DoE enquiry), suggests there was no formal indication to Forsyth that this was the case. The DoE enquiry is discussed in more detail in the next chapter but whatever the precise situation, Forsyth's actions were to have an impact on the influential position of the FSR. In a letter to the Scottish Secretary on 27 March 1985, the FSR (1985a) stated that:

'...as speedy action is vital, we would support a per capita tax as the best alternative achievable in a short time...we would be very much against the rating system being supplemented by some other form of taxation. We see that as the worst of all possible worlds.'

Thus, this is evidence of one of the first (and key) calls for the introduction of a poll tax. It is important to understand, however, that this must be seen alongside the furore from non-domestic ratepayers. It is only then that we can fully appreciate their contribution in discrediting the rating system as a whole, and also comprehend the totality of forces operating upon the Conservative Party.

Non-Domestic Ratepayers

For industrial and commercial ratepayers (in essence a range of small, medium and large capitals), revaluation was seen to be the 'last straw', coming on top of a number of other criticisms which they had levelled at the rating system.

In the first instance, Scotland was about to experience the upheaval of its second revaluation within seven years, whilst in England and Wales there had been no revaluation since 1973. Furthermore, there was some concern over the statutory obligation, under the terms of the 1984 *Rating and Valuation (Amendment) (Scotland) Act*, for local authorities to consult with non-domestic ratepayers on expenditure and rates policies. Not only was this, as the Director of the Scottish CBI argued, 'unsought and unexpected' (quoted in Martlew, 1986, p. 57), but there was widespread concern that the consultative procedures lacked any substantive basis for influence over local authority decisions. As one official in a major business organisation commented - 'The civil servants said...that consultation means the right to be heard and not to have what you say acted upon' (ibid. p. 62). In addition to this, there was the expressed concern that local authority 'overspending' was simply being passed on to ratepayers. The Scottish CBI, for example, argued that local authority spending in Scotland was higher than in England and Wales, and hence the non-domestic rating burden was higher. The impact of this, it was claimed, was that unless councils cut their expenditure, industrial costs would escalate, competitiveness would be reduced and jobs would be lost.

On top of all these pre-existing 'problems', there came revaluation. The reaction to this by the various non-domestic ratepayers was manifested in the activities of a number of organisations. It should be understood that there was (and still is) no clear dividing line between each organisation and a particular category of ratepayer (and hence a particular section of capital). For example, the Association of Scottish Chambers of Commerce represents businesses in both the manufacturing and service sectors. Overall, however, three main bodies can be identified.

First, there was the National Federation of Self-Employed and Small Businesses (NFSESB), representing in excess of 4,000 businesses in Scotland. These were largely self-employed and small, privately-owned, limited liability and domestic-orientated concerns. The NFSESB was responsible for launching a high profile, two-pronged attack, aimed at (i) obtaining selective rates relief for small businesses whose rateable values had increased by greater than 300 per cent and (ii) abolishing non-domestic rates and replacing them with a tax based upon ability to pay; underpinned by central funding of Education/Police and direct payment for such services as refuse collection. One of the key factors giving force to these criticisms was the NFSESB Scottish Secretary, Bill Anderson, arguing that the Conservative Party could no longer count on the traditional support of its members; or, as *Radical Scotland*, (1985) put it, 'threaten[ing] to remove *en bloc* their votes for the Tory Party.' The NFSESB also articulated its case through use of the media; by feeding information to the Secretary of State through his Parliamentary Private Secretary, Alex Pollock MP, and by campaigning among Tory backbenchers.

Second, there was the Scottish CBI, the largest employers' organisation, representing predominantly large industrial ratepayers in the generally ambivalent domestic/'international' position as identified in Chapter Three. During the period under discussion, the CBI adopted a comparatively low profile stance on revaluation. This was due largely to the fact that the average rates burden on individual ratepayers actually decreased in real terms when compared to the other rating sectors. Instead, the focus was on alleged local authority 'overspending' and the inadequacy of statutory consultation procedures. Despite this, however, dismay with the existing rating system still manifested itself - particularly in terms of the way in which average figures hid the fact that there were 'losers' as well as 'winners'. At a CIPFA conference in March 1985, the CBI's Scottish Director, John Davidson, argued that any change to local taxation must not be limited simply to domestic ratepayers.

Third, there was the Association of Scottish Chambers of Commerce, representing some 8,000 medium and small companies, largely in domestic-orientated services, and to a lesser extent in manufacturing. The Association campaigned publicly through the media and also privately among Tory MPs. The main thrust of its argument was that local authority spending would have to be controlled, since *only* domestic ratepayers should have been subject to an increased rates burden as a result of revaluation - *not* those in the industrial and commercial sectors. It also argued that valuation practices North and South of the Border should be harmonised in order that Scottish businesses did not suffer in comparison to their English and Welsh counterparts.

In addition to the above, and campaigning on behalf of their members, there were a number of other smaller organisations (in numerical terms), such as Commerce against the Unfair Rating Burden (CURB) representing the major stores; the Forum of Private Business, a pressure group representing 'business and professional people' and the Scottish Grocers' Federation.

Overall, the key point to be drawn out from the activities of *all* these organisations is that they are indicative of the Conservatives' 'traditional' base of support discrediting the rating system *as a whole*. Thus, criticism of non-domestic rates helped to reinforce and heighten criticism of domestic rates and vice versa. This general discrediting of the rating system was also buttressed by the reaction to revaluation by the opposition parties and the Convention of Scottish Local Authorities (COSLA).

Opposition Parties and COSLA

During this period, the Labour Party in Scotland was in the midst of a conflict between the Scottish leadership and Edinburgh and Stirling District Councils over their decisions not to set legal rate poundages. Thus, revaluation was something of a respite for Labour, in that it was provided with the opportunity to make political capital out of what Local Government spokesman, Jim Craigen, called a 'shambles' and 'the bitter results of...Scottish Office incompetence' (*Scotsman*, 5 March 1985). Thus, the focus of its attack was essentially three-fold.

First, it criticised the cuts in Rate Support Grant and the way in which this put pressure on the rating system, beyond that which it was originally designed for. As ex-Scottish Secretary, Bruce Millan, argued, 'Revaluation is simply the straw that has broken the camel's back' (HC Debates, 1984-85, Vol. 76, col. 326). Second, it argued persistently in the House of Commons for relief schemes to assist domestic and non-domestic ratepayers, and criticised George Younger's second domestic relief package of £38.5 million as inadequate. Third, it joined the calls for the rating system to be abolished, thus echoing the calls from ratepayers. By calling for abolition, Labour's own political support was advantaged and that of the crisis-ridden Conservative Party was disadvantaged. As Conservative Councillor, Paul Martin, argued, 'Many people believe that Labour has now assumed the mantle of the defender of the domestic and commercial ratepayer' (quoted in Davis-Coleman, 1985c, p. 796).

The SNP was in a similar position to Labour in terms of the political capital to be made out of the Conservatives' problems. The particular angle of its attack, however, was dominated by its nationalist ideology, focusing on the 'anti-Scottishness' of revaluation and the Labour and Conservative Parties as unionist 'partners in crime'. Thus, a number of tactics were pursued. First, it attacked both the present Conservative Government and the previous Labour Government for steadily cutting Rate Support Grant since 1975-76. Second, it attacked the 'anti-Scottishness' of a revaluation in Scotland when there had been none in England since 1973. As SNP President, Donald Stewart, argued, 'revaluation continues their policy of direct discrimination against

Scotland, using us as guinea-pigs for measures which would be unacceptable in the Tory shires of the Home Counties' (SNP, 1985a). Third, it argued that domestic relief should be doubled from 5 pence to 10 pence in the £, stating that this would cost £65 million - only two days revenue from Scotland's oil (ibid.). Fourth, it launched a campaign aimed at postponing the revaluation for at least a year. It attempted to do this by distributing 100,000 leaflets, primarily in Conservative-held seats, urging ratepayers to bring the system to the point of chaos through appeals on a mass scale. Fifth, and last, as SNP Vice-Chairman, George Leslie, argued:

'There must be a definite timescale for abolishing domestic rates entirely and replacing them, as the SNP have argued for many years, with a far fairer system of Local Income Tax. Governments, including the present one, have promised rates reform but have then found excuses for doing nothing' (ibid.).

Finally, in terms of political parties, the Liberal/SDP Alliance focused its attentions largely on the impact that revaluation would have on the commercial sector. Archy Kirkwood MP was particularly active in articulating the plight of small businesses and had links with the NFSESB. He argued that the combination of a unilateral revaluation in Scotland and reductions in Rate Support Grant, had burdened small businesses with rates increases which bore no relation to their ability to pay. Thus, he suggested that, in the short term, those with multipliers in excess of 3 should be entitled to cash relief (approximately £1,000 on average), with the proportion of rates retainable during Appeal being increased from 10 per cent to 50 per cent of total rates liability. In the long term, he argued (consistent with SDP and Liberal policy) that the rating system should be abolished and replaced by a Local Income Tax.

Turning now to consider the stance of COSLA (representing the various Regional, District and Island Councils in Scotland), its political composition was dominated by Labour, with the Conservatives in a minority. Based on the results of the previous 1982 Regional/Island elections and the District elections in 1984, control of local authorities is shown in Table 4.8 overleaf. Despite the evident Labour domination, however, the Convention was tending increasingly towards something of an eclectic stance; particularly since councils of all political colours had been subject to the same legislative attacks from the centre. Thus, for example, as Keating (1984, p. 1968) argues regarding their response to penalties for 'overspending', the 'result has been a rare display of unity of purpose among Scottish local authorities.'

Table 4.8
Control of Scottish Local Authorities as of 1984

Party With Overall Majority	No. of Regions	No. of Districts	No. of Islands
Labour	3	29	-
Conservative	2	4	-
SNP	-	1	-
Lib/SDP	-	1	-
Others	3	16	3
No Overall Majority	1	6	-

Source: *Municipal Journal*, 14 May 1982; Bochel and Denver, 1984, p. 15.

In terms of COSLA's response to revaluation, its main concerns (as expressed in correspondence and meetings with Scottish Office Ministers and officials) were three-fold. The first was that steady cuts in Rate Support Grant from 68.5 per cent in 1980-81 to 57.7 per cent in 1985-86 (i.e. as percentages of Relevant Expenditure) were putting an intolerable strain on the rating system (Scottish Office, 1986a). The Convention's request that this be increased to its 1984-85 level of 60.2 per cent was turned down by the Secretary of State. Second, there was concern about both packages of domestic relief. With regard to the first package of £50 million which was announced in December and which increased relief from 3 pence to 5 pence in the £ (only £19 million of which was being financed by the Exchequer), it was argued that this would be, as Ken Paterson (1984, p. 2003), Strathclyde Regional Council's Finance Director stated, 'merely a further transfer of the burden from the Exchequer to the local ratepayers.' The second package of £38.5 million which was announced in early March and which increased relief from 5 pence in the £ to 8 pence in the £, was also criticised as being inadequate. COSLA argued for an additional package of £100 million to be financed by the Exchequer, although this was again turned down by the Secretary of State. Third, there was a general criticism of the way that the Scottish Office had handled revaluation. As COSLA's Depute Finance Secretary, Albert Tait (1989) suggested latterly:

'One of the difficulties was that some of the horror stories started because people weren't given enough information. I don't think the publicity machine from the Scottish Office was sufficiently good to alert people to the fact that what they were going to get was a revaluation notice first of all.'

Overall, therefore, these dissatisfactions with the operation of the existing system and the experience of revaluation, led to a COSLA conference at the end of March 1985, agreeing that a letter should be sent to the Prime Minister, demanding reform of the rating system. No specific alternative was put forward, although, as the *Scotsman* (19 March 1985) noted, COSLA wants a system 'which is fairer and which gives Councillors a significant degree of control over local issues.'

Impact on the Conservative Party

The situation described so far may seem nothing unusual in that the opposition parties and COSLA were united in their condemnation of the Government. Indeed, even the criticisms emanating from the ranks of non-domestic ratepayers were not particularly unique, in that there were constant concerns about inflation, trade unions, etc. What made this situation *particularly* significant, however, was the interaction of this with the unprecedented scale of revolt from within the ranks of domestic ratepayers, and owner-occupiers in particular, who had generally been hit hardest in terms of the revaluation of rateable values (Table 4.2) and particularly in Conservative-held Parliamentary seats (Table 4.4). Domestic ratepayers (especially owner-occupiers) provided the Conservatives with their 'traditional' base of support. A study by Bochel and Denver (1983) of the 1983 General Election and voting patterns in Scotland, found a strong, positive correlation between Conservative-voting and owner-occupation. Correspondingly, there was an almost identical negative correlation for Labour-voting in the same sector (Bochel and Denver, 1983, p. 13). [7] Thus, in the first few months of 1985, at a time when the problems for the Government were compounded by conflict with the miners and the teachers, Conservative support slumped substantially in System Three Opinion Polls and was particularly poor when compared to the 1983 General Election showing, as detailed in Table 4.9 overleaf. This decline in Conservative support was exacerbated by the fact that the Party's electoral base in Scotland was already weak. As indicated previously (Table 4.8), it held overall control in only two Regional and four District councils. In addition, it held only 21 out of a possible 72 Parliamentary seats - none of these being in Glasgow, the Borders or the Highlands and Islands. Thus, with the prospect of regional elections the following year and the possibility of a

General Election the year after that, the Party's situation was extremely perilous.

Table 4.9
General Election Results and System Three Opinion Polls

Party	G.E. 1983	Dec. 1984	Jan. 1985	Feb. 1985	Mar. 1985
Conservative	28%	26%	24%	26%	19%
Labour	35%	46%	46%	44%	47%
Alliance	25%	15%	16%	16%	20%
SNP	12%	13%	14%	14%	14%

Source: *Glasgow Herald*, 9 March 1985.

As Midwinter et al. (1987, p. 37) note, 'the notion that the Government faced widespread electoral disaster in Scotland...became commonplace, and was widely alluded to in the media.' There was also the less tangible impact of a loss in confidence from its traditional support in the 'business' community. As Jim O'Neill, former Conservative leader of Renfrew District Council, stated, 'I have met many people in the business community who supported the party because it backed owner-occupation and small business. But with one move they have destroyed the dreams of many' (quoted in Midwinter et al. 1987, p. 38). It is important, therefore, to identify the impact that views such as this had at all levels within the Conservative Party.

The Scottish Conservative and Unionist Association

The SCUA is the 'grass roots', voluntary wing of the party in Scotland; traditionally supportive of Party policy. Revaluation, however, provoked a period of extraordinary turmoil from within the ranks of party workers. This was not only because of the mass criticism that was being levelled at *their* party, but also because of the effect that revaluation had on their *own* rates bills. Thus, David Scott (1985a, p. 9) noted, writing in the *Scotsman*, that 'unprecedented charges of political incompetence and ineptitude over the handling of rates reform are being made by normally uncritical constituency associations.' Edinburgh Pentlands Conservative Association, for example, issued a statement claiming that the Government had been 'uncharacteristically dilatory and incompetent' in its failure to bring about rates reform (*Scotsman*, 27 February 1985).

Certainly, most local associations favoured a postponement of revaluation until the whole 'mess' could be sorted out through a promise by the Government to abolish the rating system. When Party Chairman, Sir James Goold, tried (and failed), however, to gain a postponement (see p. 102), the pressure for reform increased. As James Highgate, SCUA Honorary Secretary, argued, 'I have no desire to be alarmist...but failure to solve the problem could seal the fate of the Government' (quoted in Parkhouse, 1985, p. 12). Seemingly indicative of this, one in five motions from constituency associations for the forthcoming Party conference in May, expressed deep concern over revaluation. Thus, by the end of March, at a meeting of the Conservative Central Council in Newcastle, the SCUA was urging that Scotland be used as a 'legislative greenhouse', the reason being that electoral disaster could be avoided only if rates *abolition* was on the statute book before the next General Election.

The Conservatives in Local Government

The uproar from the SCUA was paralleled by that from within the Party's local government ranks. An election in the Regional Council seat of North Kyle (in the heart of Scottish Secretary George Younger's parliamentary constituency), saw a Conservative majority of 1,552 overturned by a 11.6 per cent swing to Labour. Tory candidate, John Holt, blamed revaluation for the defeat (*Glasgow Herald*, 23 March 1985). In addition, Glasgow Councillor, William Aitken, accused the Scottish Secretary of mishandling revaluation. Furthermore, Newlands Councillor, John Young (1985, p. 8), said that in 26 years of Party membership, he could not recall 'such anger as has been expressed in the past few weeks.' He argued also that the second relief package of £38.5 million for domestic ratepayers which was announced on 7 March, (taking it to 8 pence in the £), did not go far enough and should have been as much as 15 pence or 20 pence in the £.

There was also widespread support for an attempt to suspend revaluation. This was not just because of the impact of revaluation itself, but also because of concerns about cuts in Rate Support Grant and the impact on rates bills. The Conservative Group on Edinburgh District Council was one of the main voices expressing this view. There was also some concern about the 'clawback' of grant. Councillor Rosemary Ferrand of Perth and Kinross said that her own council had been faced with a £275,000 clawback, despite prudency and 'good housekeeping'. By the end of March, therefore, the situation was becoming increasingly tense, due to the fact that revaluation had not been postponed and the second domestic relief package had failed to dampen the calls for rates abolition. Thus, the Conservative group on COSLA wrote to both Sir James Goold and the Prime Minister, expressing concern over the continued cuts in Rate Support Grant, and stressing that a new system of local government finance would have to be found.

In addition to all this, it is important to recognise that these general and specific concerns about the rating system were buttressed by long-standing criticisms from within Tory local government ranks South of the Border. Conservative-controlled councils as represented in the Association of County Councils (ACC) and the Association of District Councils (ADC), had persistently come into conflict with the Government over (i) Revenue Support Grant settlements, (ii) the often 'blanket' attacks on local authorities, thus regularly penalising 'prudent' councils, and (iii) the increasing centralisation of power and the erosion of local democracy. The Conservative-dominated ADC, for example, voted 49:3 to oppose rate-capping, viewing it as a 'constitutional change...a fundamental breach of local democracy and accountability and...wholly unworkable in practice' (quoted in Duncan and Goodwin, 1988, p. 182). Thus, the internal DoE enquiry into local government finance (see Chapter Three) was generally welcomed from within Tory local government ranks.

In total, therefore, all this helped to reinforce the calls from within the Party's local government ranks in Scotland, and indeed from within the Party as a whole in Scotland, that the 'rates must go'.

Conservative MPs and the Party Hierarchy in Scotland

Concern about the Party's deep unpopularity permeated it at all levels. Backbenchers intervened in almost every Commons debate on local government, making it clear that the demands for abolition of the rating system should not be ignored. The *Glasgow Herald* (8 March 1985) reported that 'Ministers are believed to have been shaken by the response from the Tory rank and file.' Party Chairman, Sir James Goold, stated publicly that revaluation was the biggest single issue facing the Party and described it latterly as 'probably the worst thing that could have happened as far as the Conservative Party was concerned' (Goold, 1991). Thus, given this strength of feeling, three main attempts were made initially to ease the situation.

First, in early February, Goold announced that two internal party enquiries (a Local Government Committee and an Arrow Group) were investigating the possibility of finding an alternative to the rates. The four options that were reported to be under consideration were a Local Income Tax, Poll Tax, Local Sales Tax and central funding of such services as Education and the Police.

Second, towards the end of February, Goold appeared to attempt to stop the revaluation via a trip to Westminster to meet with George Younger and the Prime Minister. As Councillor John Young (1985, p. 8) argued, 'I have not met a single Conservative Councillor or Party member in the past few weeks, who does not back [this].' Goold, however, had lobbied George Younger privately (and unsuccessfully) for several months on this same issue, and this was now simply the matter rearing its head in public. The media and, in particular, the *Glasgow Herald* and the *Scotsman*, were unaware of this earlier lobbying, and thus were highly critical of Goold for being 'too late' and suggested that he had been rebuffed by Younger. Certainly, this *latter* point was true. The reason that the revaluation could not be stopped, argued Younger, was that (i) it would be changing the 'rules of the game', (ii) overspending councils should be made to share the blame for rates increases, and (iii) the new revaluations had already been published and therefore the 'bureaucratic-machine' was too far advanced to be halted. [8]

Third, in early March, George Younger announced a further package of relief (£38.5 million) for domestic ratepayers. This increased domestic relief from 5 pence in the £ to 8 pence in the £, thus cutting the 27 per cent average rates bill increase to approximately 21 per cent. Nevertheless, the average increase was still more than 5 per cent in 53 out of the 56 rating authorities, with a majority (38 authorities) being in the range of 10-25 per cent (HC 328-i & ii, 1984-85, p. 6; COSLA, 1985b). It should be noted also, that the relief package did not involve any 'new money', but was to be funded by cuts within the existing Scottish Office budget.

Despite these measures, the demand for reform continued unabated from both inside and outside the Party. Thus, at the end of March, a delegation of Scots MPs (Munro, Fairbairn, McQuarrie, Hirst and Forsyth) met with the Prime Minister. They attempted to convey the depth of feeling within the Party in Scotland, and expressed the view that rates abolition was absolutely essential. Albert McQuarrie, one of the delegation, found optimism after the meeting, saying that 'something will definitely happen in the next session' (quoted in the *Scotsman*, 29 March 1985). George Younger, by-passed in this process, was nevertheless consistent with the mood of the party ranks below him, stating that 'we have had one go at trying to reform rates and everyone was against the alternatives. This time we have to deliver. Not acting at all means that there will be severe political consequences' (Channel Four News, 26 March 1985). More specifically, and in an interview several years later, he talked bluntly of the consequences being that 'the Tories would have sat at home and refused to vote for us' (Younger, 1991).

The Conservative Party at a UK Level

The Conservative Party had never been enthusiastic about domestic rates as a local tax, and the internal DoE enquiry which had been announced the previous October was yet another attempt to find a solution to this perennial problem (see Chapter Three). Initially, it looked as though the enquiry would arrive at the 'standard' conclusion. In other words, as the *Sunday Times* (10 February 1985) reported in early February, 'rates are not expected to be abolished as a result of the government enquiry since they are cheap to collect and difficult to evade.' Despite this, however, the experience of Scotland managed to give impetus to the calls for reform, urging that the Party carry out its 1974 manifesto pledge to abolish the rates. In a number of Commons debates on local government, and in motions submitted to the Conservative Central Council in Newcastle, there were calls that this be done. Certainly, calls for policy reform from backbenchers are nothing unusual, although the precise circumstances of these particular pleas were crucial.

On the one hand, the Party was facing the prospect of an electoral 'wipe-out' or 'Doomsday Scenario' in Scotland. Whilst not relying on the 21 Scottish Conservative MPs to give it a majority in Westminster, such an outcome would have seriously undermined (if not destroyed) its claim to be *the* Party of the Union, *the* Party of unity and, hence, *the* national party of government. On the other hand, the unhappy marriage of the Conservative Party and the rating system made a commitment to rates abolition, perhaps not quite as reluctant as it might otherwise have been. This was reinforced by the 'distance' of Westminster from Scotland (geographically, politically and in the media). This facilitated the view that revaluation was simply the 'last straw', piled on top of an essentially unsound system which for many years had enabled Labour councils to be profligate at the expense of ratepayers. This echoed pre-existing ideas within the ranks of capital (particularly the CBI, the Institute of Directors and the British Chamber of Commerce). It also echoed pre-exiting ideas within the Conservative Party itself, and indeed the Government had just announced the setting up of the Widdicombe enquiry into the 'politicisation' of local government and such matters as the use of rates to finance 'anti-government propaganda'. By the end of March, therefore, Local Government Minister, Kenneth Baker, announced that the DoE enquiry had reached two broad conclusions (*Scotsman*, 25 March 1985). These were crucial in setting the agenda for the subsequent development of the policy formation process. The two broad conclusions were:

- that the local tax burden was falling on too few shoulders and

- that the accountability to the electorate had become too thin.

The Prime Minister herself was also reported to have a 'new-found zeal' for reform. This was particularly so after the meeting with the delegation of Scots MPs and also after a visit to Scotland by the Deputy Prime Minister, Viscount Whitelaw. He spent three days there speaking to party activists, and described this as one of the most uncomfortable experiences of his political career. After conveying this to the Prime Minister on his return, she summoned Ministers to a meeting at Chequers the following weekend, and was reported to have given instructions for a workable alternative to be found within weeks (see the *Scotsman*, 27 March 1985), stating that 'if everyone sticks to his pet scheme, we shall not get anywhere' (HC Debates, 1984-85, Vol. 76, col. 209). Immediately after the summit and in response to Questions in the House, initiated by Labour Leader, Neil Kinnock, who accused her of 'ratting comprehensively' on previous undertakings to reform the rates, she replied:

> 'The fact is that the rating system is not a true democratic system as most of the electorate do not pay rates and, therefore, there is not proper accountability...It will take a great step to reform it, and it will be very complicated, but we hope to bring forward proposals to do just that' (HC Debates, 1984-85, Vol. 76, col. 1057).

Based on this commitment, echoed in similar statements around the time, the 'boil had now been lanced' for the Tory Party, with Scottish Party Chairman, Sir James Goold (1991) describing 'the feeling in the Party...[as] one of euphoria.'

Conclusion

This chapter has outlined the key factors, in an immediate sense, which led to the 'discrediting' of the rating system by the then Conservative Government. A fuller analysis of this will be undertaken in the Conclusion to this book. On a provisional basis, however, we can see the interaction of two main sets of forces, which 'match' with the principles of policy formation as detailed in Chapter Two.

On the one hand, there was the impetus of the 'leading capitalist forces', namely cuts in central funding, local authority spending decisions in the face of this and the impact of revaluation itself (underpinned by changes in the British economy), with there being a tendency for Conservative-held Parliamentary seats to exhibit the highest increases in rateable values.

On the other hand, however, this produced 'contradictory forces' as manifested in the ensuing 'uproar' and an unprecedented and exceptionally widespread alliance of forces, committed to the belief that the 'rates must go'. Indeed, there were no public calls at the time that the 'rates must stay'. Thus, the general alliances which buttressed the Conservative Government's attempt to 'lead' and restructure British society in favour of capital as a whole but particularly the City of London and those large capitals linked to it (Chapter Three), was being fractured because of departures (actual and potential) from its electoral base of support in Scotland, and from the rapid erosion of the links that it had forged with domestic capitals of all configurations. As a result, its legitimacy was being threatened because of the specific circumstances prevailing in Scotland. It is unsurprising, therefore, that the massed ranks of those favouring the abolition of the rating system were soon joined by the Conservative Government itself. It perceived an 'open window' that would transform its general strategy, and the basis for this was laid in the provisional findings of the DoE enquiry i.e it wanted a system of local taxation which would (i) ease the local tax burden on its supporters in the ranks of domestic and non-domestic ratepayers, and (ii) make the spending and activities of local authorities more 'accountable' to the wishes of the centre. Thus, there was a 'window' through which it perceived the potential to buttress support for its directorship of the 'leading capitalist forces' by moving the tax burden away from its middle class supporters and towards the working class, whilst at the same time suppressing the 'contradictory forces' through exercising even greater control over local authorities. There was an important practical problem to be overcome, however, because as Keating (1985b, p. 842) observes, 'the Conservatives find themselves in a quandary, agreeing with the critics of an unpopular tax but not knowing how to replace it.' In the next chapter, we will see how the Conservatives found a way out of this dilemma and decided to introduce a poll tax.

Notes

1. A number of properties such as agricultural land, Crown property and Police property were exempt from rates liability.

2. Due largely to technical difficulties and a number of associated problems, a revaluation of the domestic sector could not take place in 1983. Rather than proceed with a revaluation in the non-domestic sector only, it was agreed that a complete revaluation would be deferred until 1985 (see HC Debates, 1981-82, Vol. 28, cols. 1192-9).

3. Consistent with standard practice, all average rateable values for a particular area in a particular rating sector have been obtained by dividing the total rateable value for that area by the number of ratepayers therein. Thus, there is no averaging of averages.

4. The category of 'Others' which is referred to in some Tables, is largely that of Public Utilities, with no active role being played on behalf of these in response to revaluation. Thus, the discussion in the rest of this chapter concentrates on the three main rating sectors i.e. Domestic, Industrial and Commercial.

5. CIPFA figures give a breakdown for public sector housing, into Local Authority, Scottish Special Housing Association and New Towns. The remainder of the domestic sector is owner-occupied and private-rented housing, although the figures do not differentiate between these.

6. The latter figure was agreed eventually by COSLA and the Scottish Office as the average domestic rates bill increase.

7. The figures are 0.69 and -0.70 respectively (Bochel and Denver, 1983, p. 13).

8. It is interesting to note that an ex-Scottish Office Minister has suggested that Mrs Thatcher attempted to stop the revaluation, but 'by then it was too late. The bureaucratic machine was in motion' (see Fry, 1988). Lord Goold (1991), however, the then Scottish Tory Party Chairman, has suggested that this was not the case, and that, whilst she had strong reservations about a revaluation in Scotland alone, she was assured by Scottish Secretary, George Younger, that the situation would be worse if revaluation *did not* go ahead. This view seems to be partly borne out by Mrs Thatcher's memoirs, although it is combined with scathing criticism of Scottish Office Ministers. She argues that 'if George Younger and Michael Ancram at the Scottish Office had alerted us to the full consequences in time we could have introduced an order to stop it or mitigated its effects

by making changes to the distribution of central government grants'
(Thatcher, 1993, p. 647).

5 The Emergence of the Poll Tax

This chapter outlines the main issues and arguments which culminated in the publication on 28 January 1986 of the Green Paper *Paying for Local Government* (Cmnd. 9714, 1986), advocating the introduction of a Community Charge/Poll Tax. In this regard, the chapter covers a period from approximately the beginning of April 1985 (by which time the Conservative Government had committed itself to abolishing the domestic rating system) through to the end of January 1986.

The structure of the chapter is as follows. First, it provides a general 'political' and 'economic' context to this period, covering an initial phase from April through to September 1986. Second, it focuses specifically on local taxation and the emergence of a pro/anti-poll tax cleavage. This manifested itself within the Conservative Party and also within the Cabinet itself, where there was an initial trend towards replacing domestic rates with a dual system of a property tax and poll tax. Third, it provides a general context for a second phase from October to January and outlines the way in which the favoured option of a dual system disintegrated and was replaced by that of a poll tax alone. Finally, it integrates these in a summary and conclusion, and relates them briefly to matters of 'policy formation'.

Background (April - September 1985)

The general strategy of the Conservative Government was dominated by the need to keep down inflation which was on an upward trend because the unions had managed to obtain a general increase in the real level of wages. In May 1985, inflation stood at 7 per cent, its highest level in two and a half years (Central Statistical Office, October 1985). In an attempt to tackle this, the power of the City was ever present. In a slight shift in Government strategy (moving away from monetary targets), interest rates were raised and sterling was allowed to appreciate from an all-time low of $1.0575 in February, to $1.4590 in September (Central Statistical Office, October 1985). As the Fraser of Allander Institute (November 1985, p. 7) stated, 'this combination of high interest rates and a strong pound is unlikely to improve prospects for UK manufacturers.'

In terms of the Government's 'political' support for this strategy, it had managed effectively to 'defeat' the miners by March. Nevertheless, there was still substantial opposition to both specific policies and the nature and effects of general Government policy. In April, the National Union of Teachers voted for industrial action in support of wages and conditions, which were being threatened by the Government's attempt to bear down on public spending. The relegation of the domestic economy to the City's international position also meant that unemployment was increasing, with it reaching a new peak for April of 3,177,200 (13.1 per cent) (Central Statistical Office, May 1985).

Electorally, therefore, the position of the Conservative Party was bleak. The Conservatives lost control of eight councils in the May County Council elections, with the SDP making substantial gains. As the *Municipal Journal* (10 May 1985, p. 729) commented, 'the Conservatives must be very worried about the results.' Furthermore, in July, they were defeated by the Alliance in the Brecon and Radnor by-election, overturning an 8,784 majority in the 1983 General Election. As a result of all this, Conservative fortunes in national Gallup opinion polls declined steadily from 39 per cent in January to 24 per cent in August (Heald and Wybrow, 1985). With regard to public perceptions of the party most likely to win a General Election, the figures for the Conservative Party in the same period fell by almost one half, from 65 per cent to 34 per cent (ibid.).

In turning to Scotland, however, we find the situation even worse for the Conservative Party - with it being part of *and* heightening the 'political' and 'economic' divergence from the South. In the summer, British Steel (under pressure from the Department of Trade and Industry to put the business on a commercially-viable footing) announced its intention of challenging the position of Ravenscraig and concentrating its strip-mill production at Llanwern and Port Talbot in South Wales. This placed George Younger and the Scottish Conservatives in a compromising position, since Ravenscraig's previous three-year reprieve in 1982 was backed by the vast majority in the Party (see Dowle, 1986). Thus, after a campaign within Tory ranks and from the Unions and the Opposition Parties against this new threat (the campaign being hindered by a generally hostile attitude from Trade and Industry Secretary Norman Tebbit and Junior Minister Norman Lamont), the result was the announcement in August of another three-year 'reprieve', but at the cost of the closure of the Gartcosh rolling-mill and the loss of 800 jobs. As Dowle (ibid. p. 13) argues:

'Although Younger could technically claim to have maintained his promise to save Ravenscraig, it was seen by the unions and the Opposition as a Pyrrhic victory...thus knocking a hole in the Conservatives' claim to a commitment to an integrated steel production capacity in Scotland.'

There was also the problem for the Conservatives of the teachers' dispute in Scotland, and the lack of Scottish Office independence from Westminster in meeting the teachers' demand of an independent pay review. As McCrone (1986, p. 2), notes - 'Younger would clearly like to be rid of the teachers' dispute but is boxed in by his southern colleagues.' This was in contrast to the decision in July by the Prime Minister to implement in full, the recommendations of the Plowden Committee's report on top people's pay.

These events combined with a number of other issues, particularly the refusal of Social Security Minister, Tony Newton, and the Prime Minister to grant cold climate allowances for those suffering below-zero temperatures in Scotland, whilst payments were made to those experiencing higher temperatures in south coast resorts. Thus, as Dowle (1986, p. 17) notes again, with regard to the position of the Scottish Conservatives:

'It was becoming increasingly clear that on a whole range of fronts they were failing to gain even a grudging acceptance of their policies from a wide range of interest groups, let alone the electorate at large.'

As a result, the Conservatives in Scotland were still well behind their 1983 General Election performance of 28.4 per cent, with support in

MORI polls showing only 22 per cent in May and 21 per cent in September (*Scotsman*, 6 May 1985 and 16 September 1985).

In addition to these general pressures on the Conservative Party, it is important to recognise the persistence of specific pressures to reform the rating system *as a whole*. Thus, on top of the various arguments being put forward both for and against a poll tax (which will be dealt with shortly), a number of other factors ensured that the abolition of rates remained high on the political agenda.

First, the continual outcry from domestic and commercial ratepayers led to George Younger announcing at a turbulent Party Conference in May, yet another package of rates relief - estimated initially at £40 million. Several days later in the House of Commons, he announced that the package would be £50 million, and would give 100 per cent relief to domestic and commercial ratepayers for the portion of their valuations which was in excess of a three-fold increase. He anticipated that this would assist 250,000 domestic ratepayers (£10 million) and 50,000 commercial ratepayers (£40 million), although a survey of local authorities by COSLA revealed that in practice, it would amount to only £29-30 million. This would cover only about 200,000 properties, of which only approximately 30,000 would be in the commercial sector (see HC Debates, 1984-85, Vol. 79, cols. 175-86; COSLA, 1985b; *Scotsman*, 29 May 1985).

Second, there was the continual lobbying from non-domestic ratepayers for reform of the existing non-domestic rating system. The NFSESB pressed for a combination of central funding, direct payment for services, and a profit-related tax. The Association of Scottish Chambers of Commerce favoured a uniform business rate both North and South of the border. The Forum of Private Business did not propose a specific alternative, but argued nevertheless that 'we are against selective rates relief or tinkering with the system. That is just papering over the cracks' (*Scotsman*, 18 April 1985). Finally, the CBI at a UK level favoured a 'ceiling' on business rates, whilst the Scottish CBI gave no specific proposals but wanted reforms not to be limited simply to the domestic sector.

In total, these demands helped to maintain the pressure on the Conservatives to act on the rating system *as a whole*. Bearing in mind these general relationships, therefore, we can now turn to the specific and ongoing circumstances pertaining to domestic rates.

Attempted Resolution: A Property Tax and a Poll Tax

The previous chapter outlined the extent to which there was widespread support for the abolition of the rating system. This unity was combined, however, with a disagreement over the alternative that would be put in its place. Both inside and outside the Conservative Party, the main options put forward were a local income tax, poll tax, local sales tax and the restoration of some services to central government (and in the case of the Labour Party and COSLA, no specific alternative was being proposed). It was clear, however, that from a relatively early stage, a poll tax was emerging as a 'front runner'. As Davis-Coleman (1985a, p. 492) noted at the end of March - 'Rumours of a move to Poll Taxation are rife north of the border.'

In order to comprehend this, we must start with recognition of the work being undertaken by the internal DoE enquiry. The team was headed officially by Local Government Minister, Kenneth Baker, but day-to-day handling was charged to Parliamentary Under-Secretary, William Waldegrave, with a 'Scottish' input coming from Scottish Local Government Minister, Michael Ancram. The enquiry also comprised the leading banker Victor Rothschild; Lenny Hoffman QC; Tom Wilson, Professor of Economics at the University of Glasgow; Christopher Foster, a Director of Coopers and Lybrand and the author of a number of works on local government finance; Dr Richard Jackman, another expert in the field of local finance; Daniel Hodson; John Stancliffe; Dr Christine Whitehead, and finally a small team of civil servants who were led by Terence Heiser.

The task of *having* to find an alternative to domestic rates was an onerous one. Yet, as revealed in research undertaken by Michael Crick and Adrian Van Klaveren (1991, p. 405) for the BBC's *Panorama* programme - 'the team made progress by a simple process of elimination.' Michael Ancram (1991) suggests that a poll tax 'became a runner on its own merits.' More specifically, it was the only solution which fitted in with the two, key goals (as mentioned in the last chapter) of widening the local tax burden and, at the same time, promoting 'local accountability'. Thus, as Crick and Van Klaveren (1991, p. 405) suggest, a poll tax 'simply emerged as the option with the fewest drawbacks. Christopher Foster apparently told Waldegrave that, given the restrictions they were working under, the poll tax was probably what they were looking for.'

With regard to the timing of these events within the DoE enquiry, it is evident that even before Mrs Thatcher's public commitment to abolish the rates, a poll tax had 'won through' (at least in some form) in the relatively isolated world of a departmental enquiry (Baker, 1993, p. 122). Before long, however, this ascendancy had forged its way through to Cabinet level. Indeed, Mrs Thatcher's *public* statements on the 'death' of the rates, actually masked the fact that tentative agreement had already been reached at the Chequers meeting at the end of March, on the introduction of a poll tax in some form. Thus, Mrs Thatcher (1993, p. 649) suggests in her memoirs that it was 'at the Chequers meeting that the community charge was born.' Yet it was by no means as straightforward as this might suggest. The theoretical 'merits' of a poll tax were now confronted by the harsh realities of practical and political feasibility. Hence, from the end of March onwards, the DoE was faced with the task of producing a workable scheme for abolishing domestic rates and replacing them with a per-capita tax. As a result, under the chairmanship of Mrs Thatcher, a separate Cabinet sub-committee called E(LF) - the Local Finance Sub-Committee of the Economic Affairs Committee - held a series of meetings from May through to September, receiving regular reports on the progress of the DoE enquiry. Despite the lack of a firm commitment on the part of the Government, continual press reports did suggest that a 'solution' was emerging. It was not a poll tax *per se*, but some form of combination tax i.e. a combination of a property tax based on size of dwelling (30 per cent) and a flat-rate poll tax (70 per cent) (e.g. see *Financial Times*, 21 August 1985; *Scotsman*, 20 September 1985; *Guardian*, 24 September 1985), and this is confirmed in subsequent ministerial memoirs (Lawson, 1992, p. 576; Baker, 1993, p. 125; Thatcher, 1993, p. 650).

How, then, do we begin to consider the emergence of this *dual system* and its relationship to a later commitment to come down in favour of a poll tax alone? In order to discuss this and to provide a base for further analysis in the Conclusion to this book, it seems useful in the first instance to consider the nature of the calls from outside the Conservative Party, both for and against a poll tax. Having done this, it will then be possible to identify the relationship between these competing calls and their impact upon both the Conservative government and the DoE enquiry.

Outside the Conservative Party: Support for a Poll Tax

Support for a poll tax was minimal, with only three major groups advocating its introduction. These were the Adam Smith Institute (whose role, as we will see in a moment, seems to have been somewhat exaggerated), the Federation of Scottish Ratepayers (including some of its constituent groups, particularly RAGE - the Lothian ratepayers' group and almost certainly the most active of all the individual groups) and finally the CBI at a UK level. Briefly, each of these can be considered in turn.

The free-market 'think tank', the Adam Smith Institute, had published previously on the need for efficiency in the public sector and local government through the introduction of private sector market mechanisms. On one level, therefore, this fitted neatly into the Thatcherite strategy of (a) reducing state spending to tackle inflation and so maintaining the competitiveness of the City and British capital as a whole, and (b) eroding the power of trades unions and the Labour Party at a local level, yet at the same time consolidating domestic ratepayers as the Party's electoral base of support.

For the Adam Smith Institute, revaluation provided an 'ideal' opportunity for a further exposition of these views. In April 1985, Douglas Mason of the ASI published a work entitled *Revising the Rating System*. This argued that 'the outcry caused by the 1985 revaluation in Scotland provided a perfect measure of the unpopularity of the system' (Mason, 1985, p. 6). Thus, the rating system was described as a

'system of representation without taxation [which] has been seized on and vigorously exploited by some in local government. High-spending programmes can be adopted, inflated services introduced and generous benefits offered, in the safe and secure knowledge that someone other than the voters will have to pay for it' (Mason, 1985, p. 5).

Based on these assumptions, therefore, he advocated the introduction of a *per capita* tax (poll tax) [1] of just under £180 per head, with the intention that 'the two-thirds of voters who currently enjoy immunity from the consequences of their electoral actions would no longer be able to exploit the ratepaying minority' (ibid. p. 23). He argued also that 'it might...be thought sensible to introduce the scheme in one area of Britain first before applying it to the whole country. If so, there is an obvious opportunity to do so in Scotland' (ibid. p. 46). The 47 page work also set out broad details of how such a scheme might work in practice, and dealt with such matters as compiling and updating a register, rebates and second homes.

In terms of the influence of Douglas Mason and the ASI, it seems evident that their links with MPs and councillors helped at least in some way to build up support for a poll tax within the Conservative Party. The idea that Douglas Mason was the 'father' of the Poll Tax, however, certainly seems to be something of a myth. *Revising the Rating System* was published in April (*after* a poll tax had asserted itself within the DoE enquiry), and as Crick and Van Klaveren (1991, p. 407) suggest:

'Nobody involved in government work on the tax in 1984 and 1985 believes that the ASI had any influence. "Never heard of him", says one of the leading officials of Douglas Mason, though others were vaguely aware of his ideas.'

Further major support for a poll tax came from the Federation of Scottish Ratepayers, which continued to maintain a high public profile. Its main aim was simply to abolish domestic rates, although not only did a poll tax 'fit' with its desire to spread the tax burden more widely and increase local 'accountability', but the FSR (as mentioned in the previous chapter) had already been told by Michael Forsyth (seemingly aware of the progress that was being made on the DoE enquiry), that a poll tax was very much 'on the cards'. RAGE (1985) argued also, in its campaign literature in April 1985, that 'A Poll Tax seems the leading idea at the moment and we would certainly go along with this.' Both groups continued to encourage ratepayers through leafleting and public meetings, to put pressure on the Conservative Party at all levels to abolish the rates and replace them (preferably) with a poll tax. The leadership of both groups also continued to lobby Scottish Party Chairman Sir James Goold and Scottish Office Ministers, and arranged a fringe meeting at the Conservative Party Conference in May, where they were supported by Michael Forsyth.

The final major area of support for a poll tax came from the CBI at a UK level. Its domestic activities were under pressure from high interest rates and the gradual strengthening of sterling. At the end of April, therefore, President James Cleminson wrote to Environment Secretary, Patrick Jenkin, urging him to act swiftly by putting a 'ceiling' on business rates. The letter spoke also of encouragement at the possibility of a poll tax, stating that this 'would score very highly in promoting local accountability' (CBI, 1985a, p. 3)

Overall, these appear to have been the only major groups from outside the Conservative Party which supported the introduction of a poll tax. [2] In contrast, opposition to a poll tax was far more extensive, although very low-key. In essence, this seemed to be because the proposals were still at the embryonic stage, and also because many assumed that its impracticality would mean that such a tax would never see the light of day. It is possible to be more specific about such matters as we move on to look at opposition to a poll tax from outside the Conservative Party.

Outside the Conservative Party: Opposition to a Poll Tax

Not all domestic ratepayers supported a poll tax. The Scottish Federation of Owner-Occupiers (with approximately 6000 members) and the Federated Association of Owner-Occupiers of Glasgow (approximately 5000 members) advocated a system whereby all nationally-created expenditure was removed from the local budget and transferred to the Exchequer. The remainder would be directly 'local' and funded by wage earners, taxed on their ability to pay. Both Federations (although less influential than the FSR), lobbied the Scottish Secretary to this effect.

The Labour Party, despite having no alternative to domestic rates, condemned the possibility of a poll tax. Scottish Labour Leader, Donald Dewar, said that he would not be prepared to accept a short-term solution such as a poll tax, whilst *Scottish Labour Activist* (1985, p. 3), the paper of the Labour Co-ordinating Committee, stressed that:

> 'The Labour Party must spare no effort in making the case against a Poll Tax. It must be remembered that Poll Taxes were used by racist administrations in the Southern States of the USA, from the 1870s to the 1960s to prevent blacks from voting. The only escape that the poor in Britain would have of evading a Poll Tax would be not to register to vote.'

South of the Border, the Labour Party seemed equally opposed. Shadow Environment Secretary, Jack Cunningham, said in the House of Commons that 'the whole idea of taxing registrations to vote is abhorrent in a democratic society...if any such system were introduced, it would be abolished by the next Labour Government' (HC Debates, 1984-85, Vol. 78, col. 775).

The SNP also continued its policy of favouring a local income tax. After a 'Day of Action' at the end of April (involving distributing leaflets and questionnaires throughout Scotland), it argued that 'the Tories' fondness for a flat-rate Poll Tax is a dangerous diversion. It is regressive, hits the poor hardest and is a tax on the " right to vote", threatening the whole democratic basis of universal suffrage' (SNP 1985c). The Liberal/SDP Alliance also continued to support a local income tax and thus was opposed to a poll tax. Robert Maclennan, of the SDP in Scotland, wrote to the Prime Minister expressing horror that a Poll Tax was under consideration. Liberal Leader, David Steel, wrote to Environment Secretary, Patrick Jenkin, accusing the Government of a panic reaction, saying that a poll tax would do 'further irreparable damage to the Government' (*Times*, 10 April 1985). Also, SDP

Environment spokesman, John Cartwright, called a poll tax 'monstrously unfair', saying that 'making the poorest pay exactly the same as the wealthiest would show that this government is not interested in easing the burden on the low paid and those in need' (*Local Government Chronicle*, 12 April 1985, p. 400).

In local government (still staying outside the Conservative Party for the moment), COSLA had already rejected the idea of a poll tax when it wrote to the Prime Minister, arguing that any new tax would have to be one which increased local autonomy. Furthermore, both the Labour-controlled Association of Metropolitan Authorities (AMA) and the Association of London Authorities (ALA) met with Ministers as part of the internal DoE enquiry, to add their voices to what the *Municipal Journal* (7 July 1985, p. 910) described as 'the growing chorus of opponents to [the] Poll Tax as a substitute for domestic rates.' The AMA favoured a local income tax, whilst the ALA had not yet made any public statement on an alternative.

A number of professional bodies were also opposed to a poll tax. Speaking at the Rating and Valuation Association's annual conference at the end of April, its President, John Sharp, said that 'the R&VA as a corporate body finds itself still in favour of revaluation...[the] poll tax must be the most regressive tax that has ever been thought of' (quoted in Maclean, 1985, p. 700). In addition, the Chartered Institute of Public Finance and Accountancy (CIPFA) published an initial analysis of the impact of a poll tax, and expressed some scepticism at the possibility of a poll tax alone. Under-Secretary, Rita Hale (1985a, p. vii) suggested that 'if it will not lead to a devolution of power then there is really little point in going through the upheaval its introduction would cause.' Finally, in terms of professional bodies, the Society of Local Authority Chief Executives (SOLACE) expressed concern that a poll tax would cause substantial problems in getting people to register and was likely to lead to an increased electoral shortfall.

With regard to the Trades Union movement, public condemnation of a poll tax was almost non-existent at this stage (see Chapters Six and Seven for further discussion). The only public statement by either the TUC or the STUC was by the TUC at its conference in September, where Congress simply stated its opposition to a poll tax. It favoured a system along the lines of the Layfield Committee, which had favoured a local income tax as a supplement to domestic rates (see Chapter Three).

As far as the media was concerned, many sections of it did not yet find the prospect of reform worthy of editorial prominence. Those which did, however, did not accept the need for a poll tax. The *Glasgow Herald* favoured a system with a strong component of local income tax, whilst the *Scotsman* (1 April 1985) suggested that 'a poll tax...is not the best reform. It would bear heavily on those with less money. A local income tax would be far fairer in relating the levy to people's actual means.' Even the *Financial Times* (3 April 1985), normally a staunch supporter of the Conservative Party, argued that 'Rates are far too good a tax to throw away but they need modernising and they need supplementing with one or more extra revenue sources...[a local income tax] merits at least serious consideration.'

Finally, in terms of public opinion, the possibility of a poll tax may seem in retrospect to have been very much 'on the cards' at this time. Yet, it reality, a combination of the minor status of the various press reports and the seeming implausibility of a poll tax in 20th century Britain, meant that the 'Poll Tax' was simply *not* a major (and hardly even a minor) issue. Nevertheless, there is some evidence that public opinion was set firmly against the introduction of such a tax. In Scotland, a MORI Poll in May 1985 found only 33 per cent in favour of a poll tax, levied at £120 per head (*Scotsman*, 8 May 1985). In England and Wales in the Autumn, a MORI poll found only 24 per cent support for a poll tax of £200 per head (see the *Economist*, 1986a, p. 21). More generally, a poll commissioned in September by the AMA found three out of four people in England and Wales agreeing that local spending should be determined by local government and not by central government (*Municipal Journal*, 20 September 1985, p. 1356).

The Contradiction Within the Conservative Party

The arguments outlined so far, both for and against a poll tax, seem to represent respectively, the desirability for radical reform and the insuperability of achieving that reform. This is an important point because we find this contradiction manifesting itself at varying levels and to varying degrees within the Conservative Party. In other words, the Party was being pulled apart in ideological terms. On the one hand, it wanted radical reform by abolishing the rates and many wanted replacement by a poll tax - thus marrying with the two key principles of spreading the local tax burden and increasing local government 'accountability'. On the other hand, however, there was much resistance to/scepticism of a poll tax, on both ideological and practical grounds. This ambivalence must now be considered in more detail.

The two Party enquiries announced by Sir James Goold and also separate publications by Michael Forsyth MP and Ross Harper, Chairman of the Society of Scottish Conservative Lawyers, produced an *overall* 'contradictory' response. The strongest support for a poll tax came from Michael Forsyth. [2] He argued that

'less than half of the electorate actually pay rates. In some areas it is lower than one in ten. The majority of voters are not householders and rate rebates and the unified housing benefit scheme make sure that many millions contribute nothing to the costs of running councils they elect' (Forsyth, 1985b, p. 3).

The problem with this, he suggested, was that 'the radical left realise all too well that they can play politics with their ratepayers' cash' (ibid. p. 4), spending money whilst those who vote for them will not have to pay. In order to overcome this, therefore, he advocated the introduction of a poll tax, levied at £155 per head, and outlined how this might work in practice, suggesting that Scotland be used for a 'pilot' scheme. [3] This, he argued, would ensure that people faced the financial consequences of their actions if they voted for 'spendthrift' councils.

Further support for a poll tax came from the Conservative Local Government Advisory Committee which advocated a poll tax of roughly £175 per head, although it also put forward the suggestion that consideration should be given to central funding of education, fire, police and water services. [4]

The two remaining reports provided something of a counter-reaction to these views. The Conservative Arrow Group favoured a *per capita* rating tax paid by all wage earners, with the rating system being retained as the basis for this. A publication by Ross Harper on behalf of the Society of Scottish Conservative Lawyers, was by far the most cautious of all. It argued that 'if it is deemed politically expedient to promise change then we must hasten slowly' (Harper, 1985, p. 25). Its own proposals were highly ambiguous [5], although its view of a poll tax was clear, stating that 'the system of a Poll Tax does not have many supporters - understandably so' (ibid. p. 24). This was based on the concerns that linking taxation to voting would have a damaging effect on the electoral process; that the Tax would be regressive, and that it would be difficult and costly to administer.

Turning now to the position of the mass of Scottish Conservative activists, the view held by Party Chairman, Sir James Goold (1991), was that they would have accepted almost any alternative 'so long as it was abolition of domestic rates.' Revaluation had given birth to the Campaign for the Communication of Conservative Policies (CCCP), which Chairman, Iain Lawson (1989) described as 'borne out of the desperation of revaluation.' Fuelled further by the proposed closure of Gartcosh,

Radical Scotland (1986, p. 6) suggested that the CCCP was a 'symbol of mass disaffection on the part of the Conservative grass roots.' At its inaugural conference in June, attended by almost 200 delegates representing the vast majority of Scottish constituencies, the CCCP did not endorse a move to a poll tax. It was determined, however, that rates abolition would be on the statute book before the next General Election - thus ensuring that the CCCP was a 'thorn in the side' of the Party leadership. [6] Overall, therefore, the CCCP is illustrative of this desire for radical change but opposition to the most radical solution of all - a poll tax.

Conservatives in Local Government also produced an ambivalent response. In Scotland, a Conservative Local Government Conference at the end of April avoided taking a vote on the Advisory Committee's report which favoured a poll tax. In England and Wales, at the end of June, a meeting of Conservative delegates (representing 70 constituencies) endorsed only the need for change, but stopped short of advocating a full-blown poll tax. The *Municipal Journal* (5 July 1985, p. 1102) reported that 'while one school of thought favoured a residents' charge...[another name for a poll tax] as an alternative to domestic rates, the bulk of delegates supported the...view that a property tax should stay, but supplemented by a residents' charge.' In addition, the Conservative-dominated ADC favoured a local income tax. Indeed, its chairman, John Morgan, specifically rejected the idea of a poll tax, saying that 'getting involved with personal incomes is the job of the Inland Revenue and not the district councils' (quoted in *Municipal Journal*, 28 June 1985, p. 1062).

With regard to the position of MPs, there tended to be a slight division between those north and south of the border. The tendency was for Scots MPs to favour *any* solution to ensure that the trauma of revaluation would never be felt again. Nevertheless, personal preferences were still evident, with (for example) Michael Forsyth and Allan Stewart favouring a poll tax, Bill Walker and Michael Hirst favouring a local income tax and Lord James Douglas-Hamilton favouring a substantial increase in central funding with a poll tax being a possibility for the balance (see HC Debates, 1984-85, Vol. 76, cols. 319-55). The tendency for English and Welsh MPs, whilst also having their own personal preferences, was for much more direct scepticism of the possibility of a poll tax. For example, Robin Squire MP argued that 'the single central failing of a poll tax is that it cannot command the broad support that a fundamental reform of the rating system should have' (HC Debates, 1984-85, Vol. 78, col. 775). David Heathcoat-Amory MP also expressed concern, saying that a 'poll tax...is less attractive the closer it is studied' (ibid. col. 774). More comprehensively, one report suggested that Ministers consulted Senior Tory backbenchers on a poll tax but they were told that it would not win support (*Guardian*, 1 July 1985).

Faced with these competing calls, it is unsurprising that Scottish Office Ministers were confronted with an intractable situation. At the turbulent and highly-charged Party Conference in May, George Younger, still under pressure form all sides, reiterated the commitment to abandon the rates, saying that 'I accept on behalf of the Government that we are expected to take action on our thoroughly unsatisfactory system of local government finance. The present system as it stands is not an option' (quoted in the *Times*, 10 May 1985). The dilemma of what to do about this, however, was proving to be enormous. As an editorial in the *Scotsman* (7 May 1985) noted:

'Rarely have Government Ministers been so confused as they are over rates. Their Scottish team in particular, gives the impression of being at a complete loss as to how to deal with the revolt that is raging north of the border.'

South of the Border, however, it was up to the Cabinet sub-committee and the DoE enquiry to work through what Conservative MP Teddy Taylor (1985d, p. 5) called the 'horrendous practical problems' of actually producing an alternative system. On the one hand, the Party had committed itself to abolishing the rates. As a result, and laying the basis for an alternative, the continual signals emerging from the DoE enquiry were ones of 'fairness' to ratepayers (i.e. spreading the local tax burden), and increasing local 'accountability' (i.e. shorthand for adhering to central government's spending plans). As Junior Environment Minister, William Waldegrave (1985, pp. 1076-7) argued:

'There are 35 million local electors in England. Only 18 million are liable to pay rates. Of these, only about 12 million pay their rates in full. So about three million receive a partial rebate and the remaining three million receive full relief from their rates bills...those receiving full relief have every incentive to use their vote to maximise the level of services available to them at no cost to themselves.'

The DoE enquiry and the views expressed above were spurred on and reinforced by the Prime Minister. She was reportedly enthusiastic about reform, saying that 'we have reached the stage where no amount of patching up the existing system can overcome its inherent unfairness' (*Scotsman*, 11 May 1985). Latterly, she described the rates as 'manifestly unfair and un-Conservative' (Thatcher, 1993, p. 644). She apparently took a long time to be convinced of the practicality of a poll tax, but was lobbied consistently by Oliver Letwin (the local government adviser within her Policy Unit) who was extremely keen on the Tax (Crick and Van Klaveren, 1991, p. 410). It must be recognised, however, that in the same manner as previous attempts to reform the rating system, it may still have been possible for the proposals to be abandoned - even at this stage. Yet, not only were the pressures for reform exceptionally intense, but they were overseen by a Prime Minister who was not noted for her pragmatism. Thus, whilst it would be totally inaccurate to describe the Poll Tax as the 'child' of Mrs Thatcher, it is important to recognise her role in the entire decision making process. Thus, Sir James (later Lord) Goold (1991) described her role as 'absolutely vital' in keeping the momentum going, whilst Scottish Secretary, George Younger (1991) stated that 'she was the key to it in the sense that she was a radical...anyone else might not have been brave enough to make such a radical change.'

Thus, within a month of Mrs Thatcher's public commitment to abandon the rates, it was now evident publically that the Prime Minister and 'senior colleagues' *had* agreed that a poll tax would be involved in some form or other. By early May, the *Scotsman* (6 May 1985) stated that a poll tax 'is reported to have won favour around the Cabinet table' (see also the *Times*, 17 April 1985; *Financial Times*, 18 April 1985). Reports suggested also that other alternatives were being pushed to one side. The reasons for this seem to illustrate the incompatibility of the main alternatives with the Government's primary strategic objectives. For example, the *Financial Times* (18 April 1985) reported that a 'Local Income Tax is ruled out and no further work will be done on it.' The persistent arguments which emerged were (a) that it was impractical because Inland Revenue records were not computerised in England and Wales and (b) it would provide local authorities with a power base which would still leave them free to spend extravagantly and pass the burden on to local tax payers and impact upon the Government's macro-economic management. This also seemed to be the main reason for ruling out a local sales tax, because of the effect that high local taxes would have on inflation (Crick and Van Klaveren, 1991). Finally, in the House of Commons, Environment Secretary, Patrick Jenkin, seemed to rule out the centralising of some services, stating that he did 'not believe that the answer to the problem is simply to centralise more spending on the Exchequer' (HC Debates, 1985-86, Vol. 78, col. 772). The general argument which emerged as supportive of this, was that such a measure would effectively abdicate local authorities of any financial responsibility to the electorate.

On the other hand, and in contrast to this trend within the Cabinet towards radical reform, there were continual reports of considerable opposition to a poll tax, and sometimes even to the very need for reform at all. One report suggested that 'Many senior Scottish Conservatives at Westminster remain despondent because of the lack of sympathy in Whitehall for the...problems facing the Party' (*Scotsman*, 19 April 1985). Certainly, the Treasury's opposition to reform was well-known. It was backed by what Mackay (1985, p. 12) suggests were two 'powerful' arguments - namely (a) that control had already been established over local government expenditure and (b) an alternative was potentially more unpopular than the rates. Chancellor Nigel Lawson was undoubtedly the member of E(LF) most vehemently opposed to a poll tax. He submitted a paper to the Committee in May, arguing for a property tax based on capital values (indeed, very similar to the later Council Tax), suggesting that 'The proposals for a poll tax would be completely unworkable and politically catastrophic' (Lawson, 1992, p. 574). On a very general level, there were also reports that some Ministers were understood to have objected to a poll tax on the grounds that it was regressive and would hit 'poorer' families whilst benefiting those in upper income brackets (*Scotsman*, 21 May 1985). The *Guardian* (21 May 1985) also reported that 'some Ministers are understood to be extremely nervous of the Poll Tax idea.' Precisely who these Ministers were, however, is not particularly easy to determine, and many of the press reports at the time pertained to Ministers who were not members of the Cabinet Committee. Ministers reportedly opposed to a poll tax were Foreign Secretary, Geoffrey Howe, Defence Secretary, Michael Heseltine and Northern Ireland Secretary, Douglas Hurd (*Financial Times*, 12 August 1985; *Municipal Journal*, 27 September 1985, p. 1581). Energy Secretary, Peter Walker, (1991) also claims to have been opposed. Lawson, however, suggests that the only support he got was from Chief Secretary, Peter Rees (Crick and Van Klaveren, 1991) and then from the new Chief Secretary, John MacGregor (Lawson, 1992, p. 576). Certainly, Michael Heseltine's position was clear. He favoured local authorities being required to hold an election if their budget exceeded a figure set by the centre. He had held this view as Environment Secretary in 1981 and continued to adhere to this in the wake of the subsequent implementation of the Poll Tax (Heseltine, 1990).

There was also more indirect opposition in terms of practical matters surrounding the introduction of a poll tax. The DHSS objected to the use of National Insurance records for the purposes of compiling a register

(*Financial Times*, 21 April 1985). Home Secretary, Leon Brittan, objected to the use of the electoral register as the basis for compiling a register of those liable to pay (*Scotsman*, 10 April 1985; *Financial Times*, 18 April 1985; Crick and Van Klaveren, 1991, p. 411). It was because of this objection that the term 'poll tax' was dropped in favour of the term 'resident's charge' - thus attempting to quell any criticism of a link between payment of taxation and the right to vote.

What *all* of the foregoing seems to indicate - irrespective of the murky waters that exist in the realms of the precise decision making process - is the way in which the Cabinet embodied this contradiction of a desire for radical reform, yet the insuperability of achieving that reform on ideological and practical grounds. Based on this, it seems useful to suggest on a provisional basis, that the Cabinet was embodying and attempting to 'balance' the two forces for change. Thus, as identified previously, this gave rise to a general trend towards a dual system of a property tax and a poll tax (which had been renamed as a Resident's Charge) as put forward by Kenneth Baker who had succeeded Patrick Jenkin as Environment Secretary at the beginning of September. Otherwise, to renege on its commitment to reform would undoubtedly have led to another 'outcry' in Scotland, whilst a poll tax alone (at the time) may not have commanded sufficient support among the Party in England and Wales.

Bearing this is mind, it is important now to identify the way in which this trend towards a dual system fell apart and was replaced by the option of a poll tax alone.

The Move to a Poll Tax (October 1985 - January 1986)

Changing 'political' and 'economic' circumstances reveal the growth of a crucial divergence between the fortunes of the Conservative Party at UK and Scottish levels during this period. Until early January 1986 and the drama surrounding the Westland Affair, the period saw a marked improvement in the fortunes of the Party at a UK level. In general terms, but particularly in the South East, the ability of the Government to sustain the earlier income tax reductions (because of oil revenues and privatisation proceeds) led to a growth in real incomes and a growth in consumer spending (fuelled further by the increased availability of credit), whilst high interest rates and a strong pound helped to reverse the upward inflation trend which stood at 5.5 per cent by January (Central Statistical Office, February 1986). As a result, Conservative fortunes in opinion polls took a dramatic upswing. By December, the Party had regained its lead in Gallup polls on voting intentions, with a figure of 33 per cent (contrasting with 24 per cent in August) - largely at the expense of Labour (Heald and Wybrow, 1985). In addition, public perceptions of the party most likely to win a General Election saw the figures for the Conservatives increase over the same period from 34 per cent to 47 per cent, whilst the figure for Labour dropped from 33 per cent to 24 per cent (ibid.).

In contrast to this, the fortunes of the Party in Scotland showed no signs of improving. As well as bearing the brunt of the Government's interest/exchange rate policy which was geared largely towards the City and the more buoyant economy in the South East, there was also the delay in 'doing something' about the rates, the closure of Gartcosh, and the continuing teachers' dispute. As a result, as shown in Table 5.1, Conservative support in Scotland remained very poor and slumped to a record low immediately after the Westland Affair in January.

Table 5.1
Party Political Support in Scotland (System Three)*

Parties in Scotland	G.E. 1983	Sept. 1985	Oct. 1985	Nov. 1985	Jan. 1986
Conservative	28%	18%	22%	19%	15%
Labour	35%	41%	45%	42%	46%
Alliance	25%	28%	21%	22%	23%
SNP	12%	13%	12%	15%	16%

* There was no poll in December.

Source: *Glasgow Herald*, 19 December 1985; 17 January 1986.

It is against this general background that the final move to a poll tax (alone) came in two stages.

The Scottish 'Solution'

Two main factors resulted in a shift away from a dual system and a recognition within the Cabinet Committee that the rating system should be abolished totally in Scotland and replaced by a poll tax.

First, there was the reaction from the Conservative 'grassroots' in Scotland, to the 'horrific' possibility that rates would remain in some form. As Iain Lawson (1989), the CCCP Chairman, argued:

'They were so stunned and so concerned about the effects of the public reaction to revaluation that it was absolute desperation. There's no other description for the way that the average Party member felt. They just could not believe that their government were going ahead with this. They were putting the most massive pressure on...Ministers, both in Scotland and in England.'

When combined with the general situation facing the Party in Scotland, as one commentator noted - 'Many Conservative activists now feel that their loyal Scottish organisation is being abandoned for the greater good of the party nationally' (*Radical Scotland*, 1986, p. 6). At the Party Conference at Blackpool in October, roughly 200 Scots activists (compared to about 50 normally) turned up to lobby English and Welsh delegates outside the main hall. The thrust of their calls was that rates abolition *must* be on the statute book by the time the Party fought the next General Election. Speaking also at the conference, SCUA Honorary Secretary, James Highgate, said that speedy action was necessary, otherwise the Government's fate would be sealed. Scottish Secretary, George Younger, in an attempt to stem this tide, stated publicly that Scotland was prepared to 'go it alone' on reform. He was supported in this by the main opposition parties, although they were opposed to any move towards a poll tax. At the Labour Party Conference the previous week, Shadow Environment Secretary, Jack Cunningham, said that 'we want nothing to do with the Poll Tax. If the Tories try and impose one, then in the interim we shall oppose it in Parliament' (quoted in *Municipal Journal*, 4 October 1985, p. 1614).

The second factor, reinforcing the above, was the reaction of ratepayers. This was not only to the dual system that seemed to be emerging, but also the fact that concrete proposals were still not forthcoming and indeed there were some reports that the reforms might 'fall by the wayside' (see e.g. *Financial Times*, 11 November; *Scotsman*, 12 November 1985). The FSR (1985c) wrote to George Younger, stating that:

'Ratepayers in Scotland are becoming increasingly alarmed at the reports of lack of interest in England about the need to reform the financing of local government and the opposition you are said to be encountering in Cabinet to a UK Bill...if the proposal to abolish rates is not acceptable in England, then we would strongly support the case for action to legislate for Scotland alone.'

The Federation also encouraged members to express this view to MPs in local surgeries, and to write to the Prime Minister, reminding her of the Party's promise to abolish the rating system and her own personal commitment to do so in the October 1974 General Election. Representatives of the FSR also lobbied George Younger at the Scottish Office. In addition to this, non-domestic ratepayers were keen to ensure that reform went ahead - in Scotland at least. The most active of the non-domestic ratepayers groups, the NFSESB, urged all political parties to join forces in ensuring an end to the rating system.

These two factors acted together to rekindle the turmoil that had surrounded revaluation. When combined with the divergent fortunes of the Conservative Party at Scottish and UK levels, this seemed to provide George Younger with the ammunition to persuade his Cabinet colleagues of the 'nail in the coffin' that either a dual system or a no reform situation would bring, and that a *per capita* (poll) tax was the most feasible option, *despite* the potential electoral consequences of spreading the tax burden. As Younger (1991) argued:

'We specifically faced up to the fact that, if you're bringing a whole lot of people into paying a tax that they've never paid before, it's not going to be popular. But it...[i.e. the rating system] was violently unpopular among the few people who did pay...and they were our people...it wasn't up to us to kick them in the teeth again.'

By mid-December, therefore, the Cabinet Sub-Committee had agreed on the introduction of a Community Charge (now renamed from a Resident's Charge), and that a Green Paper would be introduced at the turn of the year. This was accompanied by Scottish Office Ministers and senior Party officials, campaigning to ensure that the whole Party united behind the proposals (*Scotsman*, 11 December 1985).

The English and Welsh 'Solution'

The position within Cabinet as far as England and Wales was concerned, was still unresolved. The basic conflict was between (a) the Prime Minister and Norman Tebbit (at least) who were determined to push ahead with the reforms on a national level, and (b) most Cabinet members, who, as the *Financial Times* (23 December 1985) suggested, 'would prefer to do nothing'. The outcome was the ascendancy of the pro-poll tax forces. This was through a compromise plan proposed by Environment Secretary Kenneth Baker (1993, p. 126), but also reported to be devised by Welsh Secretary, Nicholas Edwards (*Financial Times*, 23 December 1985). This was known as 'dual running' and involved a gradual withering away of domestic rates over many years in England and Wales. Whilst Baker (1992, p. 126) described this as essential, because otherwise 'we would run the risk of asking too much too quickly and it could bring the whole system down', the *Financial Times* (23 December 1985) reported that this was 'variously described by other Cabinet Ministers as a wheeze and not serious.' More specifically, it was seen as a ploy to satisfy the pressures for reform (both inside and outside the Cabinet), whilst delaying implementation to such an extent (i.e. coming five years later in 1990 and then a 10-year phase-in) that 'something' would come along to ensure that a poll tax was never fully implemented.

The end result of these agreements, therefore, was that on Thursday 9 January 1986, the Cabinet approved a package of reforms. This was the first time that the *full* Cabinet had discussed the poll tax proposals. Furthermore, and perhaps best described as a 'quirk' of history, this took place immediately after a break taken by the Cabinet to recover from the sudden resignation that morning of Defence Secretary, Michael Heseltine, after refusing to accept the insistence by Mrs Thatcher that all Ministerial statements on the Westland issue required prior clearance by the Cabinet Office. In the ensuing reshuffle, Malcolm Rifkind took over from George Younger as Scottish Secretary and thus was responsible for overseeing the publication at the end of January of the Green Paper *Paying for Local Government* (Cmnd. 9714, 1986). It advocated the introduction of a Community Charge to be phased in over three years in Scotland (commencing 1 April 1989); over six years in Wales, and over ten years in England (commencing 1 April 1990).

Conclusion

At the end of the previous chapter, we saw that by late March 1985, a powerful alliance of forces in favour of rates abolition was then joined crucially by the Conservative Government in an attempt to maintain its legitimacy to govern and, hence its general 'leading' strategy for the restructuring of British society. In the present chapter, however, we saw the opening up of a fundamental split in this alliance of forces - both inside and outside the Conservative Party. On the one hand, there was the desire for radical reform by abolishing the rates and replacing them with the most radical reform of all - a poll tax. Yet, on the other hand, there was resistance on both ideological and practical grounds to this solution. The Cabinet both embodied and attempted to balance these opposing forces through the moves towards a dual system of a property tax and a poll tax. As part of the 'leading capitalist forces' in society, it was imbued with the authority to *take the lead and take control* of this policy formation process and the struggle that had emerged over a new system of local taxation. It was 'leading' and helping to set the political agenda, particularly because of the provisional conclusions of the DoE enquiry that the local tax burden was falling on too few shoulders and that there had been an erosion of local accountability to the electorate. The initial trend towards a compromise between these principles and political realities was embodied in a combination tax, but was soon replaced by a movement to a poll tax alone. This arose because of a strengthening of the pro-poll tax forces as a result largely of (a) the confidence given to the Conservatives as a consequence of the beginnings of an economic upswing (particularly in the South East) and an improvement in its political fortunes at a UK level (b) the precarious position of Scottish Conservatives and the contribution from Party activists and ratepayers to the reawakening of the turmoil surrounding revaluation, and (c) the reaching of a compromise agreement within the Cabinet on the need for the introduction of a poll tax in England and Wales.

A more comprehensive analysis of all this will be conducted in the Conclusion. In the meantime, however, we can move on to the next stage in the policy formation process and look at the Government's Green Paper (containing a firm commitment to introduce a Poll Tax) and the reaction/responses to this and the ensuing 'consultation' exercise. We also see in this, how the process of 'consultation' allowed the state to take the lead and take control *even more*, of the entire policy formation process

Notes

1. With regard to non-domestic ratepayers, he argued that 'A national assessment should be made of the benefits non-domestic ratepayers such as businesses receive from local government and the costs involved in providing them. That assessment should be used as the basis for fixing a new national rate poundage, indexed for inflation, to be applied to all non-domestic ratepayers' (Mason, 1985, p. 46).

2. Douglas Mason of the Adam Smith Institute (ASI) was also a Conservative councillor. Given that he was writing on behalf of the ASI, however, it is assumed here that his ideas were 'outside' the

Conservative Party. It is recognised, of course, that his personal contact with Party members (including the undertaking of research work for Michael Forsyth) means that, in practice, it is not possible to draw such a clear dividing line. Another way of arriving at the same conclusion is via a close reading of Mason's (1985) *Revising the Rating System* and Michael Forsyth's (1985) *The Case for a Poll Tax*. An examination of both reveals a *remarkable* similarity in terms of the style, structure and content of many passages. Private information in the hands of the author of the present work reveals that Douglas Mason did in fact write both publications. This is confirmed in research undertaken for BBC *Panorama* by Crick and Van Klaveren (1991), who came to the same conclusion on the basis of information obtained from two separate sources.

3. He argued also for a fixed, national non-domestic rate poundage, or fixed rates for each of the separate parts of the UK.

4. Its proposal for non-domestic rates was the same as (3) above.

5. Apart from rejecting a poll tax, the report seemed to find attraction in a number of possibilities and was by no means clear on which one was favoured. On *page 16*, it suggested that 'it would be possible to alter the present system but retain property as its base...a switch to capital values may involve practical difficulties of implementation, but the obstacles do not appear to be insuperable if it is ultimately decided to take the plunge' (Harper, 1985, p. 16). On *page 25*, however, in its 'Conclusions', it stated that 'Developments in advanced technology may well provide easier solutions to problems presently encountered when considering alternatives to the rates system. For example, it is projected that every national income tax payer will be monitored on a computer basis by 1987 and accordingly it could well be possible for a system of local income tax to be organised on this computer basis by the early 1990s' (ibid. p. 25). In addition to this, another 'Conclusion' on the *following page* proposed 'changing the basis of valuations so that they are based not only on the notional rental value of the property but also on the number of adult occupants' (ibid. p. 26). Finally, yet another 'Conclusion' on the *same* page recommended 'Considering the transfer of responsibility for funding education and police to the National Exchequer' (ibid. p. 26).

6. Iain Lawson himself was undoubtedly a 'thorn in the side' of the Party hierarchy. As Lawson (1989) commented 'I was summoned to a meeting to meet Goold and was basically told that I was finished in the Tory Party unless I gave up on Gartcosh' (Lawson, 1989). At the beginning of October 1985, Lawson resigned as CCCP Chairman and the CCCP folded, although the underlying discontent of many Party activists remained. The following year, Lawson joined the SNP.

6 The Green Paper and Public 'Consultation'

This chapter outlines the main elements of the Green Paper *Paying for Local Government* (Cmnd. 9714, 1986) and identifies the main thrust and the context of the varying reactions to it. In this respect, the chapter covers a period from the end of January 1986 through to the end of November 1986, when the *Abolition of Domestic Rates Etc. (Scotland) Bill* received its First Reading in the House of Commons.

The structure of the chapter is as follows. First, it provides a general 'political' and 'economic' background to the period under consideration, focusing particularly on the continued divergence between the fortunes of the Conservative Party at Scottish and UK levels. Second, it identifies the main findings and proposals contained in the Green Paper. Third, it considers the reaction to these in two main phases within the consultation period. Fourth, it provides a summary of official responses and identifies the reaction to these by the Conservative Party in terms of its decision to proceed swiftly with the introduction of a Bill. Finally, it takes a brief overview of the chapter in terms of matters pertaining to 'policy formation'.

It should be noted that the chapter will concern itself with the reaction to the Green Paper *as a whole* (thus including the non-domestic rating reforms). The reason for this is that the Government used support from the non-domestic sector for a Uniform Business Rate, as justification to proceed with the reforms in general.

Background (January - November 1986)

The Westland Affair and its aftermath plunged the Conservative Party into an acute political crisis (see Dunleavy, 1990). It is worth quoting, at length, the comments of the *Economist* (1986, p. 12) at the beginning of February. These link the Westland Affair to the Government's general strategy and its effects, by stating that:

> 'The Westland affair has stripped Margaret Thatcher's leadership of vital authority. Her hesitant handling of a rebellious colleague, her misleading explanations to Parliament, the departure of two good cabinet ministers, taken together in just a few weeks, these mistakes have given her government a shiftiness reminiscent of the later years of Mr Harold (now Lord) Wilson's Labour administrations.
>
> The weakening of Mrs Thatcher comes at a bad time for the British economy. The pound has been under pressure this month and interest rates have risen. Growth is slowing, industrialists are grumbling and the trade-off between unemployment and wage inflation is becoming even worse. Some of these economic weaknesses are inevitable in the fifth year of a recovery. But the others will go untreated if what is left of Mrs Thatcher's toughness has to be devoted to the duller task of political survival.'

The political reverberations of this continued for several months, with Conservative support in Gallup polls on voting intentions, falling from 29.5 per cent in January to 27.5 per cent in May (Craig, 1989, p. 110). Throughout this period, the Party sat in third place behind Labour and the Alliance. Also, in May, it lost over 200 seats and control of 29 Councils in the municipal elections in England and Wales. Furthermore, in Parliamentary by-elections, it lost control of the previously Conservative-held seats of Fulham and Ryedale, whilst retaining a third (West Derbyshire) by only 100 votes.

Underlying these political troubles, however, the immediate post-Westland period and beyond actually saw the beginnings of a partial turnaround in the fortunes of the economy. Financed again by oil revenues and privatisation proceeds, the March Budget saw a further reduction in the Basic Rate of Income Tax from 30 per cent to 29 per cent. Thus, whilst the real value of incomes for those in work was maintained (especially in and around London and the South-East), a City-orientated policy of high interest rates and the stabilising of sterling around the $1.40 mark, meant that inflation fell to a low of 2.4 per cent in July and August (Central Statistical Office, January 1987). Essentially, this was because of the impact of the exchange/interest rate policy in deflating much of the outlying regions, with seasonally adjusted unemployment increasing by an average of 15,000 per month for the first six months of the year (Fraser of Allander Institute, November 1986, p. 15).

Despite these figures, however, as the *Economist* (1987a, p. 21) noted - 'comfortable voters overlooked the one out of eight workers on the lengthening dole queue.' Thus, the Conservative Party, assisted also by a partial collapse of the Alliance vote because of a split over defence policy, was able to strengthen its vote in the South and so strengthen its overall fortunes from July onwards. In Gallup polls, support increased from the May figure of 27 per cent, to 36 per cent in November (although this still put it slightly behind Labour, who stood at 39.5 per cent) (Craig 1989, p. 110). Significantly, however, public perceptions of the Conservatives' electoral strength also took a substantial upswing. For example, in March, 36 per cent of voters expected the Conservative Party to win the next General Election and 40 per cent thought that Labour would do so. By November, however, the figure for the Conservatives had increased dramatically to 65 per cent, and support for Labour had slumped to 18 per cent (Gallup, November 1986).

The fortunes of the Conservative Party in Scotland, however, continued to show no signs of paralleling such successes. As McCrone (1987, p. 7) comments - 'Nineteen eighty-six was not a year of miracles. Scotland slid further into the pit of economic recession.' In 1986, seasonally-adjusted unemployment figures for the UK as a whole, fell by 2.7 per cent, whilst in Scotland they actually increased by 2.5 per cent (Central Statistical Office, February 1986 and 1987). [1] Future employment prospects also indicated that this gap would increase. A collapse in world oil prices led to a fall in the 'spot price' of North Sea Oil by roughly 50 per cent between January and October. Salmond and Walker (1986, p. 87) estimated that this would lead to an increase in the Scottish unemployment rate of between 0.9 per cent and 1.3 per cent over the next two years. The slump in oil prices also put further pressure on the coal industry, with British Coal proposing to close one pit (Comrie) and rationalise four others (Monktonhall, Bilston, Killoch and Barony) with a projected 21 per cent fall in employment within the industry in Scotland (Fraser of Allander Institute, November 1986, p. 30).

In addition, Gartcosh rolling mill finally closed on the 31 March with the loss of 800 jobs. The teachers' dispute rumbled on, with the EIS voting at the end of November to reject a 16.4 per cent pay offer, phased in at a much slower pace than had been recommended by the Main enquiry (announced by Malcolm Rifkind in March). Furthermore, there was some concern that the proposal to introduce a poll tax would prove to be far worse than domestic rates (see rest of chapter). As a result, 1986 saw the Scottish Conservatives continuing to struggle for electoral support. In the Regional elections in May, they suffered badly when compared to the previous Regional elections in 1982 - both in terms of percentage voting patterns and seats won. The results were:

Table 6.1
Regional Election Results *

Party	1982 % of Vote	1982 Seats Won	1986 % of Vote	1986 Seats Won	Change in Share of Vote	Change in Seats Won
Cons	25.1	119	16.9	65	-8.2%	-54
Labour	37.6	186	43.9	223	+6.3%	+37
All	18.1	25	15.1	40	-3.0%	+15
SNP	13.4	23	18.2	36	+4.8%	+13
Ind	5.1	87	4.8	79	-0.3%	-8
Others	0.6	1	1.1	2	+0.5%	+1

* Percentage figures do not add up to 100 because of rounding.

Source: Bochel and Denver, 1987, pp. 28 and 30.

In addition to the Regional election results, opinion poll showings remained poor. In the last System Three poll of 1985 (in November), Party support stood at 19 per cent. Exactly one year later in November 1986, and in contrast to the improved fortunes of the Conservatives south of the border, the level of support remained at 19 per cent - still well below the 1983 General Election performance of 28 per cent (System Three, 1988). It is against this general background of both uneven economic development and Conservative Party support, that we can consider the publication of the Green Paper and the determination by the Conservative Government to press ahead with a Bill for Scotland - abolishing domestic rates and replacing them with a poll tax.

The Green Paper

The Green Paper *Paying for Local Government* (Cmnd. 9714, 1986) was published on 28 January 1986. [2] Himsworth and Walker (1989, Section 47-3) describe it as 'a document which knew where it was going and went there in a no-nonsense manner.' Prior to detailing what it called 'the most radical reform of local government finance in Great Britain this century' (Cmnd. 9714, 1986, p. 76), it portrayed a general picture of the activities of local government, echoing much of the Government's thinking on legislation since 1979. This contained two main elements.

First, it stressed the link between local spending and macro-economic policy. By 1979-80, local authority expenditure constituted 28 per cent of public expenditure in the UK (Cmnd. 9714, 1986, p. 3). The impact of spending of such magnitude, it suggested, was that:

- since capital expenditure was financed largely by borrowing, this had an impact on the Public Sector Borrowing Requirement (PSBR)

- this also affected the rate of monetary growth

- both the PSBR and monetary growth affected interest rates

- local expenditure would have to be reduced if the Government was to be successful in reducing inflation and producing sustained economic growth

- local taxation affected the overall tax burden on the economy, which the Government had sought to reduce in order to enhance individual freedom of choice.

Second, and linked to this, it stressed the general importance of reducing local expenditure, but suggested that Government initiatives to do so since 1979 had met with only limited success. Overall, it deployed *three different arguments* to justify this in England, Scotland and Wales. In England, the average growth in local authority expenditure was 5.5 per cent in the 1960s; 5 per cent in the 1970s, and 1.5 per cent in the 1980s (Cmnd. 9714, 1986, p. 4). It saw this as a 'limited' success, however, because of (a) the existence of a minority of 'overspending' authorities, and (b) authorities becoming 'adept at manipulating expenditure between financial years to minimise grant losses' (Cmnd. 9714, 1986, p. 5). For Scotland, the Green Paper gave no evidence of an aggregate growth in local expenditure. Instead, it justified the need for restraint by saying simply that the Secretary of State had used his rate-capping powers and that planned expenditure by local authorities in 1985-86 was 3.2 per cent in excess of Government guidelines (Cmnd. 9714, p. 62). With regard to Wales, it conceded that council spending was no more in real terms than it was in 1979, and that in actual fact, rates had risen by roughly seven percentage points *less* than the rate of inflation (Cmnd. 9714, 1986, p. 5).

Faced with these three different sets of circumstances, the Green Paper's justification for proceeding with reform (even in Wales where local government could not be accused of 'overspending') is particularly interesting. The reason for this is that it redefines the 'problems' to be tackled. The essence of this is that there is a shift in *emphasis* - away from the 'affordability' of local government in terms of its impact on macro-economic policy, and towards 'accountability'. Thus, the Green Paper (Cmnd. 9714, 1986, p. vii) argued that 'effective local accountability must be the cornerstone of successful local government...The present local government finance system does not strengthen local accountability.' According to Midwinter and Mair (1987a, p. 117), however, this vision of accountability is 'couched in terms equating with the preferences of the centre.' In other words, 'accountability' means a view of local government whereby it fits with the Government's overall strategy of protecting the ranks of capital from excessive tax burdens, whilst at the same time buttressing its support from domestic and non-domestic ratepayers, and suppressing any challenge from 'local socialism'.

Based on this, therefore, the 'problems' as identified by the Government have their corollary in a need for reform which tackles them head-on. Thus, the Green Paper justifies the need for reform because even a country such as Wales which satisfies the criterion of 'affordability', cannot possibly satisfy the criterion of 'accountability' because it is the basic system of local government finance which is seen to be problematic. As the Green Paper (Cmnd. 9714, 1986, p. 67) argues, 'The need for a self-regulating local government sector underpinned by a measure of local accountability is as pressing in Wales as in England and Scotland.' Thus, revolving around the concept of 'accountability', the Green Paper identified what it considered to be the three main problems with the existing system.

First, there was the extent to which non-domestic ratepayers funded the marginal expenditure of local authorities. Non-domestic ratepayers provided 54 per cent of rating income in England, 56 per cent in Wales and 64 per cent in Scotland (Cmnd. 9714, 1986, p. 5). This meant that local authority spending at the margins was financed largely at the expense of the non-domestic ratepayer who did not have the protection of voting rights in local elections. The Green Paper suggested that 'This provides little incentive to economy' (Cmnd. 9714, 1986, p. 6).

Second, there was the mismatch between those entitled to vote in local elections; those benefiting from local authority services, and those actually paying domestic rates. To illustrate, the Green Paper quoted figures showing that in England, 34 per cent of the electorate paid full rates; 9 per cent paid partial rates by virtue of rates rebates, 8 per cent paid no rates at all, due to receipt of full rebates, and 49 per cent were non-householders who also paid no rates (Cmnd. 9714, 1986, p. 6). In reality, the latter figure of 49 per cent is highly misleading and exaggerates the extent to which individuals did not contribute to domestic rates payments. The reason for this is that although in practice the 'head of household' paid rates, he/she may have had a partner or other tenants who contributed to this, or even had non-employed dependants with no independent income and hence no means to make a payment anyway. Nevertheless, the Green Paper was undeterred and used these figures to identify two main failings with domestic rates. These were (a) that the system didn't take into account varying household compositions or the consumption of local authority services which were increasingly 'people' rather than 'property' orientated, and (b) that more than half of the electorate paid nothing or only a portion towards local authority spending, whilst about one third bore the full brunt of local authority spending increases financed from the domestic sector.

Third, and on a more technical note, the Green Paper suggested that there were inadequacies in the method of calculating central government grants. It suggested that matters such as assessing the cost of providing a reasonable standard of service in different local authorities and compensating for variations in domestic rateable values, simply 'conceals the real cost of local services from the local electorate' (Cmnd 9714, 1986, p. vii).

Based on these perceived inadequacies (with the focus firmly on 'accountability') and with the impetus given by the 1985 property revaluation being relegated solely to the section on Scotland, the Green Paper proposed two central reforms and a number of other secondary changes. [3] The two main reforms were as follows:

Domestic Rates

- to be phased out over ten years in England, six years in Wales and three years in Scotland

- this would commence on 1 April 1990 in England and Wales and one year earlier on 1 April 1989 in Scotland, due to the conviction that there was a demand for early action in Scotland

- domestic rates would be replaced gradually by a flat-rate Community Charge, payable by all adults [Note: no estimate was given for this]

- proposals for Social Security reform (Cmnd. 9691, 1985) would require every householder to pay a minimum of 20 per cent

- the Community Charge would be set by the relevant local authorities and they would be responsible for administration and collection procedures

- an estimated 51 per cent of households in Great Britain would be better off with the Community Charge, and 49 per cent would be worse off (Cmnd. 9714, 1986, p. 125)

Non-Domestic Rates

- a national non-domestic rate poundage (Uniform Business Rate [UBR]) would be set by central government (as opposed to local authorities), and would be index-linked to inflation

- this would commence with a revaluation in England, Wales and Scotland on 1 April 1990

- all proceeds would be pooled by central government and redistributed to local authorities on a per capita basis

- more bills would be increased than reduced, but increases would generally be small

- businesses in the South of England and the West Midlands would tend to lose out, whilst those in London and the North would tend to benefit.

The Green Paper requested comments on these proposals by 31 July. Roy MacIver, however, about to become General Secretary of COSLA, suggested that 'it is really a White Paper with one or two green parts in it' (quoted in Davis-Coleman, 1986a, p. 490). As the *Scotsman* (4 February 1986) commented, 'it is clear that Ministers are not prepared to reconsider the main proposals...though they are willing to look at points of detail.' Linked to this, was the speed of reform. Scottish Secretary, Malcolm Rifkind, made a statement in the House of Commons (the day after the Green Paper was published), saying that because of the extent of the dissatisfaction in Scotland with the system of domestic rates, 'we...are, therefore, at present planning for early legislation in the current Parliamentary Session to abolish the domestic rating system in Scotland' (HC Debates, 1985-86, Vol. 90, col. 949). It was clear, therefore, that contrary to the expectations that would normally surround a Green Paper, the consultative nature of this particular publication was severely limited.

Reaction to the Green Paper

Reaction to the proposals can be broken down into two main phases. First, the immediate reaction. Second, the longer term reaction as the impact of the Westland affair began to die down and the detailed implications of the reforms began to emerge.

Short-term Reaction

From outside the Conservative Party, there were no new converts to the proposals (at least in public). The reforms were welcomed in particular by the CBI in Scotland; Commerce Against the Unfair Rating Burden (CURB); the Association of Scottish Chambers of Commerce and the Adam Smith Institute. The abolition of domestic rates was also welcomed by the Federation of Scottish Ratepayers (FSR). Indeed, Chairwoman, Mary Whitehouse (1990) commented that:

'When the Green Paper came out, the Scottish Office made absolutely sure that I and Richard Adlington of RAGE got advance copies. We were supplied with every bit of information we could ask for. If I wanted to know anything, I had the private numbers of the civil servants in the Scottish Office. I got the most amazing amount of help.'

When we turn away from this support for the Poll Tax and towards opposition to it, we find once again that a 'quirk' of history helped slightly to lower its profile. The Green Paper was published on the same day as the Space Shuttle Challenger blew up, thus understandably, dominating the media the following day. Nevertheless, lurking underneath the headlines, it was evident that there was a welter of opposition to the

Poll Tax. The *Local Government Chronicle* (1986, p. 111) commented that 'if any government wanted to upset a large part of the electorate it would find it hard to surpass the proposals outlined in *Paying for Local Government.*' The *Guardian* (29 January 1986) suggested that 'Mr Baker has given the opposition parties a gift issue and it is hard to imagine that they will fumble it.' The *Economist* (1986c, p. 22) suggested that 'Thank goodness, the Government may reflect, there is an election or two before any of this has to happen.' The prospect of a Poll Tax was also condemned by, among others, both the *Glasgow Herald* and the *Scotsman*. The *Glasgow Herald* (29 January 1986) called it from 'bad to worse.'

Several different ratepayers' groups were also less than enthusiastic. Bill Anderson, Scottish Secretary of the National Federation of Self-Employed and Small Businesses (NFSESB), said that a UBR would have a devastating effect on his members in rural areas, with rate poundages and bills being moved upwards. The Scottish Landowners Federation was disappointed that the proposals did not include the abolition of sporting rates. The National Union of Ratepayers Associations (NURA) favoured a Local Income Tax. Deputy Chairman, Roland Rench, said that 'we are extremely disappointed...this could prove to be the biggest banana skin they have slipped on. It's a double backwards somersault' (*Municipal Journal*, 31 January 1986, p. 134). Finally, CBI Director-General Sir Terence Beckett, said that 'we have not advocated a uniform business rate...and it was not supported when it was debated at our annual conference' (*Municipal Journal*, 31 January 1986, p. 134).

The reaction of the vast majority in local government (with the exception largely of Scottish Conservatives) was of public hostility to the reforms. They were rejected by the non-Conservative-dominated bodies of the AMA, ACC, ALA and COSLA. The Chairwoman of the ALA, Margaret Hodge, said that 'A Poll Tax and centrally fixed business rate would be impossible to operate in London...They will increase Whitehall's grip on local authorities, cause endless headaches for those who have to collect poll taxes, encourage widespread evasion and destroy people's incentive to vote in elections' (*Local Government Chronicle*, 31 January 1986, p. 113). The Conservative dominated ADC was no less critical. Chairman, John Morgan, said - 'A poll tax, that's what it is, would be an utter nonsense as a substitute for the present domestic rating system...It would become both an attack and a tax on local democracy' (*Local Government Chronicle*, 31 January 1986, p. 113). Opposition also came from the Conservative-dominated London Boroughs Association, which was opposed to a UBR, and favoured instead a 'cap' on the business rate. Westminster Leader, Lady Shirley Porter, warned of the 'dire effects' that a UBR would have on industry in the South-East (*Municipal Journal*, 7 February 1986, p. 174).

A number of professional bodies were also critical. CIPFA maintained its preference for a combination tax and argued that domestic rates should be retained - at least in part. The Rating and Valuation Association (R&VA) argued that an essentially fair and logical system of taxation was being replaced by one which was grossly unfair.

The Trades Union movement was surprisingly quiet on the prospect of a Poll Tax, with no public statements being issued by the TUC or STUC. Nevertheless, NALGO General Secretary, John Daly, called the Community Charge 'a poll tax by a different name with no place in 20th century Britain' (*Local Government Chronicle*, 31 January 1986, p. 113). Furthermore, Hugh Wilson, the TGWU's Agricultural Trades Group General Secretary, condemned the Poll Tax as being regressive and taking no account of ability to pay.

Unsurprisingly, all the opposition parties were horrified at the proposals. In Scotland, Labour Leader, Donald Dewar, focused on the Poll Tax, arguing that it was 'unfamiliar, unjust...lacking in popular support...and socially divisive' (HC Debates, 1985-86, Vol. 90. col. 951). He also expressed concern at the rush to legislate in Scotland, and asked that a White Paper be issued to deal with the many practical problems. At a UK level, the focus of the Labour Party was not only on the regressive nature of the Tax, but also on what was perceived to be self-destructive proposals which would rebound on the Tories. Shadow Environment Secretary, John Cunningham, called the Poll Tax 'a time bomb ticking away under them...[i.e. Conservative MPs] in their constituencies' (HC Debates, 1985-86, Vol. 90. col. 801). Even Denis Skinner, an MP not known normally for his accommodation with the Labour leadership, argued that 'during the course of the Green Paper consultation and up to the next general election, we shall be able to tell every constituent in every target seat how much the rates [sic] will go up as a result of this latest blunder by the Tory Government' (HC Debates, 1985-86, Vol. 90, col. 812). For the Alliance, Liberal Environment Spokesman Simon Hughes called the Poll Tax 'the most reactionary proposal since 1601' (HC Debates, 1985-86, Vol. 90. col. 805), whilst John Cartwright of the SDP called it 'unfair, complicated and expensive to administer' (HC Debates, 1985-86, Vol. 90, col. 802). More generally, the Alliance in Scotland pressed for the Secretary of State to be open-minded about the responses to consultation and to listen carefully to the calls for a local income tax. Also in Scotland, the SNP saw the Green Paper as a missed opportunity to introduce a local income tax. The self-destructive capacities of the Tax, however, were also evident. As Andrew

Welsh, the SNP's Vice-Chairman for local government, commented, 'This damaging and divisive scheme is not so much a Poll Tax as a Polecat Tax - no sane government would go near it, were the Scottish Tories not fighting for their political lives' (SNP, 1986).

Faced with this largely hostile reception, the vast majority of the Conservative Party - with the exception of the Conservative-dominated ADC - were actually (or at least gave the impression of being) in favour of the reforms. The precise reasons for this, revolve around four main factors.

First, the Party was still living through the experience of the Westland affair, and Trade and Industry Secretary, Leon Brittan, had resigned only four days prior to the publication of the Green Paper. Thus, as the *Economist* (1986c, p. 20) argued with regard to the cheers of Tory Backbenchers - 'having just survived the parliamentary turmoil of the past few weeks, they would probably have cheered almost anything.' Second, the Government had finally 'done something' about the whole issue of local government finance, which the *Economist* (1986a, p. 21) described as 'an issue on which Conservative Ministers fear their own supporters more than the opposition.' Only the previous week, in a vote in the Commons on the 1986-87 Rate Support Grant, 33 Tory MPs voted against the Government whilst another 20 abstained. Third, in Scotland, the support from Scottish Conservatives was, to a large extent because the Party had finally 'done something' about the rates and about the uproar from its traditional supporters in response to the 1985 property revaluation. For example, MP Bill Walker, who had previously favoured a local income tax, now favoured the Poll Tax and criticised a local income tax, saying that 'there is not just the fact that there would be 56 different varieties of tax; there is the problem that the people of Scotland would not take kindly to having those employed in local authorities knowing what their income was' (HC Debates, 1985-86, Vol. 90, col. 95). Fourth, the proposed reforms helped partly to mitigate the unrest from Party activists over not just the 'rates', but also the closure of Gartcosh. In other words, the Green Paper was seen as evidence that the Party *was* able to respond to the particular problems facing it in Scotland.

Taken together, these factors seem to indicate the main reasons for a generally positive response by the Conservative Party to the Green Paper (albeit with a strong dose of pragmatism), in the face of a largely hostile reception elsewhere. It is important to move on, however, and consider the development of these relationships during the bulk of the 'consultation' period and the succeeding months until the First Reading of the *Abolition of Domestic Rates Etc. (Scotland) Bill* at the end of November that year.

Long-term Reaction

In the wake of the initial reaction to the Green Paper, a number of clarifications/modifications took place to the Government's original schedule. Estimated levels for the Poll Tax were made public. For Scotland, it was estimated that a hypothetical Poll Tax, fully operational in 1985-86 would have been £207 (HC Debates, 1985-86, Vol. 92, cols. 341-2w). For Wales, it was estimated that a fully operational Poll Tax in 1984-85 would have been £106 (HC Debates, 1985-86, Vol. 93, cols. 290-3w). No estimate was given for a likely Poll Tax in England.

With regard to Scotland, the Scottish Office also issued a series of consultation papers to COSLA, colleges, universities and various professional bodies, in an attempt to 'flesh out' the practical details of compiling a register; registration procedures; treatment of students; collection procedures etc. The timetable for submissions was also amended. In England and Wales, the DoE seemed to take a fairly relaxed view about the timetable for the consultation process. The deadline for submissions was extended to 31 October, after lobbying by a number of local authorities, the CBI and the Association of British Chambers of Commerce (although Environment Minister, William Waldegrave, indicated that he would prefer to have the submissions by 1 October). In Scotland, however, Scottish Local Government Minister, Michael Ancram (determined that there should be no delay in introducing a Bill for Scotland) initially rejected COSLA's request for a similar extension. It was only latterly, towards the end of the consultation period, that COSLA *alone* was granted an extension until the end of August.

These clarifications/modifications aside, both the 'pro' and 'anti' Green Paper stances gained in strength. The 'anti' Green Paper lobby was by far the largest of the two. It should be noted, however, that the public profile of both was still extremely low. In terms of the reasons for this, it seems reasonable to suggest that not only would it be difficult for *any* issue to have a sustained high profile over a period of several months, but many people/organizations assumed that the Government could not possibly proceed with such a scheme, once it had time to appreciate both its impracticality and the sheer strength of the arguments against it.

Looking first of all at the 'pro' Green Paper forces, the FSR (1986) was fully supportive of a Poll Tax and suggested, with regard to potential administrative problems, that 'these difficulties seem to have been much exaggerated, and the Glasgow Finance Director, Mr Bill English, speaking at a meeting in Edinburgh on 4 June, admitted that it would be perfectly possible to carry out the requirements of the Green Paper if it were to become necessary.' In terms of responses submitted to the

Scottish Office as part of the consultation exercise, further support for the Government's proposals came from 'smaller' bodies of ratepayers, such as the Sandyhills Owner Occupiers' Association, the Renfrew Owner Occupiers' Association and the Helensburgh Ratepayers' Association.

In the non-domestic sector, the Association of British Chambers of commerce joined the Association of Scottish Chambers of Commerce in its support for a UBR. A UBR was also welcomed by both Esso and Shell. The latter paid £62.5 million in both commercial and industrial rates over 640 locations. It welcomed a UBR as 'much fairer than the existing very wide spread of poundages' (Shell, 1986, p. 1). Support came also from the Scottish Branch of the Institute of Directors. Peter Cross, West of Scotland Branch Chairman, said that 'all members welcome the proposals. They are concerned at the way local authorities do not consult with them about the rates or, when they do consult, do not listen to them...There are too many cases of Scottish businesses having to pay far higher rates than similar ones in England' (quoted in the *Scotsman*, 13 May 1986). In addition, the CBI (Scotland) (1986, p. 3), which had been supportive of a UBR, was now joined in this by the CBI at a UK level. In doing so, it changed its earlier position which rejected a UBR and favoured a 'cap' on business rates. In its response to the Green Paper, it now accepted a UBR, although it did so subject to the conditions of an introduction of gradual derating; primary legislation which limited UBR increases to the rate of inflation, and the phasing-in of revaluation and a UBR to ensure that no business faced a rates rise in excess of 10 per cent in any one year (*Local Government Chronicle*, 31 October 1986, p. 1238). In formal responses to the Green Paper, a UBR was also supported by such bodies as the Scotch Whisky Association, CURB, ICI and the National Association of Steel Stockholders. Finally, with specific regard to the Poll Tax, and unlike a non-committal stance on this by its Scottish counterparts, the CBI at a UK level was explicit in favouring the introduction of the Tax (*CBI News*, 24 October 1986, p. 5).

In contrast to the above, there was detailed and much more extensive criticism of the reforms from a growing 'anti' Green Paper lobby of professional bodies, local government associations, ratepayers, trades unions and political parties.

With regard to professional bodies, none gave anything which might sensibly be called 'support' for the Green Paper. In terms of a UBR, this came under fire from management consultants, Coopers and Lybrand. It argued that a UBR 'has no real advantages over the present system in terms of simplicity and ease of operation, administrative costs and its perceptibility. It will...significantly reduce local authority autonomy and democratic accountability...the link between local businesses and local government would effectively be broken' (quoted in *Municipal Journal*, 23 May 1986, p. 809). In addition, a report by Chartered Surveyors, Debenham Tewson and Chinnocks, concluded that most businesses could not expect to benefit from a UBR. In an analysis of 22 industrial locations in England and Wales, it found that about two-thirds of rates bills would be higher. In only three centres (Tower Hamlets, Harlow and Bristol), would rates be cut by 10 per cent or more (*Local Government Chronicle*, 12 September 1986, p. 1017).

With regard to a Poll Tax, the independent Institute for Fiscal Studies (IFS) published a report entitled *Who Will be Paying for Local Government?* The *Municipal Journal* (28 March 1986, p. 485) suggested that this 'effectively demolishes the Government's case for rating reform.' Whilst the Green Paper had argued that ability to pay was no worse under the Poll Tax than under the rates, authors Smith and Squire (1986, p. 20) of the IFS concluded that richer households actually stood to benefit substantially from the Poll Tax. In addition, the Society of County Treasurers criticised the Poll Tax for being highly regressive and said that the increased central control over local authority funding meant that the Poll Tax was not buoyant enough to cope with the strain placed upon it. Furthermore, the Scottish Consumer Council produced an extensive seventy five page report (conducted by three academics in the Law Faculty of Dundee University) on the technical adequacy and fairness of the Green Paper. It concluded that:

'For once, study of Government proposals raises countless questions and brings few answers. The gaps speak eloquently of work being done in a hurry. The main conclusion of the SCC's study is that the problems associated with implementation are insuperable' (Scottish Consumer Council, 1986, p. iv).

Similar points were also made by the Scottish Branch of the Rating and Valuation Association and CIPFA. The latter, in a response to the Scottish Office on operational matters, commented that 'We have severe reservations about the practicability of the Community charge. We think it will be difficult and expensive to collect and will create public resentment far greater than the present domestic rate' (CIPFA, 1986a, p. 1). On a more general level, John Banham (1986, p. 2), Controller of the Audit Commission, published figures which showed that, in real terms over the period 1980-85, local government spending in England and Wales actually *decreased* by 4.6 per cent, whilst central government spending actually increased by 11.9 per cent. As the *Economist* (1986d,

p. 26) asked, 'If anybody needs to be kept in check by Kafkaesque mechanisms of distribution and control, is it the town and county halls?'.

In local government, the long-term reaction was similar, as detailed criticisms began to emerge. In Scotland, only 3 out of the 65 local authorities expressed support for a Poll Tax. COSLA's (1986a, p. 8) formal response to the Green Paper found the extension of tax liability and the limiting of relief to those on low incomes 'utterly repugnant'. Furthermore, based on calculations of the wide range of Poll Tax levels that would exist before and after the three-year transition period at both regional and district level, 'it is difficult to see how a sensible progression to full implementation will ever take place' (COSLA, 1986a, p. 12). Also, COSLA's Depute Finance Secretary, Albert Tait (1989), commented with regard to meetings with the Scottish Office on the series of consultation papers, that:

'Most of these meetings used to end up with people rolling around on the floor - not literally, but some of the proposals seemed so ludicrous that, rather than being any sort of formal sensible meeting, they became sort of a laughing shop about how things were actually going to operate.'

Remaining within local government for the moment, a report by Strathclyde Regional Council (1986) predicted that the Poll Tax in Strathclyde would be £246 a year, when compared to the Scottish Office estimate of £229. In Glasgow, it would be as high as £296. Residents in Glasgow would pay an increase of 14 per cent on their contribution to the Regional Council's funds, whilst those in the areas of Eastwood and Bearsden & Milngavie would enjoy reductions of 40 per cent and 42 per cent respectively. As Finance Director, Ken Paterson argued, 'Once the proposed reform is fully phased in by 1991, and Glasgow has to bear its full cost, the effect will be dramatic' (quoted in the *Evening Times*, 3 April 1986).

South of the Border, the AMA focused on the administrative difficulties that would be encountered. Chairman, Jack Layden, said that:

'Constantly updating a register based on individuals rather than households is going to cost a fortune in staff time. Unless extensive checks are introduced which will invade the privacy of honest, law-abiding citizens, evasion will be widespread and the poll tax will quickly become absurd' (quoted in *Local Government Chronicle*, 12 September 1986, p. 1017).

The AMA also suggested that the Poll Tax would be much more regressive than the Green Paper had suggested. It estimated that roughly one third of those with a nett income in excess of £200 per week would gain by more than £2 per week, whilst 3.2 million of the poorest households would be £2 a week worse off (*Local Government Chronicle*, 12 September 1986, p. 1052). Also, Steve Hughes (1986, p. 183), Finance Adviser to the Association of London Authorities, argued that a small increase for commercial ratepayers in London actually masked a much more worrying redistribution of the rates burden. In eighteen out of the nineteen London Boroughs, commercial ratepayers would face increased bills. The highest increases would be 43 per cent in Ealing and 42 per cent in Kensington and Chelsea. He also argued that, when combined with the Poll Tax and the problems of administration and collection in London, 'it is difficult to believe that these proposals will ever be implemented' (Hughes, 1986, p. 183).

Opposition to the Green Paper also came from a variety of domestic and non-domestic ratepayers. For example, in terms of domestic ratepayers, the National Union of Ratepayers Associations continued to object on moral grounds to the Poll Tax. Deputy Chairman, Roland Rench (1986) argued that 'the inescapable conclusion must be that the cause of equity and justice has come a very poor second to political expediency.' Caravan park operators in Scotland also mounted a strong campaign against the Poll Tax because it would hit the industry through caravans being treated as 'second homes', with owners being liable to pay the equivalent of two Community Charges for this (in addition to their normal place of residence). The Poll Tax was also opposed by the Scottish Crofters Union because no special exemption was being made for crofters, who had previously been allowed a 50 per cent derating on their croft houses. Finally, in terms of domestic ratepayers and formal responses submitted to the Scottish Office, the Poll Tax was opposed, for a variety of different reasons by (among others) the Esk Place Tenants Association; the Lower Woodburn Tenants Association; Cross Stobbs Ratepayers; Muirend Residents Association; Govan Community Council; Bearsden Community Council; Loanhead Community Council; Westfield Community Council; the Federated Association of Owner-Occupiers of Glasgow and the Scottish Federation of Owner Occupiers.

Turning now to criticism from non-domestic ratepayers, British Petroleum (1986, p. 2), unlike Esso and Shell, favoured the retention of non-domestic rates with firm central control over poundages. It paid £55 million in rates and was concerned that a UBR would break the business/local authority link - stating that 'The degree of increased centralism implied by the UBR cannot be justified...in the context of encouraging responsible local government.' At a UK level, the Institute of Directors differed from its Scottish counterparts in being opposed totally to a UBR, seeing it as a 'policy of despair'. In its response to the Green Paper, it said that it would reduce business protection under an unsympathetic central government; it would be easier politically to increase it than to increase other national taxes such as VAT and Income Tax; it would make consultations virtually impossible, and 'Business would be forced to revert to national lobbying to protect its local interests' (quoted in the *Times*, 19 May 1986). A UBR was also opposed by such bodies as the NFSESB, the Forum of Private Business, the British Retailers Association and the Scottish Licensed Trade Association.

The trades union movement (primarily in the form of the TUC, STUC, NALGO and NUPE) continued to oppose the Poll Tax, although this opposition was limited simply to responses submitted to the Scottish Office as part of the consultation exercise. There was no attempt to launch any sort of pre-emptive campaign against its introduction. As John Henry (1989), the then Deputy General Secretary of the STUC argues:

'There was this feeling in the movement that it...[i.e. the Poll Tax] would never get off the ground. That certainly mitigated against a sort of revulsion getting mounted on the scale of the Gartcosh campaign...When they were making up the agendas for the joint liaison committee, that was way down at the bottom...what was dominating the scene was trying to protect the Scottish economy in all its shapes and forms.'

Thus, the STUC (Scottish Trades Union Congress, 1986b, p. 8) confined itself to responding formally to the Green Paper and calculated that those with nett weekly incomes of between £100 and £400 would pay a higher percentage of income than under domestic rates. With regard to the Government's notion of 'accountability', it argued that 'we would adhere to the principle of the ballot box as the instrument of test applying to any elected representative, at either local or national level (ibid. p. 8).

Finally, in terms of political parties, Labour provided the main opposition to the Green Paper, although this bore some similarities to the STUC in being decidedly weak. In March, at the annual Conference in Scotland, Labour Leader, Neil Kinnock, told journalists (although not the Conference itself) that a Scottish Assembly would be set up when Labour came to power after the next General Election - likely to be 1987 or 1988. This seemed to take priority over an alternative to the Poll Tax, as the slow process was begun of agreeing to the mechanics of devolution and the role and financing of local government within this. Two other important factors were also combined with this. First, there was the belief that the proposals for a Poll Tax would, according to Scottish Labour Leader, Donald Dewar, 'collapse under the weight of [their] own application' (quoted in the *Scotsman*, 28 February 1986). Second, there was the potential electoral benefit to Labour. As Murray Elder (1989), ex-Scottish Secretary of the Labour Party, argues:

'I think we probably always took the view that it was all tied up with the General Election and the Poll Tax would be introduced after the General Election. Therefore, what one had to do is convince people that if they didn't want the Poll Tax, they ought not to vote Tory.'

This rather confused mixture of ideas resulted in an equally confused opposition to the Poll Tax. The resolution carried on local government at the Party Conference in March 1986, did not even mention the Poll Tax. Apart from occasional mentions in Parliamentary debates, the main opposition was from Shadow Scottish Secretary Donald Dewar. At the beginning of July, he wrote to Scottish Secretary, Malcolm Rifkind, urging him to abandon the Poll Tax, and warning him that the Opposition would examine the proposals in 'stringent detail'.

Faced with this largely hostile reception (irrespective of whether or not some elements of it were 'weaker' than they might have been), the Conservative Government (buoyed by its resurgence in opinion polls and the drop in inflation) was undaunted at the prospect of proceeding with reform. In Scotland, Party support for the proposals was maintained. The continually low opinion poll support and the poor results in the Regional elections were used by the Party as justification that (more than ever) 'something should be done' for Scotland. In this instance, of course, that 'something' was rates reform. Since becoming Secretary of State in January, Malcolm Rifkind had adopted an aggressive stance - setting a target of 30 per cent support in Scotland. Rates abolition was seen as a necessary condition for this and three main tactics were used in order to ensure that it was followed through.

The first was to focus on Scotland and present the case for the introduction of a Poll Tax by drawing on what support existed for non-domestic rates. For example, Malcolm Rifkind suggested that:

'It is interesting that, among those who have welcomed the proposals for a community charge and the Government's other proposals are the ratepayers' associations in Scotland, the Chambers of Commerce, which represent small businesses and the CBI in Scotland, which represents industry. These organisations have all given a full welcome to the Government's proposals. As they represent pretty well all the ratepayers of Scotland, that is something from which we can take great satisfaction' (HC Debates, 1986-87, Vol. 106, col. 253).

The second tactic was to put down the opposition as coming from 'predictable' sources. In other words, a variety of vested interests whose position would be threatened by reform. The most 'predictable' of these was seen to be the Labour Party, which Malcolm Rifkind accused of being 'entirely wedded to the existing system of domestic rates, because it suits their political requirements' (HC Debates, 1985-86, Vol. 90, cols. 951-2). The fact that Labour did not have an alternative to domestic rates made it particularly easy for this argument to be used. The third and final main tactic was to attack what was seen to be the 'superficial' attraction of a local income tax. Malcolm Rifkind argued that this would act as a disincentive to those in work; discourage inward investment in some areas; administrative problems would be immense, and it would do nothing to promote local accountability. Furthermore, in view of the fact that only about two-thirds of the electorate would pay local income tax, 'if we are to have any hope of giving democratic accountability a higher profile, local authorities with only one course of taxation open to them must have a tax which is easily visible and affects virtually every elector' (Rifkind, 1986).

In England and Wales, the Government was more relaxed about the timetable for reform (i.e. contemplating whether to issue a White Paper or a Bill), although there was no evidence of deviating from the desire to press ahead with the reforms. On a general level, Party unity was maintained in the wake of the Westland affair and then latterly with the upturn in the economy and a marked improvement in opinion polls. The adversarial nature of electoral politics meant that dissent from the Party line would not have been particularly rewarding under either set of circumstances. On a more specific level, two factors seemed to reinforce the desire to proceed. First, Environment Secretary, Kenneth Baker, was replaced in May by Nicholas Ridley, who was enthusiastic about the Poll Tax (more so than Baker) and pledged that 'rates reform will be our top priority in Scotland' (quoted in the *Scotsman*, 9 October 1986). He was supported in this by the Prime Minister who told the Backbench 1922 Committee that she was determined to press ahead with reform. She suggested also, in an interview on Scottish Television that rates were a 'very special reason' for her unpopularity in Scotland (quoted in the *Scotsman*, 5 September 1986). Second, the Government overturned a defeat on the *Social Security Bill* in the House of Lords, which would have entitled householders to 100 per cent rates rebates. Social Services

Secretary, Norman Fowler, argued that 'every household receiving a rebate - about 5.5 million, on the basis of our illustrative figures - would no longer have any financial interest in the spending policies of its local authority' (HC Debates, 1985-86, Vol. 102, col. 412).

Both in Scotland and also in England and Wales, this evidence of a commitment to reform was undeterred by the official responses to the Green Paper.

Official Responses to the Green Paper

A breakdown of official responses for England, Wales and Scotland is given in Tables 6.2, 6.3 and 6.4, respectively. Three main points should be recognised prior to discussing these.

First, the responses for England and Wales are based on figures provided by the DoE (1986) and the Welsh Office (1986). As a result, the composition of figures is limited to the particular categorisations employed by both. In addition, the way in which both tended to present the figures was misleading (see note [4]). Thus, whilst still operating with overall figures given, these have been reclassified in Tables 6.2 and 6.3 in order to give a fair and accurate impression of support or otherwise for a Poll Tax.

Second, the figures for Scotland are based on a first-hand examination by the author of the responses lodged for public access in the Scottish Office. This has been necessary because, unlike the DoE and the Welsh Office, the Scottish Office has not compiled (for public consumption, at least) a detailed breakdown of the responses. In a written Commons reply requesting such information, Local Government Minister, Michael Ancram, said that 'most of the responses to the Green Paper include comments in favour of some of the detailed proposals and against others. It is not, therefore, possible to provide separate lists in the form requested' (HC Debates, 1986-87, Vol. 106, col. 447).

Finally, it should be recognised that the responses are simply a 'count' of the main thrust of the formal responses to the Green Paper. This means that, for example, a Chamber of Commerce, representing several thousand members, carries the same 'weight' as a small business. This can work both ways, however. This is particularly the case with regard to domestic ratepayers, where support for a Poll Tax was boosted substantially by responses from a large number of individuals. In general, however, the overall thrust of the results seems consistent with opposition/support which existed at the time and as detailed in the previous section.

Table 6.2 *

England

Breakdown of Responses to the Green Paper 'Paying for Local Government'
(Attitudes to a National UBR, and Preferences for Particular Local Tax Systems)

	National UBR		Domestic Rates and Alternatives							
Category	For	Against	Retain With Rental Values	Retain With Capital Values	Retain With Other	Local Income Tax (LIT)	Rates and LIT	Local Sales Tax	Poll Tax	Other
Local Authorities, Parishes etc.	31	296	67	60	2	84	39	1	44	-
Ratepayers, Individuals etc.	33	21	22	9	10	43	6	10	178	-
Non-domestic Ratepayers	46	47	-	-	-	-	-	-	-	-
Others	25	43	18	19	3	28	3	1	61	-
Totals (as a %)	135 (25%)	407 (75%)	107 (13%)	88 (11%)	15 (2%)	155 (19%)	48 (6%)	12 (1%)	283 (35%)	102 (13%)

* See Note [4] for an explanation of the category of 'Other'.

Source: Adapted from DoE (1986).

Table 6.3 *

Wales

Breakdown of Responses to the Green Paper 'Paying for Local Government'
(Attitudes to a National UBR, and Preferences for Particular Local Tax Systems)

| Category | National UBR | | Domestic Rates and Alternatives | | | | | |
	For	Against	Retain With Rental Values	Retain With Capital Values	Local Income Tax	Central Funding	Poll Tax	Other
Local Government	-	24	3	8	4	-	1	-
Private Individuals	5	1	1	-	4	1	25	-
Businesses	9	2	-	-	-	-	5	-
Others	3	8	1	4	2	0	1	-
Totals (as a %)	17 (33%)	35 (67%)	5 (6%)	12 (14%)	10 (11%)	1 (1%)	32 (37%)	27 (31%)

* See Note [4] for an explanation of the category of 'Other'.

Source: Adapted from Welsh Office (1986).

Table 6.4 *
Scotland
Breakdown of Responses to the Green Paper 'Paying for Local Government'
(Attitudes to a National UBR, and Preferences for Particular Local Tax Systems)

Category	National UBR		Domestic Rates and Alternatives							
	For	Against	Retain With Rental Values	Retain With Capital Values	Retain With Other	Local Income Tax (LIT)	Rates and LIT	Central Funding	Poll Tax	Other
Local Government	7	41	13	3	4	8	-	1	7	24
Ratepayers & Individuals	6	15	4	1	2	8	-	1	27	91
Non-domestic Ratepayers	17	44	-	1	0	-	-	2	3	4
Others	7	22	4	3	1	9	3	0	4	24
Totals (as a %)	37 (23%)	122 (77%)	21 (8%)	8 (3%)	7 (3%)	25 (10%)	3 (1%)	4 (2%)	41 (16%)	142 (57%)

* See Note [4] for an explanation of the category of 'Other'.

Source: All figures calculated on the basis of the author's examination of responses to the Green Paper. These are lodged with the Scottish Office Library.

Turning now to the figures themselves, two features are particularly striking. The first relates to the UBR, with this being important because support for it was used to buttress support for a Poll Tax. The figures reveal that a UBR did not have majority support - being favoured by only 25 per cent, 33 per cent and 23 per cent in England, Wales and Scotland respectively. What is also important, however, is that this support was dominated by the category of 'businesses'. In particular, support came from the major Chambers of Commerce and the CBI in England, Wales and Scotland. The opposite of this, of course, is that in terms of responses, there was only minority support for a UBR from business in Great Britain as a whole; and from the vast bulk of local authorities, professional bodies and individuals.

The second feature relates to the Poll Tax. Certainly, the figures show that a Poll Tax obtained more support than any other alternative. Given the wide range of alternatives, however, the overwhelming majority in each instance *did not* support a Poll Tax. In England, the figure was 65 per cent; in Wales, it was 63 per cent; and in Scotland, it was a staggering 84 per cent, with the Poll Tax receiving only 16 per cent support. Again, what is of importance is that this support was composed largely of ratepayers (both individually and collectively - the 'flagship' being the Federation of Scottish Ratepayers). In addition, the Poll Tax was supported by almost one half of 'business' ratepayers who commented on it.

Decision to Proceed with a Bill for Scotland

The response by the Conservative Party (seeing a revival in its opinion poll showings and a drop in inflation) was to sweep aside this ideological and practical opposition. Malcolm Rifkind said that 15,000 people had written to George Younger to protest at the time of revaluation, and 'the opposition we have had pales into insignificance beside [this] groundswell of popular opinion' (quoted in the *Scotsman*, 8 August 1986). The Bill was received at the Scottish Office some four weeks later and the decision was taken to exclude the non-domestic reforms from it and to include them in national legislation at a later stage. Malcolm Rifkind was then given a high-profile slot at the Tory Party Conference in October, where all ten motions from Scotland supported the Government's proposals for a Poll Tax.

Latterly, in a debate on the Queen's Speech in November, Environment Secretary, Nicholas Ridley, promised that rates reform would be a top priority in England and Wales, after the next General Election (HC

Debates, 1986-87, Vol. 105, col. 337). This was combined with a step up in the attack on local government via the pledge to extend compulsory competitive tendering into new local authority service areas, because of 'The fact that there is a vast amount of waste and misuse of resources, especially in Labour local authorities' (HC Debates, 1986-87, Vol. 105, col. 333). In debates, this was linked continually to the Poll Tax, with the emphasis on the Government being forced into having to legislate in order to make local authorities more 'accountable' to the electorate.

In response to all this, both the Labour Party and the main local authority associations made the only attempts to block the Poll Tax prior to the introduction of a Bill. First, Donald Dewar again called on the Government to abandon the Poll Tax, whilst John Maxton, Labour's local government spokesman said that Malcolm Rifkind 'should not waste Parliament's time putting through a measure that will cause so many problems' (quoted in the *Scotsman*, 26 September 1986). When this did not work, Donald Dewar wrote to Malcolm Rifkind, suggesting that the Standing Committee scrutinising the Bill should be constituted as a Select Committee in order to take advice from professional bodies. This was brushed aside by Malcolm Rifkind as being totally unnecessary. Second, Leaders of COSLA, AMA, ADC and ACC met with Mrs Thatcher in a last-ditch attempt to persuade her that the Poll Tax should be dropped. Again, the Government's response was dismissive. Environment Secretary, Nicholas Ridley, (echoing the continual Government response since the publication of the Green Paper), said that 'Everyone was agreed that the present system was not working well. We are prepared to talk about improving the details but the Government is long past the point of changing its mind' (quoted in the *Municipal Journal*, 28 November 1986, p. 2106).

Conclusion

This chapter has detailed the content of, and varying reactions to, the Green Paper *Paying for Local Government* (Cmnd. 9714, 1986). It has shown, set in its historical context, a relatively unified Conservative Party, brushing aside substantial opposition to the Poll Tax - both on grounds of ideology (that the Poll Tax was unfair, undemocratic etc.) and on the interrelated grounds of practicability (severe collection problems, the burden and costs of administration etc.). A fuller discussion of this in terms of 'policy formation' will be conducted in the Conclusion to this book. In the meantime, however, we can identify some of the main elements of this.

Using the autonomy vested in it by Parliament, the Government *took the lead* in the policy formation process through a 'consultation' exercise. This proved to be a highly suitable strategy for it to employ, in view of the fact that it was keen to integrate a poll tax into its leading strategy. Given the sovereignty of Parliament and its hegemonic 'lead' in being the focus for political opposition, then 'consultation' could provide the Government with a measure of the opposition that the Poll Tax would encounter, whilst at the same time it would allow it to proceed with the introduction of the tax - subject to conditions being conducive to this. In practice, circumstances were indeed suitable, and the Government was assisted particularly by the interaction of two key factors. First, and in addition to specific support for the Poll Tax from the FSR, it was able to draw on support for a UBR from key representatives of domestic capital in the form of Chambers of Commerce and the CBI. The Conservative Government utilised this as evidence of support for the reforms in general, and so for the Poll Tax. Second, there was the low-key response from the trades union movement and the Labour Party, which was caught up in the interaction of a variety of conflicting processes i.e. devolution as a response to the uneven political and economic development of Scotland; the need to find an alternative to the Poll Tax; a belief that it would never work in practice; and an abhorrence at the very idea of a Poll Tax, yet a perceived electoral benefit to Labour as long as the Conservative Party was prepared to go ahead with it. By November 1986, therefore, the Government could (quite legitimately in constitutional terms), sweep aside the opposition which manifested itself in the consultation exercise, and decide to bring a Bill before Parliament. Thus, it *took the lead and took control of the policy formation process* to such a degree that it could propose to pass legislation through an institutional structure where *it* commanded an overall majority.

Initially, it may have seemed that this would not prove unproblematic for the Government. With the prospect of MPs now actually having to vote for a Poll Tax, there was a re-emergence of some uneasiness within the Party. As Robin Oakley (1986b, p. 7) commented, writing in the *Times* at the end of November:

> 'The first mutterings are already reaching Tory Whips that a number of Conservative MPs are deeply unhappy about the planned reforms and that they would see it as inconsistent to vote for them in a Scottish Bill when they may be forced to refuse to support their implementation in England and Wales. They will not be enough to lose the Government its Bill, but there is clearly trouble ahead.'

As we will see in the next chapter, however, the Government's working majority of 137 ensured that it had little cause to be alarmed.

Notes

1. In *absolute* terms, unemployment rates are only of limited value, because of the numerous changes in the calculation of 'unemployment'. Despite this, however, the universality of the revisions means that *relative* comparisons between Scotland and the rest of the United Kingdom are still possible. The figures given here have been obtained by calculating the changes (for Scotland and the UK) between the seasonally adjusted unemployment figures for the year January 1986 to January 1987.

2. The Scottish Office (1986a) also produced *Paying for Local Government: The Scottish Approach.*

3. (i) 'The grant system should be radically simplified. It would consist of needs grant, which would compensate for differences in what authorities needed to spend to provide a comparable standard of service and standard grant, which would be paid to all authorities as a common amount per adult. The formula for assessing authorities' relative spending should also be reviewed, with a view to making it less complex and more stable' (Cmnd. 9714, 1986, p. 76).

    (ii) Distributional changes resulting from the new grant system and the non-domestic changes to be offset by a system of self-financing adjustments

    (iii) A separate consultation paper to be produced on the possibility of a 'rolling revaluation' of non-domestic property

    (iv) A review of specific grants to local authorities

    (v) Reform of the system of controls on capital expenditure in England and Wales

    (vi) A review of centrally-determined fees and charges

    (vii) Duties to be placed on local authority treasurers with regard to the budgets of their authorities.

4. The DoE, for example, was misleading in two main ways with regard to the way in which it presented the responses to the Green Paper. First, views on the existing domestic rating system were presented. Given the depth of dissatisfaction with the system, it is unsurprising that the majority favoured abolition. It then dispensed with the 'rates' and considered support for the various alternatives. In this, the Poll Tax came out with the most support i.e. 57 per cent. This gives a misleading impression, however, because it (and all other options) should be considered simply as that i.e. options - whether or not they favour the rating system in one form or another. Thus, Table 6.2 does just this and corrects this misleading impression. Second, the DoE did not list a category where respondents commented on the Poll Tax and either rejected it or simply did not specify an alternative when they criticised the tax. Again, Table 6.2 rectifies this by utilising figures given for the total number of respondents (in other words, by subtracting those specifying a favoured system from the total number of respondents who commented on domestic rates). Such respondents are contained in the category of 'Other' alongside support for alternatives which are not listed in the main columns. Overall, therefore, a more accurate picture of support is obtained at 35 per cent rather than 57 per cent.

7 The Bill: Parliamentary Passage

This is the fourth and final 'empirical' chapter, and outlines the main issues, events and arguments surrounding the passage through Parliament of the *Abolition of Domestic Rates Etc. (Scotland) Bill* - a title suggested to the Scottish Office by the Federation of Scottish Ratepayers. In this respect, the chapter covers a period from the First Reading of the Bill on 27 November 1986, through to its Royal Assent on 15 May 1987.

It should be noted that it is *not* the intention to focus here on the various arguments and intricacies of a Bill with thirty four clauses and numerous Schedules; dealing with the setting up of a register, the role of the registration officer, standard and collective community charges etc. There are two main reasons for this. First, such an exercise has already been undertaken by Himsworth and Walker (1989) of the Department of Constitutional Law in the University of Edinburgh. They do so on a clause by clause basis, and produce a guide to the main debates surrounding these. Second, it is beyond the scope of the present work to deal with such essentially 'administrative' matters in any depth. The main concern of the present work regarding such issues, is whether or not (despite a number of potential administrative problems) the Government saw it as actually *possible* to implement a Poll Tax. The answer is 'yes'. There was never any serious doubt that administrative problems could not be resolved. This was confirmed by COSLA, which intimated that 'All the professionals...will no doubt do all they can to ensure that, if the Bill is enacted, the appropriate arrangements will be in place for 1st April 1989' (quoted in HL Debates, 1986-87, Vol. 486, col. 366)

The focus of this chapter, therefore, is on two central characteristics of the Poll Tax. The first of these is the feature that it is essentially a *flat-rate charge per head*, thus spreading the local tax burden and attempting to appease the Conservative Party's electoral base of support. The second and related characteristic is that there is liability for a *minimum payment of 20 per cent*, thus intending to restrain the spending of Labour-controlled councils (because of the threat of an electoral backlash), and at the same time reducing inflation and enhancing the competitiveness of British capital. [1] It should be noted that the 20 per cent figure was not particularly 'scientific' in terms of its relationship to local 'accountability'. Ex-Scottish Secretary, George Younger, (1991) suggested that 'we just thought that "twenty" was the lowest that was something. There's nothing magic about it.'

Focusing on these two principles, the structure of the chapter is as follows. First, it provides a general 'political' and 'economic' background to the period under discussion. Second, it considers the Bill in its first period in the Commons. Third, it considers its movement to the House of Lords. Fourth, it looks briefly at its final return to the Commons prior to Royal Assent. Finally, it concludes by drawing out the main points from the Parliamentary passage of the Bill, and relates them briefly to matters of 'policy formation'

Background (November 1986 - May 1987)

At a UK level, this period was again dominated by the consumer boom, which was mostly in the South East. This was assisted by a boost to domestic exporters because of the depreciation of sterling against the Deutschmark, and also because of a further reduction in the Basic Rate of Income Tax (in March) from 29 per cent to 27 per cent. Overall, therefore, the apparent strength of the economy was sufficient for the *Economist* (1987a) to suggest in early January, that economic indicators pointed to a General Election in the summer. After this, it was likely that inflation would exceed 5 per cent and hence squeeze the growth in real incomes.

Whilst one might have expected these economic indicators to have resulted in an increase in Conservative support, this did not happen at first, since elements of Government policy were rebounding on it for several months. It had given tacit support to Rupert Murdoch's News International in its year-long attempt to enforce new working practices on the NGA printworkers at the Wapping Plant (culminating in violent clashes towards the end of January), whilst it became embroiled at the same time in the Zircon Affair, over its withholding of information about a £500 million spy satellite from the House of Commons Public Accounts Committee. Conservative Party support fell as a result of this in the first two months of 1987, but then recovered, more or less in parallel to economic performance. Previously, in November 1986, Conservative support in Gallup Polls on voting intentions had stood at 36 per cent, just behind Labour at 39.5 per cent. By May, however, this had increased to 39 per cent, whilst Labour had slumped to 28 per cent, largely to the benefit of the Alliance (Craig, 1989). Furthermore, the May municipal elections in England and Wales produced a generally favourable result for the Conservatives. They made a nett gain of 78 seats and won control of three more councils. The Alliance also made substantial gains. Labour, however, lost a total of 220 seats and overall control of six councils.

In terms of Scotland, both the Scottish economy and the fortunes of the Scottish Conservatives continued to develop out of step with the UK as a whole. The *Quarterly Economic Commentary* of the Fraser of Allander Institute (February 1987, p. 2) suggested that:

'the issue of the increasing regional imbalance in economic activity within the UK cannot be...easily dismissed. To believe that reference to "areas of prosperity in the north", or "success in attracting inward investment", are an adequate response to the accumulating evidence, is tantamount to the belief that a man in need of open-heart surgery will feel reassured when complemented on his ruddy complexion or his fine head of hair.'

For the period under discussion, the unemployment rate was roughly one third higher in Scotland than in the UK as a whole (Central Statistical Office, December 1986 and July 1987), and a growth in service sector employment masked both a continual decline in manufacturing and the effect on jobs of the 1986 slump in oil prices. Between November and February, there were at least 12 major redundancy/closure announcements involving 100 workers or more. The highest profile of these was the decision by American multinational, Caterpillar, to shut its factory in Uddingston. The result was a 14-week occupation of the factory by the workforce and an issue, which the *Economist* (1987c, p. 29) described as 'a dispute [which] has become a symbol of Scotland's claim for more control over its own economy.' Thus, when combined with the Zircon affair, the imminence of the Poll Tax and the general state of the Scottish Economy, the Conservative Party was unable to obtain any long-term increase in its support in Scotland. In System Three (1988) opinion polls on voting intentions from November until May, the Party started and finished the period at a level of 19 per cent.

This uneven development of Scotland continued to create pressure on the Government to ensure that a 'Poll Tax for Scotland' was on the statute book prior to the next election. Before turning to the specifics of the legislative passage of the Bill, however, it is important to recognise a number of *additional* factors which helped to maintain the pressure for rates reform. In particular, three main factors can be identified.

First, there was another revolt in the Commons over the 1987-88 Rate Support Grant settlement. Senior Tory Backbencher, Bernard Braine (MP for Castle Point in Essex) said that 'it is best to be honest about this, none of the County's backbenchers will go into the division lobby tonight' (*Guardian*, 26 March 1987). In addition, Conservative MP, Simon Coombs commented that 'it must be the profoundest hope of all hon. Members who have spoken in the debate that the days of the rate support grant system are numbered' (HC Debates, 1986-87, Vol. 113, col. 510). Second, there was another uproar from Scottish ratepayers as rates increases for 1987-88 were announced. The average domestic increase throughout Scotland was 15.1 per cent and the highest was 32.9 per cent in Edinburgh (Scott, 1987, p. 4). COSLA argued that this was due to (a) inflation and the teachers' pay deal/other settlements which were not recognised in the Rate Support Grant, and (b) former administrations having used up their financial surpluses. The Scottish Office, however, reinforced the notion of a discredited system by attributing the increases to local authority 'overspending'. Third, there was a clear commitment by the Government to introduce the Poll Tax in England and Wales. This was confirmed by Environment Secretary, Nicholas Ridley, in a written Commons reply on 15 December (HC Debates, 1986-87, Vol. 107, col. 392w). It is against the background of these pressures that the Parliamentary passage of the *Abolition of Domestic Rates Etc. (Scotland) Bill* can be discussed in depth.

The House Of Commons

From the outset, the main priority of the Government was to ensure that the Bill was on the statute book by the summer, when a General Election would be a distinct possibility after four years in a second term of office. If the Bill were not completed by then, it would be 'lost' as Parliament dissolved in preparation for the General Election. The Minister charged with overseeing the Bill through the Commons was Scottish Local

Government Minister, Michael Ancram. The Opposition was led by John Maxton for Labour and Robert Maclennan for the Alliance.

The only organisation lobbying throughout the entire Parliamentary passage was COSLA. It sent a seven-strong Bill team to Westminster, with its members being based in the AMA offices. Their role was one of briefings, providing supporting material, drafting amendments and general lobbying. On 8 December, COSLA (1986b) President, Ken Fagan, wrote to all Scottish MPs and informed them that the Bill team would be available to offer assistance in 'opposing it...[the Bill] throughout the legislative process.' Not a single Conservative MP contacted COSLA, whose main point of contact was with the Labour Party. COSLA also undertook a co-ordinating role with the Scottish Council for Voluntary Organisations (SCVO), which represented such bodies as Shelter, Age Concern Scotland, the Scottish Convention of Women, the Scottish Council for Single Parents, the Scottish Council for Single Homeless, and the Scottish Society for the Mentally Handicapped.

Second Reading and Committee Stage

After a formal First Reading on 27 November, the Bill was pushed swiftly to a Second Reading on 9 December. At this stage, MPs were lobbied by several bodies. In *opposition* to the Bill were COSLA, a number of local authority bodies and the Forum of Private Business. This last body were opposed to the Bill because it contained one clause which pertained to non-domestic rates and sought to fix non-domestic poundage increases to the rate of inflation. It was opposed to this because it paved the way for the introduction of a UBR, rather than a non-domestic tax which was based on ability to pay. Lobbying *in favour* of the Bill, was a delegation from the Federation of Scottish Ratepayers. Chairwoman, Mary Whitehouse (1989), commented that 'we were very conscious that we were the only people, more or less supporting it.'

The Second Reading provides the opportunity for major debate on the principles of a Bill, and it is here that a Bill is most likely to be voted out, prior to extensive Committee work. Only one Bill, however, (the *Shops Bill*), had fallen at the crucial Second Reading stage since 1979. The *Abolition of Domestic Rates Etc. (Scotland) Bill* was to be no exception to this general trend.

During the debate, the Opposition parties put forward the (now familiar) arguments that the Poll Tax was regressive; would benefit only the rich at the expense of the poor; would cause administrative chaos, and would damage local democracy. It is important to note that Labour, in particular, displayed a contradictory response in being opposed totally to a Poll Tax, yet committing itself to working within the parameters of Parliamentary procedures, dominated numerically by the Government with a working majority of 137. Thus, on the one hand, Labour Leader, Donald Dewar, argued that 'it is misconceived in principle, regressive in impact and unworkable in practice. *None of us want anything to do with it*' (HC Debates, 1986-87, Vol. 107, col. 222). [2] On the other hand, however, less than one hour later, he affirmed the Party's intention to participate in the legislative process by saying that 'I warn the Minister that there will be no easy passage for the Bill. We will fight tooth and nail on every sentence and every clause, and we will table thousands of amendments' (HC Debates, 1986, Vol. 107, col. 233).

The Government's response to this and the general Opposition argument was also now familiar. It attacked a local income tax, accused Labour of not having an alternative to the old rating system, and propounded the merits of a Poll Tax. In the words of Michael Ancram, the Poll Tax 'means the end of a system that has underwritten profligacy at local level, which has drained ratepayers, which has milked businesses and destroyed jobs' (HC Debates, 1986-87, Vol. 107, col. 275). Not all Conservative MPs, however, were in agreement with the proposed 'solution'. Robin Squire suggested that 'it is precisely because these proposals are being trailed as a pilot for England and Wales that some of us are most unhappy and cannot find ourselves able to support the Bill' (HC Debates, 1986-87, Vol. 107, col. 2020). The *Guardian* (10 December 1986) reported that 'a handful of English MPs are understood to have abstained in protest at plans to extend the community charge system to the rest of the country.'[3] Nevertheless, the Second Reading was passed by 258 votes to 204. Not a single Conservative MP voted with the Opposition.

The Bill then moved quickly to Committee (First Scottish Standing Committee) on 16 December. In terms of direct and indirect lobbying at this stage (which lasted some two months) there was almost unanimous opposition to the Bill, either in whole or in part. Representations came from COSLA and the SCVO, AMA, ACC, Scottish Action on Dementia, Strathclyde Poverty Alliance, Scottish Council for Single Homeless, NFSESB, Scottish Womens' Aid, Scottish Consumer Council, NFU, National Union of Ratepayers Associations and the Scottish Association of Citizens Advice Bureaux. [4] More indirectly, there were a number of reports produced which were utilised by the Opposition as further evidence of the failings of the Bill. One of the main studies was commissioned from researchers at Dundee University by COSLA and the Scottish Consumer Council. It concluded that the new system was likely to be highly expensive and fraught with administrative problems

(McManus et al. 1987). The only public evidence of direct support for the Bill at this stage came via delegations from Edinburgh and Glasgow Chambers of Commerce who lobbied the Committee in an attempt to ensure that the proposals for limiting business rate rises stood as part of the Bill.

From the very beginning of the Committee stage, the Government's haste was clearly evident. Michael Ancram took the unusual step of moving a Sittings Motion for the committee to meet twice-weekly in both morning and afternoon sessions. Labour's John Maxton described this as 'astonishing...I accept that there are precedents, but the precedents for having morning and afternoon sessions this early in a parliamentary session are very few indeed' (HC Debates, 1986-87, Vol. IV, col. 4). There was also concern that the Bill was simply an 'enabling' Bill which would be fleshed out at a later stage by delegated legislation. On 23 occasions, the Bill contained the phrase 'as may be prescribed'. John Maxton argued that the Government had produced 'a Bill as vague as a White Paper which did not contain any of the necessary detail about what should be included' (HC Debates, 1986-87, Vol. IV, col. 757). Indeed, a substantial number of Labour and Alliance amendments were simply 'probing' amendments - designed to extract information from the Government as to how the Poll Tax would operate in practice.

Despite this frustration, Labour's commitment to Parliamentary principles meant that it opposed the Bill within a committee where the Government possessed an 11:7 majority (excluding two non-voting Labour Chairmen). [5] The only departure from this occurred on 18 December in the last sitting before the Christmas recess. At 7 pm., Deputy Chairman, Hugh McCartney, surprised everyone by wishing Members a Merry Christmas and a Happy New Year [!], and then suspended the sitting until 13 January. After a two-hour suspension and some procedural wrangling, the Government accused the Deputy Chairman of exceeding his powers and responded by placing Conservative MP Albert McQuarrie in the Chair. This led to Labour MP, Dennis Canavan (not a member of the Committee) who was viewing from the public benches, taking a seat on the Committee and refusing to move. He accused the Government of having no mandate to impose the Poll Tax on the people of Scotland, and that his fellow Labour MPs should be fighting and not 'sucking up to the establishment' (*Scotsman*, 19 December 1986). After a further one and a half hour period of further suspensions/ resumptions, Dennis Canavan was persuaded to leave, much to the relief of other Labour Members. Labour's John Maxton said that he could not condone the actions of an MP acting alone in such a manner.

Given, therefore, that Labour (and also the Alliance) opposed the Poll Tax strictly within the confines of Committee procedures, the corollary of this is, as John Maxton commented, that 'the opposition always have [to] work on the basis that legislation will go ahead' (HC Debates, 1986-87, Vol. IV, col. 273). Thus, a number of amendments were tabled which were underpinned by this assumption. [6] Focusing on the two key principles of the Poll Tax, these amendments required that:

- (Labour) domestic rates should be abolished only after the practicality and value of the rating system/alternative property tax/local income tax/local sales tax/combination of local income tax and local sales tax/poll tax have been considered by the Select Committee on Scottish Affairs hearing evidence from experts in local government finance and with the Report being debated in the Commons

- (Labour) the Community Charge should be renamed a 'Poll Tax'

- (Labour) students should be exempt if their only source of income is a student grant

- (Labour) there should be exemptions for those on Income Support; in receipt of state pensions; on YTS/MSC schemes, or in receipt of severe disablement allowance

- (Labour) Poll Tax liability should be reduced according to income, with rebates being permitted of up to 100 per cent

- (Alliance) the Poll Tax should be graduated according to ability to pay

The response from the Government side to all of these was generally dismissive. On a specific level, the idea of a Select Committee investigation was seen essentially as a waste of time since the Government had already investigated the matter thoroughly and the Poll Tax was the only workable system which would promote 'accountability'. In addition, renaming the Tax as a 'Poll Tax' was seen to be an Opposition ploy to mislead the Scottish people into thinking that it was a tax on the right to vote. Finally, with regard to the amendments which would have reduced or eradicated personal liability, the main argument used was that the principles of the Bill were not negotiable. For example, as Michael Ancram argued with regard to Labour's attempt to obtain up to 100 per cent rebates:

'there needs to be a relationship between the services that local authorities provide and the willingness of their local taxpayers to meet the costs. If a significant proportion of local taxpayers bear more of the burden of meeting those costs, that relationship is broken...On the Second Reading, I said that I did not deny that the amounts that we were asking people to pay were significant. There would be no point in trying to create accountability if that were not so' (HC Debates, 1986-87, Vol. IV, cols. 1293-4).

On a more general level, the Labour opposition was attacked continually for colluding with COSLA which was not making its services available to Conservative Members (an allegation which was simply untrue); failing to have an alternative to the Poll Tax, and for providing a generally weak and ineffectual opposition to the Bill.

This latter accusation did not emanate simply from Conservative Members. A major opinion poll on the Poll Tax had been conducted in January (by System Three on behalf of the Scottish Local Government Information Unit (1987)), and it showed considerable opposition to the Tax. Only 37 per cent considered the Poll Tax to be 'very fair' or 'quite fair', whilst 80 per cent thought that it should not be introduced in Scotland in advance of England and Wales. Buoyed by this, some sections of the media opposed to the Poll Tax, were highly critical of Labour's failure to capitalise on this in Committee. The leader comment in the *Evening Times* (5 February 1987) argued that 'the Labour opposition to the Bill has been pathetic. The party which glorifies and delights in its overwhelming lead in opinion polls should perform better on such crucial issues.' The *Daily Record* (described on several occasions by Conservative Members as the equivalent of *Pravda*) stated that 'Labour's promise to give rates reform a rough ride has never really materialised' (quoted in HC Debates, 1986-87, Vol. 110, col. 361). Also, the *Glasgow Herald* (26 January 1987) said that 'The promised major offensive has failed to materialise...the result is another piece of ineffectual opposition.'

These criticisms of the Labour opposition will be discussed in more detail, shortly. There seem little doubt, however, that persuasive argument had little impact on voting in Committee. Throughout the entire Committee stage, not a single Opposition amendment was passed. They were either withdrawn as the Opposition felt it of little use to force a division, or they were voted down when a division was pressed. All amendments accepted were Government-initiated, as it sought to put in place more detailed mechanisms to ensure that the Poll Tax could be put into practice. There was not a single instance of a Conservative Member voting with the Opposition.

In addition to all this, the Government (with one eye on a possible General Election and the other on a potential delay for the Bill in the Lords) took the decision to guillotine the Bill. This was the tenth guillotine of that Parliament and the fifth involving local government. Conservative Committee Member, Michael Hirst, summed up the general feeling from the Conservative benches when he suggested that 'many of the interventions and speeches in Standing Committee were no more than a lot of time wasting' (HC Debates, 1986-87, Vol. 110, col. 340). Thus, the Bill was guillotined after 101 hours debate in Committee and only 20 out of the 34 clauses discussed. One hour was allocated for discussion of each of the remaining 14 clauses. In the final minutes of the Committee on 19 February, Labour's John Maxton said that 'this has been one of the most unpleasant committees that I have served on. I would not want to finish without saying that' (HC Debates, 1986-87, Vol. IV, col. 1373).

Report Stage and Third Reading

On 4 and 5 March 1987, just prior to the Report Stage, Scottish Secretary, Malcolm Rifkind announced that instead of a three-year phase-in of the Poll Tax, there would now be a one-stage transition from domestic rates to a Poll Tax on 1 April 1989. He acknowledged that he was responding to the views of a number of organisations (particularly COSLA, CIPFA, R&VA and also the Labour Party) who argued that running two systems in tandem would be highly expensive and enormously difficult to administer. Rather than this being a reluctant Government 'concession', however, Malcolm Rifkind argued that it actually represented 'a major improvement with regard to the administration of the Bill' (HC Debates, 1986-87, Vol. 111, col. 889).

Turning now to the Report and Third Reading Stages, both returned the debate to the Floor of the House. The Report stage is a 'report' to the Commons on the Committee stage, but also allows both the Government and Opposition to table and vote on further amendments. The Third Reading then provides the opportunity for a short debate before sending the Bill to the Lords. Both stages were subject to some lobbying of MPs by a number of organisations. The only evidence of support for a Poll Tax came from Mearns Community Council. It wrote to Conservative MP, Allan Stewart, objecting to the 'wholly unjustified' rates increases by Strathclyde Region. Counter to this, COSLA, AMA and ACC lobbied the view that the Poll Tax was unfair, would result in a growth of bureaucracy and would erode local democracy. Representations came also form the SCVO and the Scottish Society for the Mentally Handicapped, with both expressing concern that members/clients would have to pay a

20 per cent minimum. From the Government's point of view, however, certainly the most embarrassing opposition came from the Tory Reform Group (TRG). A major paper produced for it by Chris Mockler (1987, p. 1) argued that the '"community charge" is misconceived and will undermine local self-government.' It perceived that it would involve excessive centralisation of power in Whitehall; would fail to achieve the necessary accountability, and would be administratively expensive.

Utilising all this opposition, Labour and the Alliance proposed a number of major amendments to the two central principles of the legislation. These required that:

- (Labour) the Poll Tax should be implemented in one local authority, only. The extension of this to other authorities would be contingent on the Secretary of State considering the findings of an independent commission which would survey the operation of the scheme. This would consist of representatives of COSLA, Scottish Office, STUC, Valuation Officers and the Law Society.

- (Alliance) as above, plus CIPFA and the Institute of Local Government

- (Labour) no-one in the following categories should pay any more in Poll Tax than under the rating system, i.e. recipients of Supplementary Benefit, Supplementary Pension, Family Income Supplement and students (including student nurses).

- (Labour) public bodies (such as the Scottish Agricultural Wages Board) should increase the minimum wage rate for employees in tied accommodation in order to compensate for liability to pay the Poll Tax.

- (Labour) student grants should be increased to compensate fully for payment of the Poll Tax.

- (Labour) 100 per cent rebates should be granted if level of income warrants it.

Some of these amendments did arouse marginal sympathy from the Conservative benches. Barry Henderson and Allan Stewart urged the Scottish Secretary to exempt the 'mentally retarded' and the 'mentally handicapped' from the Poll Tax (HC Debates, 1986-87, Vol. 111, cols. 1115 and 1119-20). Nevertheless, the dominant view on exemptions was akin to that of Bill Walker who argued that it was 'only 20 per cent' and that it would 'give voters an interest' (HC Debates, 1986-87, Vol. 111, col. 1122).

Furthermore, Michael Ancram said that the Poll Tax was a personal liability and that it was not the duty of the state to increase student grants or the wages of those in tied accommodation in order to negate this liability. The idea of a 'pilot' scheme was also dismissed as impractical, likely to produce distorted results/conclusions and was, according to Michael Ancram, about 'procrastination and delay' (HC Debates, 1986-87, Vol. 111 col. 907). With regard to the criticisms from the Tory Reform Group, Michael Ancram dismissed these by saying that they referred only to England and Wales. Michael Forsyth, however, went as far as to say that one good reason for supporting the Bill was precisely because the TRG was opposed to it (HC Debates, 1986-87, Vol. 111, col. 1124).

All Opposition amendments at the Report stage were voted down either after a verbal vote of 'aye' or 'no', or after a vote in the division lobby. Then, at the Third Reading, the Bill was sent on its way to the Lords with a 204:150 majority. Yet again, not a single Conservative MP voted against the Government. The Opposition was unable to do anything other than submit to this, with the Bill, according to Labour MP, Dick Douglas, 'dragooned through because the Government have an overwhelming majority' (HC Debates, 1986-87, Vol. 111, col. 1126). As the *Scotsman* (6 March 1987) commented:

'it is beyond doubt that Mr Rifkind has failed to carry Scottish opinion, lay or expert, with him...he will carry the day on the back of Conservative MPs representing constituencies which will be unaffected by the Bill's provisions...There is every possibility that these same MPs, when it comes to applying the Poll Tax in England and Wales, will have none of it.'

The House of Lords

The movement of the Bill to the House of Lords was undoubtedly more worrying for the Government than in the Commons. There were four main reasons for this. All are interlinked. First, the working attendance of the Lords (as opposed to its total membership of over 1100) did not provide the Government with an inbuilt majority. For the 1986-87 Session, the 'working House' (i.e. Peers who attended at least one third of Sittings) was:

Conservative	173	
Labour	82)	Total of
Liberal	36)	Opposition
SDP	15)	206
Independent	73)	

Source: House of Lords Information Office, 1989.

Second, the experience of voting in the Lords suggested that there was no guarantee of a Government majority. During the 1986-87 Session, the Lords registered roughly 100 defeats against the Government, and it was only the previous year that they had voted in the *Social Security Bill* in an attempt to ensure that householders receive 100 per cent rates rebates (Dowle, 1988, p. 19). Third, there was what Kay (1990, p. 1) calls the 'independent-minded membership' of the Lords. As FSR Chairwoman, Mary Whitehouse (1990) commented with regard to a meeting that the FSR had with Peers, 'The Lords is rather different...they wanted to know the answers to questions.' Fourth, and unlike the Commons, Parliamentary procedure dictated that a Bill could not be guillotined in the Lords. Thus, any major delay was likely to put the Bill in jeopardy if a General Election were called.

The Lords stage was also subject to both direct and indirect lobbying. Working directly to oppose the Bill (in whole or in part) was COSLA and the SCVO, AMA, ACC, TGWU, Forum of Private Business, NFSESB, Royal College of Nursing, Scottish Consumer Council, Social Security Consortium, Age Concern Scotland, Scottish Womens' Aid, Scottish Action on Dementia, NUS Scotland, Shelter, Scottish Association of Citizens Advice Bureaux, Scottish Landowners Federation, National Trust for Scotland, Strathclyde Poverty Alliance, National Federation of Retail Newsagents and the Principals of Universities in Scotland. More indirectly, a number of studies were published which seemed to reinforce the 'unfairness' of the Tax. In particular, a study published by NALGO was used by the Opposition on a number of occasions as evidence of this. It was carried out by Professor Hughes of Edinburgh University, and one of its main conclusions was that there would be more 'losers' than 'winners' in all Income Tax groups, with the only exception to this being in the income band which averaged £558 per week.

In contrast to all this, the only evidence of support came from two organisations. First, there was the Scottish CBI, which had written to Conservative Peers, expressing its support for the Bill. Second, there were domestic ratepayers in Scotland. Baroness Carnegy said that 'I have had any number of letters from people begging me to say that the unfairness which the present domestic rates produce in Scotland shall stop' (HL Debates, 1986-87, Vol. 486, col. 368). Reinforcing this, the FSR sent a delegation to meet approximately 30 Peers in order to put forward the case on behalf of Scottish ratepayers. The meeting was arranged through the Government Whip, Lord Dundee.

Second Reading and Committee Stage

After a formal First Reading on 9 March, the Bill moved to a Second Reading on 17 March. The essence of the debate was essentially the same as the Commons. Leading the Labour Opposition, Lord Ross described the Bill as 'the biggest bribe Tory voters have ever had' (HL Debates, 1986-87, Vol. 485, col. 1328). It was seen also as rooted in a crisis of the Government's own making, through an antagonistic attitude to local authorities and years of underfunding. The 'solution' (the Poll Tax) was seen to be conceived in haste, administratively complex and grossly unfair. Particular emphasis was given to this latter aspect in view of the numerous representations from bodies such as Age Concern and Scottish Action on Dementia. For the Alliance, Lord Wilson said that:

> 'The view that this is a fatally flawed measure does not rest merely on the representations of these various special interests...it is difficult to avoid the conclusion that this time the Government really have got it wrong. So wrong indeed that but for the now well-established convention of our constitution, I venture the view that on a free vote, noble Lords who had weighed the argument and the evidence would refuse the Bill a Second Reading' (HL Debates, 1986-87, Vol. 485, cols. 1334-5).

The reaction to this from the Government side (led by Lord Glenarthur) was somewhat more measured than the Commons, with the tendency being to reply in detail to each point in turn - rather than relying largely on political rhetoric. Nevertheless, the substance of the response was the same, with Lord Glenarthur saying that 'exemptions and reliefs from the personal community charge must be kept to an absolute minimum...[and] the one group that both noble Lords failed to consider was the ratepayers. He [sic] will find that groups representing Scottish Ratepayers have expressed strong support for these reforms' (HL Debates, 1986-87, Vol. 485, cols. 1394 and 1398). There was, however, some dissent from the Conservative benches. Lord Ellenborough, for example, was blunt in describing the Poll Tax as 'unsound and unfair and may be virtually impossible to implement' (HL Debates, 1986-87, Vol. 485, col. 1368).

Nevertheless, the Government had imposed a three-line whip and the Second Reading was accepted without a formal division.

The Bill then moved on to the Committee Stage, where, consistent with normal practice, this was constituted as a Committee of the Whole House. Here, the Opposition proposed a number of major amendments to the two central principles of the Bill:

- (Labour) the community charge should be renamed a 'personal poll tax'

- (Labour) exemptions should be made for the severely disabled and the severely mentally handicapped

- (Labour) exemptions should be made for those in receipt of Income Support; State Pensions or Severe Disablement Allowance, and on YTS/MSC schemes

- (Labour) 100 per cent rebates should be granted for those in receipt of Income Support or with an equivalent level of income

- (Labour and Independent) student grants should be increased to compensate for payment of the Poll Tax

- (Labour and Independent) the Poll Tax should be paid only by those who have attained the age of 21

- (Alliance) the Poll Tax should be graduated according to ability to pay

- (Alliance) domestic rates should be abolished, only if a scheme for a Local Income Tax has been established

- (Alliance) the Poll Tax should be introduced as a 'pilot' scheme in one area, with the Secretary of State being bound to consider the findings of its review by an independent Commission, comprising representatives of COSLA, Scottish Office, Valuation Assessors and the Law Society

- (Alliance) the Act should come into force, only if a simple majority of the people of Scotland have approved it in a referendum

- (Alliance) 95 per cent rebates should be granted, dependent on incomes

The Government's response to these continued to be more detailed and measured than the Commons, but (again) the substance was the same. Exemptions and anything related to ability to pay other than an 80 per cent rebate (despite George Younger's statement that there was nothing 'magic' about the figure) were seen as undermining 'accountability'. A pilot scheme would be unnecessary as the Bill would be fair and workable. The 'Community Charge' could not be renamed a 'personal poll tax', because, according to Lord Glenarthur, it was 'in no sense a tax upon the right of people to vote' (HL Debates, 1986-87, Vol. 486, col. 551). Furthermore, with regard to a referendum, Conservative Peer, Lord Boyd-Carpenter, said that 'The idea of expecting the whole population of Scotland to take a snap decision on the simple issue of whether or not to have it is to bring the whole legislative process into a state of mockery' (HL Debates, 1986-87, Vol. 486, col. 1203).

These amendments were all withdrawn, with the exception of the request for the introduction of a local income tax, which was defeated 139:93, without a single Conservative Peer voting with the Opposition. Despite an apparently unyielding stance by the Government, however, there was actually a distinct shift in one area. Lord Glenarthur said that:

> 'on the whole substance of the disabled - the physically disabled, the mentally handicapped, residents in homes and all the categories that have been incorporated in Lord Henderson's amendment - may I say that I certainly recognise that there are real difficulties for all those categories of people...I should like to take away this amendment and consider it in the whole context of this particularly difficult area' (HL Debates, 1986-87, Vol. 486, col. 785).

He said also that he would be prepared at least to consider the matter of students.

The precise reasons for this shift in position have a very definite basis, since altruism on the part of the Government must be discounted (otherwise there would have been a 'shift' at Committee stage in the Commons when the Government was pushed on these same issues). Thus, in the Lords and unlike the Commons, there seemed to be substantial reservations from the Conservative side to the Government's unilateral stance of no exemptions. For example, Baroness Carnegy (in conjunction with Lady Soulton, a Cross-Bencher) tabled an amendment which requested exemptions for 'persons suffering from a state of arrested or incomplete development of mind which includes significant impairment of intelligence and social functioning' (HL Sessional Papers, 1986-87, Vol. 1, First Marshalled List of Amendments, p. 16). Another amendment by Lord Campbell (with Lady Soulton) required that couples in receipt of maximum rates rebates should not be put at any financial disadvantage as a result of the passing of the Act (HL Sessional Papers, 1986-87, Vol. 1, First Marshalled List of Amendments, p. 29). Neither amendment was 'pressed', although with rumours emerging of a possible General Election in June, there was little doubt that these posed problems for the Government. As the *Glasgow Herald* (8 April 1987) commented, 'Senior Government Ministers are said to be concerned at the prospect of defeats in the Lords if no concessions are made - a move which could delay seriously the Bill's progress.'

Report Stage and Third Reading

At both stages, the Opposition continued to push forward a number of major amendments, as it was evident that the Government *may* be prepared to make some concessions. The Opposition's stance was fuelled by the NALGO study which showed the extent of the 'losers' throughout Scotland. Concentrating on amendments where concessions were a *possibility*, there were attempts to require that:

- (Labour) 100 per cent rebates should be available, dependent on income

- (Alliance) exemptions should be made for those undertaking a full-time course of education, or full-time industrial or professional training

- (Alliance) Income Support should be enhanced so that those in receipt of same and paying a 20 per cent minimum would be no worse off

These amendments were all withdrawn. The Government, however, did announce a number of concessions at this stage. These can be broken down into two categories. First, total exemptions were granted for the severely mentally handicapped and residents in nursing and residential homes. Second, it was announced that students and those on Income Support would be liable for only 20 per cent, with the Government taking the latter into account when setting Income Support levels.

Again, there were further concrete circumstances which lay behind this. Several newspaper reports suggested that Government Whips were now 'clearing the decks' for a General Election. In conjunction with this, the continual concern of some Conservatives in the Lords was proving to be potentially fatal to the Bill - none more so than ex-Prime Minister, Lord Home, who, according to the *Scotsman* (1 May 1987), had 'set alarm bells ringing at the Scottish Office...if senior Tories such as Lord Home were unhappy, then the potential for revolt was strong.'

As the Bill moved on to the Third Reading before going back to the Commons, the Opposition continued to press for further amendments:

- (Labour) exemptions should be made for the mentally handicapped (i.e. not simply the severely mentally handicapped)

- (Labour) the maximum rebate for the most 'vulnerable groups' should be 100 per cent. The term 'vulnerable groups' should be arrived at after discussions with associations (including COSLA) who are knowledgeable about the needs of these groups

By this stage, however, the reservations of Conservative Peers had largely subsided. There were two main reasons for this. First, the concessions at Report Stage had been enough to quell the threat of a large-scale revolt. Second, the local elections the previous week in England and Wales (see p. 163), had produced a favourable result for the Conservatives. Further dissent, therefore, would hardly be conducive if a General Election announcement were to follow in the wake of this.

As a result, the Government could quite easily afford to brush aside the amendments - both of which were withdrawn. On the mentally handicapped, Lord Glenarthur said that this was not an easy condition to define and that many such conditions were often temporary. On the matter of 'vulnerable groups', he said that many of these were covered already in the 'concessions' and that further exemptions would undermine 'accountability'. Thus, the Bill was returned to the Commons without recourse to a vote. For the Labour Opposition, Lord Ross concluded by saying that, 'it was...such a terrible Bill. Anyone who has anything to do with the making and passing of the Bill will rue it. The Scottish People will not forget' (HL Debates, 1986-87, Vol. 487, col. 481). Fairley (1988, p. 60) comments that 'Most political commentators judged that Lord Ross's contributions in the House of Lords were far more pointed and effective than anything heard in the Commons.'

The Final Stage: Back to the Commons

On 11 May, on the crest of improved opinion poll showings for the Conservatives and favourable results in the municipal elections, the Prime Minister announced that a General Election would be held in exactly one month's time. On 13 May, two days after the announcement, the Bill returned to the Commons for a debate on the Lords' Amendments. The floor of the House was virtually empty and there was only one MP representing a constituency in either England or Wales (Labour MP, Andrew Faulds). The Government introduced a further guillotine motion, which limited the debate to three hours. Scottish Labour Leader, Donald Dewar, called it a debate 'taking place in injury time' (HC Debates, 1986-87, Vol. 116, col. 295). The Opposition welcomed the concessions in the Lords, but said that they did not go far enough in terms of reducing or eradicating the liability of 'vulnerable' groups. Thus, Labour tabled a last-ditch series of amendments which would have exempted the mentally handicapped, registered disabled persons and all students in full-time education. These were dismissed by Michael Ancram, however, who said that they would simply erode 'accountability' and that 'many handicapped people play an active part in the life of their communities and are quite capable of appreciating the issued of local authority accountability' (HC Debates, 1986-87, Vol. 116, col. 337).

The Opposition response to this was a flurry of anger. Labour MP, George Home-Robertson told Ancram to 'Go to hell' (HC Debates, 1986-87, Vol. 116, col. 337). Labour's Dick Douglas found it 'absolutely nauseating' (HC Debates, 1986-87, Vol. 116. col. 338). Robert Maclennan of the Alliance found the judgment of whether or not people were 'severely' mentally handicapped (this being a judgment on whether or not they could participate in the democratic process), as like 'procedures...operated in Nazi Germany' (HC Debates, 1986-87, Vol. 116, col. 340).

At the end of three hours, the division lobbies filled up as the 'last-ditch' Opposition amendments were voted down by 227:115 and the Lords' Amendments were approved. Again, not a single Conservative MP voted with the Opposition. Two days later, on 15 May, the Bill received Royal Assent along with 42 other Bills, as Parliament dissolved in preparation for the General Election.

Conclusion

This has been the last of four 'empirical' chapters, detailing the development of the Poll Tax policy formation process and the gradual integration of a Poll Tax into the Conservative Government's reformulated strategy. The Conclusion to this book will take a wide-ranging overview of this in terms of matters pertaining to policy formation. In the meantime, however, it seems useful to locate this present chapter within the context of the previous three empirical excursions. Chapter Four looked at the 1985 property revaluation in Scotland, and showed how the contradictions of the Conservative's 'leading strategy' became condensed in a particular geographical location and at a particular point in time. These produced an 'uproar' and a consequent powerful alliance of forces (joined latterly by the Conservative Government), committed to abolishing domestic rates. Chapter Five then showed how these forces split initially into pro/anti-poll tax camps, but that a shift in the balance of forces led ultimately to the Government using its 'leading' constitutional authority to take the decision to proceed with a Poll Tax alone. Chapter Six then showed how the Government adopted a 'leading strategy' of public consultation, using its constitutionally legitimate powers to sweep aside substantial practical and ideological opposition to the Poll Tax.

The present chapter completed this process, through an outlining of the manner in which the *Abolition of Domestic Rates Etc. (Scotland) Bill* survived its Parliamentary passage with considerable ease. Throughout the passage of the Bill, the two central principles of a flat-rate 'head' tax and a 20 per cent minimum liability remained intact, with marginal concessions occurring on the latter, primarily for reasons of political expediency. The entire process pivoted around the constitutional sovereignty of Parliament, and the ideological 'lead' provided by this. Thus, the commitment of the Opposition to working within the confines of Parliamentary procedures meant that opposition to the Poll Tax and the scrutiny and passage of the Bill was dominated by a government which possessed a working majority of 137 in the Commons. This was utilised by the Government to its greatest advantage, not only because of the use of the Whip, but also because of the relative lack of interest by English and Welsh Tory MPs. To a large extent, they accepted the Government's insistence (both implicit and explicit) that legislation was necessary for Scotland in order to 'do something' about Conservative Party support there and to promote the 'accountability' of local authorities to the electorate. But at the same time, they saw the introduction of the Poll Tax in England and Wales as something which may or may not happen in the dim and distant future.

The nett result of all this was that the Poll Tax became an Act of Parliament, whilst the labour and trades union movements did little, in practical terms, that would have blocked it or even turned it into a major issue in Scotland. Ken Fagan, the President of Labour-dominated COSLA, likened the whole thing to the legislation which introduced the deregulation of buses. He said that public outcry materialised only after it was clear that buses were not going to turn up on time. By then, of course, it was too late to stop the legislation. Furthermore, the STUC's conference at the end of April, carried, for the *first time*, a Resolution specifically on the Poll Tax. It called on the 'use of every means possible to publicise the gross inequalities of the community charge and prevent the implementation of the legislation' (Scottish Trades Union Congress, 1987, p. 233). By this stage, however, the Bill was about to enter its final stages in the Lords. With regard to the Parliamentary Labour Party, it did of course oppose the Poll Tax within Parliament. In terms of the Party as a whole, however, it was never a *major* issue. Thus, there were similarities with the STUC, in that the 1987 Conference in March carried the first Resolution even to mention the Poll Tax. A combination of Labour's commitment to constitutional politics, the priority of devolution, the perceived unworkability of the Poll Tax, the lack of an agreed alternative, the perceived electoral liability to the Conservatives and the corresponding benefit to Labour, resulted in what was acknowledged widely as an ineffectual Opposition and the failure to capitalise on what the *Guardian* (29 January 1986) had called a 'gift issue'. As Adrian Ham, argued (writing in *Tribune*):

'The failure to push home the sheer awfulness of the new poll tax was one of the great missed opportunities. Few governments this century anywhere in the world have brought forward tax proposals which introduced an enormous financial incentive for people to disenfranchise themselves...but the issue was presented in a way which made hardly a ripple of interest' (quoted in Fyfe, 1987, p. 9).

Notes

1. Much to the dismay of the Opposition, the figure of 20 per cent was never actually made concrete in the Bill itself. The liability for a minimum payment of rates was one component of the Social Security reforms which were due to come into operation on 1 April 1988. The Government had still to set a figure for this and argued persistently that the *Abolition of Domestic Rates Etc. (Scotland) Bill* should not pre-empt this decision. Nevertheless, all indicators from the Government were that it would be inconceivable for the figure to be anything other than 20 per cent. It is understandable, however, that the Opposition should be dismayed at such a key principle being the subject of separate legislation.

2. Emphasis added.

3. It should be noted that Parliamentary records do not record 'abstentions'.

4. There was some conflict between NURA and its Scottish counterparts, the FSR. Members of the FSR had, on several occasions, contacted NURA to express their disappointment that NURA should be opposing a Bill which the FSR supported on behalf of Scottish domestic ratepayers.

5. The membership (excluding Chairmen) was Conservative (11), Labour (6) and Alliance (1).

6. Throughout this chapter it has been necessary to be selective in identifying the amendments which were tabled around the two central principles of a flat-rate 'head' tax and a minimum 20 per cent liability. This is because (i) of the sheer volume of amendments, (ii) there was a considerable overlap between many which differed only marginally from one another, and (iii) many amendments were simply 'probing' amendments i.e. designed to extract more information as to how the Poll Tax would operate in practice. Thus, amendments have been 'selected' in order to indicate the main ways in which the Opposition parties attempted to oppose the Tax at each stage. Following on from this, it should be understood, of course, that it has been necessary to select virtually identical amendments when they were tabled at different stages in the legislative process.

Conclusion

The main purpose of this Conclusion is to integrate theory and practice. More specifically, it is to utilise the principles of policy formation which were developed in Chapter Two, in order to explain the Poll Tax policy formation process. In seems useful in the first instance, however, to briefly restate these principles. Having done this, we can then look in turn at each stage of the policy formation process, as detailed in the previous four chapters.

Policy Formation: A Brief Restatement

Chapter One identified how existing theoretical perspectives on 'policy formation' were beset by a series of problems. These were rooted largely in the fact that analysts tended to neglect this broad area of study in favour of other concerns. In order to illustrate this, a series of writings was tested against a 'skeleton' definition of policy formation which encapsulated the processes which this book sought to address. These writings tended to devolve into two main categories. First, there were number of perspectives whose focus was on a range of matters from policy cycles to the state, and which dealt with *some* aspects of policy formation as a by-product of this. This refers to (among others) the works of Downs, Simon, Lindblom, Bachrach and Baratz, Richardson and Jordan, Miliband, and Poulantzas. Second, there were the works of

Bauer, Claus Offe and John Kingdon. Each *did* attempt explicitly to deal with policy formation, but still fell short of providing an integrated view of the policy formation process as a whole.

Chapter Two then recognised that whilst there are a problems in developing 'general' principles of policy formation, the shortage of existing theoretical materials lends itself to laying down some tentative markers in the ground. The basis for this, it was argued, rests with Marxist dialectical principles. The very essence of these is that we should understand society as the dynamic interaction of opposing forces. Chapter Two argued that the most useful way of conceptualising policy formation processes was in terms of the contradiction between the 'leading capitalist forces in society' (in essence, *all* those relationships buttressing the pursuit of private profit and the accumulation of the ownership and control of material resources into 'private' hands), and the 'contradictory forces in society (in essence, a range of forces continually reacting against *all* or *some* components of the 'leading capitalist forces'). The corollary of this is that the domination of the former is never complete. Thus, the ruling class rules, but in a *contradictory* way. The remainder of Chapter Two explored these matters by discussing the contradictory nature of policy and policy formation. Analysis of these was expanded upon by looking at the leading and controlling roles of the liberal-democratic Parliamentary state - situating these in the wider context of dynamic societal contradictions. Thus, to recap, the 'general' principles of policy formation that should be considered as applicable to liberal-democratic societies are as follows.

1. 'Leading capitalist forces' in society are continually confronting and creating 'contradictory forces'.

2. Policies are part of these leading forces, although these forces can develop to such an extent that the 'contradictory forces' (with policies also being part of these) may hold back the development of the leading forces to the extent that key decision-making actors within the state perceive a particular policy to be incompatible with their strategy.

3. A commitment may then be made to begin a process with a view to producing a replacement policy.

4. This gives rise to a struggle between an array of interests, with the state being part of and mediating between these as it attempts to take the lead and take control gradually of the policy formation process.

5. In terms of the British Parliamentary state, it does so through (i) the capitalist parameters set by liberalism, (ii) the sovereignty of Parliament which acts as a focus for expressed interests, (iii) the dominance of the Executive in terms of decision-taking and the legislative passage of Bills, acting as a vehicle for 'getting things done' in the policy formation process, and (iv) the autonomy of key state actors in deciding the particular type of strategy used to 'lead' the policy formation process i.e. consultation, imposition etc.

6. The end result is a 'new' policy - containing within it the seeds for further development as it operates in the context of the pressures of a contradictory class society.

Having reminded ourselves of these general principles, we are now in a position to apply them to each stage in the Poll Tax policy formation process.

The Poll Tax and State Policy Formation

Chapters Four, Five, Six and Seven, all dealt with separate but interlinked stages in the policy formation process which culminated in a Poll Tax for Scotland being enshrined in an Act of Parliament. Each of these stages can be considered in turn, although first of all they must be placed in the wider political and economic context of the origins and initial development of the Thatcher Government.

The Thatcher Government and its Contradictions

Chapter Three illustrated the way in which the Thatcher Government in the period 1979 to 1984-85, held the directorship of the 'leading capitalist forces', and this helped create a series of 'contradictory forces'. Each of these can be outlined briefly.

The 'leading capitalist forces' were focused on what Woolfson and Foster (1988, p. 11) describe as a conscious attempt 'to change the balance of class forces in Britain.' In essence, the Government's initial 'lead' in terms of its general strategy, comprised three main components. First, it was able to forge its 'political' strategy on the back of (i) a widespread public antipathy and hostility towards the Labour Party and the trade union movement after the experience of the Wilson/Callaghan Governments and (ii) the ascendancy within the Tory Party leadership of the radical 'right' and its reaction against Heath's 1972 U-turn from free market polices. In addition to this, there was a shift in some skilled working class votes to the Conservatives. The Government was able to 'appeal' to this class of voter - particularly in the South-East - through the 'right to buy' and income tax reductions, these being financed to a large extent by oil revenues and privatisation proceeds. The Government, therefore, had the 'political' basis for governing, and this was assisted further from 1983 onwards by a splitting of the Opposition vote by the SDP. Furthermore, the vagaries of the first-past-the-post electoral system enabled the Conservatives to govern with a massive 144 majority and only just over 42 per cent of the vote.

The second key component of the Government's 'lead' was the use of interest and exchange rates (in conjunction with the abolition of exchange controls) to promote the international interests of the City and those elements of large industrial capitals linked to it. In the short term, and with controlling inflation being put forward as the key aim of Government policy, this was intended to provoke a massive 'shakeout' of domestic-oriented capital.

The third key component was (according to the Government) that this would be to the long-term benefit of domestic-oriented capital for a number of key reasons. It would force the trade union movement along a 'flexible' path (buttressed by legislation restricting its activities). This would be complemented through an assault on the labour movement and state provision and spending levels in the areas of welfare benefits, nationalised industries etc. Then, after all this had happened, conditions would be favourable for reinvestment in the domestic economy. Scotland, of course, was also 'led' by the effects of all these processes, although apart from an encouragement of inward investment, the only other major 'lead' for Scotland was cuts in regional policy and what Balchin and Bull (1987, pp. 52-3) describe as 'the spatial manifestation of...monetarism and free-market economics.'

The 'lead' for local government was deployed through what Stallworthy (1989, p. 23) describes as a 'vast panoply of legislative tinkerings', designed to limit the finances and autonomy of local authorities. In effect, local authorities were viewed as having the potential to drive *political* and *economic* wedges in the heart of the new-found Conservative philosophy. This was because of their ability to '*extend* service provision...[and] demonstrate *alternative* policies' (Duncan and Goodwin, 1988, p. 113), and to spend at levels which would breach the Government's public expenditure targets and hence its anti-inflationary strategy. The Government's use of the rating system was an important component of these 'leading' forces. Not only was it to continue to perform the pre-existing roles as detailed in Chapter Two (i.e. managing the uneven development of capitalism, reproducing people as 'fit to work', financing local infrastructures and contributing to social stability), but it was also placed at the forefront of the Government's 'leading' strategy. On the one hand, the legislative controls and cuts in central funding were intended to suppress public spending and inflationary pressures. This would assist in the general revival of the fortunes of British capital, and some capitals would benefit particularly from low rates bills. On the other hand, these were also intended to suppress the challenge from 'local socialism', and to buttress the Government's electoral base of support in the form of domestic ratepayers.

In terms of theorising this 'leading' strategy of the Thatcher Government, it is all too obvious that it has been the subject of considerable and often heated debate. On one level, for example, there is the work of Stuart Hall, Martin Jacques et al., where post-Fordist, individualised and flexible production processes are seen as having been harnessed by the 'authoritarian populism' of Thatcherism and its 'populist' appeal...orchestrated with the imposition of authority and order' (Hall and Jacques, 1983, p. 10). On another level, for example, there is the work of Jessop et al., (1988). This sees Thatcherism as operating within the limits of a City-dominated power bloc, utilising 'relative autonomy' to construct a 'two nations project' of productive/parasitic, rich/poor, North/South, employed/unemployed etc. It must be clearly understood that it is not the intention here to enter into this debate because it is beyond the scope of the present work and would simply distract us from a focus on policy formation. It must be said briefly, however, that neither of these seems particularly attractive. In the former, 'technology' rather than 'class' seems to be the foundation of society. Whilst, in the latter, the influence of Poulantzas looms large, and the autonomy for state actors is effectively dehumanised through it being somehow 'assigned' by power bloc and associated relationships.

Whichever way we wish to theorise the nature of the Thatcher Government, Chapter Three illustrated the way in which it produced a whole series of 'contradictory forces'. These created the pressures which reached a critical point in Scotland in early 1985. There are several reasons for this. Scotland was removed geographically from the economic activity around the City and the emerging consumer boom, whilst not benefiting to the same degree as the South from increased defence spending. Furthermore, Scottish-based industrial capital suffered from cuts in regional policy and a heavier reliance on a (contracting) industrial base, with the consequence of this being higher levels of unemployment. This was compounded by a feature of the domestic economy as a whole i.e. the unattractiveness of domestic reinvestment by the City because of the technology gap between Britain and its main competitors, Japan and Germany. This comparative uneven economic development of Scotland was translated into a weakening of Conservative Party support in Scotland. Thus, there was an even 'political' development when contrasted with the much higher level of Conservative support South of the Border. In addition to this, both in Scotland and elsewhere, there were the 'contradictory forces' within local government, and a whole series of pressures building up within the rating system itself. Resistance from the 'left' in local government meant that changes in local finance had not been able to suppress the challenge from 'local socialism'; domestic and non-domestic ratepayers were being squeezed by high rates bills, and the system was coming under attack from within Tory Party ranks and from the Government-created Audit Commission.

Overall, therefore, it was the 'leading capitalist forces' under the directorship of the Conservative Government, and the ensuing 'contradictory forces' manifesting themselves particularly in Scotland, which provided the impetus and the wider context for the demise of domestic rates and the advent of the Poll Tax.

Stage One: The 1985 Property Revaluation in Scotland

In Chapter Four, we saw how layer upon layer of 'contradictory forces' were converging at a particular historical and geographical point. The Government's promotion of private sector housing through the 'right-to-buy' and restrictions on local authority capital spending, were creating above average increases in domestic rateable values, with this being felt particularly in areas with sitting Conservative MPs. When combined with local authorities increasing rate poundages in order to recoup the losses from cuts in Rate Support Grant, the result was a backlash from the Tories' electoral base of support in Scotland, whom Scottish Secretary George Younger (1991) had called 'our people'.

On top of this, there was an above average increase in the rateable values of non-domestic ratepayers in the constituencies of the 21 sitting Conservative MPs. When combined with increases in rate poundages, representatives of the bulk of Scottish-based capital (NFSESB, Association of Scottish Chambers of Commerce, Scottish CBI, CURB and the Forum of Private Business) were criticising the Government and the existing rating system. With all this reinforced by the support given by the Opposition Parties and COSLA, the 'fright' given to the Tory Party in Scotland permeated it from the 'grass roots' of the SCUA through to Scottish Secretary, George Younger.

Why, might it be asked, was the Government in the position that a 'policy formation process' was set formally in motion? The answer seems to be that the contradictions of its 'leading' strategy were threatening that self-same strategy. With its massive Parliamentary majority in excess of 140, it did not actually *need* the 21 seats in Scotland to sustain this. The crucial matter seems to have been one of legitimacy. A key ideological theme of the Thatcher Government was the need for 'unity' in the fight to suppress inflation, and this meant curbing the trade unions, cutting public spending etc. Thus, it already had the ideological ammunition to cope with the backlash against its radical strategy. With the uproar surrounding the property revaluation in Scotland, however, it was faced with a situation where the backlash was from the very interests that were crucial to the legitimacy of its general strategy. In other words, homeowners, and what we might loosely call the 'business' community. Certainly, there had been 'uproars' at the time of previous revaluations, but this was the first time that any government since 1601 had experienced an overwhelming problem with regard to 'consent' to be taxed under the rating system. It was not that there was a non-payment campaign. It was simply voices from crucial foundations of Government support, indicating that they were *not* prepared to be taxed under the existing system. Thus, albeit that the uproar was in Scotland, the Party (if it did not commit itself to abolishing the rating system), would have had extreme difficulty in proclaiming itself to be *the* Party of the Union, *the* Party of unity, and hence *the* Party of Government. Yet the situation was not so bleak for the Conservative's that they had to take a gigantic leap of faith to avoid such a scenario. There had been long-standing reservations from within Tory Party about domestic rates. Furthermore, the uproar surrounding revaluation had opened up a 'window' of opportunity for the Government, because it saw the potential to transform its general strategy by incorporating into it a system of local taxation which would (a) ease the tax burden on its supporters in the ranks of domestic and non-domestic ratepayers, and (b) make the spending and activities of local authorities more 'accountable' to the wishes of the centre. Viewed in this light, therefore, it seems understandable and perhaps unsurprising that the Government committed itself to abandoning the rating system - thus giving birth to what Scots Party Chairman Sir James Goold (1991) described as 'euphoria' within the Party ranks.

In summary, therefore, this initial stage of the policy formation process was rooted in the 'leading capitalist forces' (dominated by the City and large industrial capitals with a similar international orientation) creating a concentration of 'contradictory forces'. This then created a crisis in the Government's general strategy, which it sought to exploit. It did so by taking the first steps (underpinned by the capitalist parameters set by both liberalism and private property rights) to reformulate its strategy and move it to the 'right'. This would shift the tax burden away from the middle class and towards the working class, whilst at the same time exercising even greater central control over local authorities.

Stage Two: The Emergence of the Poll Tax

During this stage, we saw how the Parliamentary state gradually took the lead in the struggle over the content of the 'new' policy and hence the content of a transformed strategy. In terms of this struggle, we saw in Chapter Five that there was the emergence of essentially two sets of forces.

On the one hand, there were the pro-poll tax forces of the Adam Smith Institute, Federation of Scottish Ratepayers, the CBI at a UK level, and sections within the Conservative Party up to Cabinet level. In essence, they favoured a radical shift in the tax burden towards working class people, and a local tax which would tie local authorities inexorably to low spending programmes (because of the electoral repercussions of doing otherwise). This would consolidate the Conservatives' electoral base of support, allowing the local tax system to perform its 'traditional' roles. Crucially, however, it would do so by shifting the balance of power towards capital and away from trades unions and the labour movement. Thus, not only was a Poll Tax seen as being able to 'head off' any labourist challenge at a local level, but lower local tax bills and a lower level of domestic inflation were also seen as benefiting all sections of capital. In particular, it would strengthen the dominance of the City of London and those large domestic capitals linked to it. It would do so through the maintenance of a Government which allowed it to invest abroad, and which was prepared to use interest and exchange rates to protect the City's position as a leading European Banker.

On the other hand, there were the anti-poll tax forces of some ratepayers' associations, the Opposition parties, most local authority associations, the trades union movement, the media, 'public opinion' as expressed through opinion polls, and sections within the Conservative Party up to Cabinet level. Some of these had their own preferred alternatives to domestic rates, whilst others did not. Common themes, however, were the effective denouncing of a Poll Tax on the grounds of it being impractical and/or on the grounds of introducing what the Child Poverty Action Group described as 'a proposal which so blatantly favours the rich over the poor' (quoted in COSLA et al. 1987).

As part of the 'leading capitalist forces' in society, the Parliamentary state (and in practice the Cabinet) was imbued with the authority to *take the lead and take control* of this policy formation process and the emerging struggle taking place over a new system of local taxation. It was also 'leading' because of the provisional conclusions that the DoE enquiry had reached with regard to a replacement system - thus setting the parameters for the relevant 'policy community', and running counter to the dominant role given to policy communities as suggested by Richardson and Jordan (Chapter One). In other words, it took the 'lead' through the two conclusions specified by Local Government Minister Kenneth Baker (*Scotsman*, 26 March 1985) at the end of March 1985:

- that the local tax burden was falling on too few shoulders, and

- that accountability to the electorate had become too thin.

As we saw in Chapter Five, a poll tax had 'won through' on these grounds and hence on what Scottish Local Government Minister Michael Ancram (1991) had described as 'its own merits within the Committee.' Yet, by exhibiting an initial tendency towards a dual system of a property tax and poll tax, the Cabinet seemed to be embodying and attempting to balance these conflicting forces. The reason for this is that it seemed to be in an otherwise insuperable position. To favour a poll tax alone would probably not have commanded sufficient support from within the Party as a whole, whilst to remain simply with a property tax was likely to lead to another 'uproar' in Scotland and a re-opening of the cracks in its overall strategy.

This situation was then transformed because of a changing 'political' and 'economic' environment which was conducive to the ascendancy of the pro-poll tax forces. On the one hand, the beginnings of a consumer boom in the South East (supported by tax cuts which the Government had been able to pay for through oil revenues and privatisation proceeds) was leading to a resurgence in the fortunes of the Tory Party at a UK level. On the other hand, Scotland continued to bear the brunt of the Government's interest/exchange rate policy and suffered because of the proposed closure of British Steel's Gartcosh rolling mill and the continuing teachers' dispute. The result was the inability of the Scottish Conservatives to parallel the Party's success South of the Border. Acting in conjunction with a rekindling of the earlier uproar by the Federation of Scottish Ratepayers and the Tory 'grassroots' over the possibility that rates might remain in some form, this was enough to create the conditions for the Cabinet Committee to approve a Poll Tax in order to 'do something' about Scotland. It was then subsequently approved for England and Wales, seemingly because of the pragmatism of many Ministers - unable to resist the pressures for a Poll Tax, but devising what some had described as the 'wheeze' of a ten-year phase-in (*Financial Times*, 23 December 1985).

In this second stage of the policy formation process, therefore, the 'leading force' of the Parliamentary state, used its constitutionally legitimate authority and autonomy to make the initial moves towards a poll tax and towards the reformulation of (and shift to the 'right' in) its general strategy. As we can now see, it began to *take the lead and take control even more*, as it sought to make moves towards putting this on a concrete footing.

Stage Three: The Green Paper and Public 'Consultation'

As we saw in Chapter Six, the 'lead' taken by key actors within the Parliamentary state, was one of 'consultation' through a Green Paper. As Roy MacIver of COSLA, suggested - 'it is really a White Paper with one or two green parts in it' (quoted in Davis-Coleman, 1986a, p. 490). The malleability of Green Papers, therefore, meant that this was a highly suitable 'leading' strategy for the Government to employ. Given the sovereignty of Parliament and the 'lead' provided by it in terms of being the prime channel for political expression seeking to influence state policy, 'consultation' could provide the Government with a measure of the opposition to the Poll Tax and would enable it to say that it had 'consulted', whilst at the same time allowing it to proceed regardless. This would depend, of course, on circumstances being favourable to this. Briefly, we can consider the support/opposition that the Government confronted in this consultation exercise, and how conditions were indeed favourable for it to proceed with plans to produce a Bill for Scotland. It should be noted that the 'reactions' will be considered (as before) in terms of the Green Paper, rather than simply the Poll Tax. The reason for this is that the malleability of 'consultation' allowed the Government to utilise support for non-domestic rating reforms as justification for the reforms in general, and so for introducing the Poll Tax.

The main organisations in favour of the measures contained in the Green Paper were those integral to its overall strategy namely the Federation of Scottish Ratepayers, and the bulk of domestic-based capital i.e. the major Chambers of Commerce, the major divisions of the CBI, and the Scottish Branch of the Institute of Directors. The main organisations now *opposed* to the Green Paper were (apart from some such as the National Federation of Self-Employed and Small Businesses) what might be termed 'traditional' opponents of much of Government policy, and support from these was not *necessary* if it was to develop a political alliance around which the reforms could be based. Thus, opposition to the Green Paper came from all the main local authority associations, professional bodies such as CIPFA and the R&VA, the trades union movement, all the Opposition parties, and the National Union of Ratepayers Associations (which the Government seemed to consider as something of a 'maverick' and unrepresentative of the views of most domestic ratepayers). Also, in terms of opposition, there was what might loosely be called 'public opinion'. Certainly, there seemed to be a substantial bedrock of opposition to the principle of a poll tax. There was never, however, any organised campaign against its introduction. The reasons for this, it might be suggested, were because of a combination of a generally low level of interest in engaging in 'political' activity, the perception that no government could possibly introduce such a blatantly 'unfair' tax, and finally a reliance on the trades unions and labour movements to spearhead any opposition if there was ever any danger of the Government actually deciding to proceed with the Tax.

As a result of both this general support and opposition, the 'leading forces' (under the directorship of the Thatcher Government) were in the position to *take the lead and take control* of the policy formation process to an even greater degree by making a firm commitment to legislate. This would depend, of course, on the 'political' and 'economic' environment being conducive to this. As we saw in Chapter Six, the impact of the Government's developing strategy produced four such conditions.

First, its mishandling of the Westland Affair had the by-product of producing a Tory Party (in early 1986) which the *Economist* (1986c, p. 20) suggested would probably have cheered almost anything. Second, the oil reserves and proceeds from privatisation had been able to create a consumer boom in the South East and a revival of Tory fortunes in opinion polls. Third, the continuing uneven 'economic' and 'political' development of Scotland helped to perpetuate the idea that 'something' should be done for Scotland. Fourth, the trades union and labour movements were unable to offer the 'lead' that might have been expected from them. Why was this the case? With regard to the unions, the answer seems to lie in the fact that they had been weakened by the 'axe through the door' legislative onslaught of the Thatcher Government. Thus, they had limited resources to devote to constructing barriers to prevent the 'axes' of trade union restrictions, social security reforms, protection of the industrial base etc. As a consequence, one of the many potential 'axes' being wielded on the other side of the door (i.e. a Poll Tax), seemed hardly worth the time of devoting resources to. This was especially given what STUC Deputy General Secretary John Henry (1989) described as 'this feeling in the movement that it would never get off the ground.' The Labour Party was in a similar position, although this was compounded because the quest for an alternative to the rates was subordinate to working out the practicalities of devolved assemblies for Scotland and the regions. This matter aside, however, the Labour Party actually saw the Poll Tax as something positive for the labour movement, in the sense that it was seen as harbinger of electoral disaster for the Tories. Thus, extra-Parliamentary activity was never a serious option, and a commitment to opposing the Poll Tax within Parliamentary parameters ensured that the Government (with its massive majority) would have little trouble in steering a Bill through Parliament.

Faced with this 'weak' opposition and the conditions favourable for the incorporation of the Poll Tax into a transformed strategy, the Government had the confidence to declare its commitment to introducing a Bill (doing so by utilising key sections of the non-domestic respondents as justification for proceeding with the reforms in general). Thus, in this crucial stage of policy formation, we find key actors in the Parliamentary state, *taking the lead and taking control* to an even greater degree of the policy formation process. They did so by using the vehicle of a Green Paper to 'soak up' opposition to a Poll Tax and then (in a constitutionally legitimate way) use their authority and autonomy to press ahead regardless. At a theoretical level, of course, this runs counter to the view of Downs and Dahl that potential electoral repercussions would ensure that no government could realistically proceed on this basis.

Stage Four: The Bill: Parliamentary Passage

In this final stage as detailed in Chapter Seven, we saw the Parliamentary state at the apex of its *leading and controlling* roles as the Bill passed through Parliament and the very structure of a pivotal element of the state apparatus. The sovereignty of Parliament was essential to this. It acted as a focal point for the expressed interests of pressure groups and political parties. This then allowed the structure and procedures of Parliament to perform key leading and controlling roles, as a means of getting things done' in terms of the passage of legislation.

Illustrating this, and with regard to the House of Commons, the Government's working majority of 137 on the floor of the House and a proportionate majority in Standing Committee, ensured that the Bill was never in any danger, as long as Conservative MPs voted 'with the Party'. Given the largely pragmatic support by English and Welsh Conservative MPs, and factors mentioned in Chapter Two which facilitate the subservience of backbenchers to the dominance of the Executive within the Parliamentary structure, then the Bill was undoubtedly 'safe' in this respect. Understandably, therefore, and given its commitment to the sovereignty of Parliament, the Labour Party and others had little choice but to table a raft of amendments in an attempt to undercut the key principles of a Poll Tax, but with no realistic chance of them ever being passed.

In terms of the House of Lords, the factors contributing to its 'independence' (as outlined in Chapter Seven) made it something of a weak link in terms of the 'control' exercised by the Parliamentary state. Since the 1911 Parliament Act, the Lords has generally been 'mindful' of its position as a Second Chamber, and as Adonis (1990, p. 167) notes - 'The peers are only concerned that proper procedures are followed, constitutional etiquette respected, and existing rights maintained.' Thus, despite some pragmatic concessions regarding exemptions and rebates on the part of the Government in order to clear the way for the announcement of a General Election, the Bill was never in any serious danger of being 'sent back' to the Commons.

Overall, therefore, this is the final stage in a policy formation process which started off from a very broad base, with the Parliamentary state doing little to 'manage' the uproar surrounding the property revaluation. From thereon, however, it gradually *took the lead and took control* of the policy formation process. It did so particularly through setting the parameters for a new tax; deciding the strategy to be employed (i.e. consultation), and utilising the consultation process itself as a springboard for introducing a Bill. Now, in this final stage, we saw the Parliamentary state at the apex of its *leading and controlling* roles. It provided the focus for the representation of expressed interests, and organised these around a structure and procedures, geared to 'getting things' done and producing legalisation amidst the conflicts of a class society. The end result was a Bill which Scottish Local Government Minister Michael Ancram (1991) described as 'not a very difficult Bill to get through.' Thus, a policy which the Tory Reform Group had called as 'fair' as the Black Death (HC Debates, Vol. 105, col. 349) became an Act of Parliament in 20th Century Britain.

Conclusion

As specified in the Introduction, this book has two interrelated aims. The first is to comprehend 'how the Poll Tax came about', and the second is to comprehend general processes of state policy formation. We can now see quite clearly that each of these aims has been fulfilled.

First, there is the Poll Tax. Based on the uniting of theory and practice as contained in the present chapter, it can be suggested that the Poll Tax was far from an 'aberration'. The Poll Tax was consistent, although not in a deterministic sense, with the domination of the City of London and large industrial capital with similar international orientations (heightened by a Government particularly enthusiastic and determined to shift the balance of power further in this direction). It was also consistent with the contradictions that emerged from this, and which the Government then exploited by utilising the 'weakness' of the Labour movement to produce a shift to the 'right' in a reformulated strategy.

Second, there is the attempt to comprehend general processes of state policy formation in liberal democracies and the British Parliamentary system in particular. As detailed in Chapter Two and as restated briefly at the beginning of this present chapter, the theoretical basis put forward for comprehending these was one which rested on general dialectical principles whereby 'leading capitalist forces' continually confronted and created 'contradictory forces'. These often reached the stage where key decision-making actors perceived the situation to be incompatible with their general strategy and the further development of the 'leading forces'. The result was a quest to find an alternative policy, and a struggle between an array of interests, with the state being part of and mediating between these as it attempted to take the lead and take control gradually of the process of policy formation. In doing so, it upheld the 'leading capitalist forces' in this process, with the end result being a 'new' policy and hence a further development in the contradictory rule of one class over another.

In terms of the particular experience of the Poll Tax, this seems to indicate in a highly revealing manner, both the 'strengths' of the Parliamentary state in being able to push through blatantly unpopular policies, and the 'weaknesses' of a reliance on constitutionalism and Parliamentary politics to prevent this. It must be stressed that there is nothing deterministic about this. Also, it is not to advocate a particular political strategy. Rather, it is simply to highlight crucially important tendencies within the British Parliamentary system. Whatever our ideological predilections, however, it apparent that 'leading strategies' *do* have their contradictions. Nowhere is this more evident than with the swift demise of the Poll Tax. With barely any assistance from the 'official' labour movement (subscribing to the existing constitutional framework), the contradictions of the Poll Tax were able to provoke what Hoggett and Burns (1991-92, p. 95) describe as 'possibly the largest mass campaign of civil disobedience in modern British history...[and the] revenge of the poor.'

Appendix: A Summary of Local Taxation from Feudal Times to 1970

This Appendix provides additional, background material on the historical development of local taxation until 1970. This date has been chosen because the period thereafter is covered in some detail throughout the main body of the book. It must be noted, however, that there is an extreme shortage of writings on the history of local taxation. There are essentially two 'classic' texts in this field. The first is Edwin Cannan's (1927) *The History of Local Rates in England*, published originally in 1898. The second is Turner's (1908) work *The History of Local Taxation in Scotland*. The undernoted summary of the main stages in the development of local taxation is derived from both of these works and a variety of additional sources. For present purposes, this development can be divided into four main stages.

The Rise and Fall of Feudalism: 1000s - Late 1500s

Headed by the Monarchy in alliance with the Church and the nobility, both the Church and fiefholders (usually a noble himself, or a local lord or rich free peasant) were granted the right to raise 'local' taxes i.e. taxes levied by different taxing authorities and varying from place to place. Landlords would use their receipts largely to increase their income and to help subsidise the taxes they paid to the King. The position with regard to the Church was similar, although it also used its tax-raising powers to pay for church repairs. For example, John Stratford, Archbishop of Canterbury, decreed in 1342 that all those with 'possessions, lands or revenues' in the parish 'shall be obliged to pay...all the charges which are either of common right or by custom incumbent on parishioners for the repair of the church and the ornaments belonging thereto, according to the quantity of the possessions and revenues which they have in the said parishes, as often as there shall be need for the same' (quoted in Cannan, 1927, p. 15). The towns, under Royal Charter, also had tax-raising powers, sometimes resulting in poll taxes (see Cannan, 1927, pp. 17-20) which were used mostly for the maintenance of roads and bridges in order to support local trade. These features of local taxation applied both in England & Wales and Scotland, with the only major difference being that, in Scotland, the bulk of income for local administration was derived from the 'Common Good' i.e. revenue comprising mostly court fines, petty customs and income from land bequeathed by the King.

The Rise of Capitalism: Late 1500s - 1830/1840s

With the demise of feudalism and the rise of market and capital/wage labour relations, as Morton (1979, p. 166) notes, 'the peasantry had to be broken up into solitary and defenceless units, before they could be reintegrated into a mass of wage labourers taking part in capitalist production.' The result was land enclosures and begging on a massive scale as men were driven to the towns to find work (see Turner, 1908, pp. 10-11). The 'management' of this was tackled via Acts of Parliament in 1574 (Scotland) and 1601 (England and Wales), which formalised earlier conventions in a parochial 'poor rate', for what the 1574 Act describes as the 'punishment of strong and idle beggars, and provision for sustenation of the poor and impotent' (quoted in Turner, 1908, p. 14). As Hill (1969, p. 45) notes, therefore, 'wage labour and the Poor Law rise together and complement one another.'

Liability for payment of rates fell on *occupiers* of property, and assessments were determined by church wardens, 'overseers of the poor', and sometimes even 'neighbours'. Assessments varied considerably from one local administration to another (because of varying local interpretations), and indeed a succession of vague and ambiguous Acts of Parliament in Scotland meant that in practice, payment was often not compulsory and the principal method of 'poor relief' was via church collections. In Scotland, for example, assessments were based on such nebulous guidelines as 'means and substance', 'goods and substance' and 'estates and conditions'. This meant that assessments were on the basis of what a later Royal Commission described as 'a kind of local income tax' (quoted in Foster et al. 1980, p. 160), which was levied on the basis of measuring a whole spectrum of indicators from personal belongings and immovable property through to movable property i.e. stock-in-trade.

Rapid industrialisation then saw the advent over time of a whole series of rates which, as Cannan (1927, p. 2) observes, 'have names of their own...[yet which] are in reality nothing but additions to the poor rate.' The twin focus of these rates was mainly on (i) minimal infrastructural spending for the transport of goods, and (ii) the 'policing' of an increasingly urbanised working class, and the attendant problems of sanitation, overcrowding etc. Thus, by the early 19th century in England and Wales in the counties, boroughs, parishes and independent districts, there were (at various levels of local government), 'rates' for highways, militia, jails, police, drainage and inclosures, sewers and workhouse building. Similarly, in Scotland, in the counties, burghs and parishes there were (again at various levels of local government) 'rates' for turnpike roads, highland roads and bridges, rural police, town police and prisons.

Ascendancy of Industry over Agriculture: 1830s/40s - 1920s

This period saw further developments in local taxation and the gradual unleashing of three main processes which are central not just to an understanding of the rating system at the time, but also to its subsequent development.

First, because of the sheer scale of state action required to tackle the effects of advancing industrialisation and urbanisation, there was the rationalising of the structure of local administration and the gradual (although not total) merging of the multiplicity of rates and uniformity of assessments. This started with the 1836 *Parochial Assessments Act* and the 1840 *Poor Rate Exemption Act* - the latter being described by Thornhill (1971, p. 122) as 'one of the landmarks in the history of rating', since it abolished the rating of stock-in-trade for the Poor Rate. Other rates gradually followed suit and were also assimilated with the Poor Rate, although it was only with the 1925 *Rating and Valuation Act* in England and Wales and the 1929 *Local Government (Scotland) Act* that most rates were merged into one general rate. Provision was also made for five-yearly revaluations by each rating authority, whilst a new grant system (a diluted version of that recommended by the Balfour Report in 1901) attempted to take into account the differing spending needs and rateable values of local authorities. In terms of assessments, parish rates in England and Wales after 1836, were levied only on immovable property and on the basis of 'net annual value' - specified by the 1836 Act as 'the rent at which the [hereditament] might reasonably be expected to let from year to year' (quoted in Widdicombe et al. 1968, p. 376), with a similar 'net value' basis applying in Scotland after the 1845 *Poor Law Amendment (Scotland) Act*. Other rates again gradually followed suit, although Richards (1988, p. 27) notes that even after the 1925 Act, the subjectivity of valuation ensured that it was still 'subject to local traditions and processes.'

Second, there was the matter of the financial burden for this increased state role. Some of this burden was borne by national taxpayers as the state began to fund aspects of local authority activities (see e.g. Foster et al. 1980, p. 174). In terms of locally-borne taxation, however, and despite the assessment of rates being based essentially on annual 'property' values (with a rate poundage being applied by the local authority in order to arrive at the sum due), legal liability continued to remain on the 'occupier'. In an attempt to enforce this on an impoverished and increasingly mobile working class, 'compounding' was born i.e. a situation whereby property owners were paid allowances to collect rates from occupiers. In addition to this, the actual incidence of rates (whether compounded or not), was spread unevenly throughout the population. As Offer (1981, Ch. 18) notes, the poor spent a higher proportion of their incomes on rates (and indeed rent as well), and the tax base was smaller in poorer areas whilst the need to spend was higher. As Englander (1983, pp. 53-4) suggests, therefore, 'the contribution of the working class family to local taxation was no less than that of the middle-class family, and a good deal in excess of the contribution of the families of the wealthier classes.'

By comparison, the burden on capital was generally much lighter and in fact by 1927, the total rates paid by agriculture, manufacturing, railways, docks, canals and harbours was only one fifth of all rates revenue (Mair, 1986, p. 162). Furthermore, as a result of the gradual decline of agriculture (both in its influence over state policy and in practical terms as it commanded less and less of the economy's employment and suffered more and more from cheap imports), it was derated partly in 1896 and 1923 and then derated entirely in 1929 i.e. it became exempt from payment of rates. Industry also benefited latterly from similar measures. The return to the Gold Standard in 1925 in order to maintain the City's international profitability, resulted in deflation and a severe impact on industrial capacity and profitability. Thus, in order to reduce unemployment, lower industrial costs, boost the balance of payments and so strengthen sterling, Churchill derated industry and freight by 75 per cent in 1928 (see Mair, 1986).

The third and final main process unleashed in this period was the 'politicisation' of rates. This took a number of forms. The 'left' particularly under the influence of the Fabians (and particularly Sidney and Beatrice Webb), saw local tax autonomy as a means of providing the power base to build some form of 'municipal socialism'. Unsurprisingly, however, this also released two counter-forces. The first of these emanated from vociferous ratepayers' groups (see Englander, 1983; Offer, 1981) intent on preventing what they perceived to be 'fiscal extravagance'. The second was the reaction to local financial autonomy from central government at Westminster, because of the potential to obstruct nationally-set policies. Chamberlain, for example, talked of authorities as 'Bolshie Paradises' (quoted in Keith-Lucas and Richards, 1978, p. 88).

By 1930, therefore, the foundations of the modern rating system had been laid. Local government was no longer highly fragmented. Rates levied on occupiers were calculated on a 'rental' basis (with a poundage applied to this) and were virtually merged. The general rates burden was being tempered through national funding although the remaining burden was felt particularly by the working class, whilst rates had also become highly 'politicised' in the sense that they were utilised by the left, and decried by both ratepayers groups and national government. Thus, the 'rates' were now a fairly centralised method by which the state could attempt to 'manage' and 'police' the social and infrastructural impact at a local level, of an increasingly (although of course not exclusively) industrialised economy, whilst generally minimising the tax burdens of capital in paying for this.

Changes at the Margins: 1930s -1970

Developments in the final period discussed here revolve around four main factors. First, in conjunction with changes in grant equalisation, an Act of Parliament in 1948 authorised the 'nationalisation' of valuations for rating purposes, although the differing nature of institutions North and South of the Border resulted in this being carried out by the Inland Revenue in England and Wales, and Assessors in Scotland. This move to 'nationalisation' was rooted partly in the post-war egalitarian mood, and the idea that there was much that the state could and should do in the interests of post-war reconstruction. Keith-Lucas and Richards (1978, p. 173) also argue, however, that 'valuation for local rating had to be removed from local authorities because the distribution of Exchequer aid to compensate for low rateable values would have given local valuers a powerful incentive to under-assess.'

Second, the 1950s and 1960s saw further developments in the rating of industry. Industrial derating in England and Wales was reduced from 75 per cent to 50 per cent in 1958 and was then abolished completely in 1961. The reason for this was that the balance of forces had shifted away slightly from industry, since as Richards (1988, p. 30) suggests, 'in a period of full employment the arguments used thirty years before about the need to use the rates as means to reduce unemployment no longer had any force.' Derating for Scotland was continued at 50 per cent - not because of any special assistance for Scottish industry, but because of different valuation practices.

Third, in 1967-68, 100 per cent rebates were introduced (dependent on income) and an 'across the board' domestic rates relief was initiated. This was fixed in terms of pence per £ and payable through an adjustment to the new Rate Support Grant (i.e. the 'domestic element' at 5 old pence in England and Wales and 10 old pence in Scotland), and followed on from the recommendations of the Allen Report (Cmnd. 2582, 1965), which had been set up after the protests from ratepayers at the 1963 revaluation. One of the main findings of the report was that rates were 'certainly regressive in their impact on one-person and two-person households. In the lowest group, rates represent some 5 per cent of income (after taxes and benefits) of the one-person households and account for up to one-third of all taxes on expenditure' (quoted in Travers, 1986b, p. 15). This finally put the regressive nature of rates into the public domain and 100 per cent rebates were introduced to combat this. In terms of the reasons for this, however, any concern for 'social justice' was undoubtedly bound up with short-term political considerations. As Housing and Local Government Minister, Richard Crossman (1979, p. 150) explained to the Cabinet in 1965, 'we had lost five hundred seats in the local elections last May and...we should lose another five hundred if we didn't give some relief to the ratepayer.'

Fourth, and finally, the 'flexibility' of the rating system and its continual rebirth in new forms, also resulted in a number of investigations into alternative systems of local finance, with these investigations being initiated as a result of particular problems that had arisen. In other words, the aim was to find a system that would achieve such goals (however incompatible they might be) of being popular, fair, avoiding the disruption of revaluation, easy to administer, enhancing local democracy, limiting local autonomy, increasing central control etc. These investigations, however, all concluded that no acceptable alternative was available. The 1956 revaluation had to be carried out at hypothetical 1939 rental values in order to avoid a public outcry at substantially increased assessments. The outcome of the Government's investigation into a longer term solution in a White Paper (Cmnd. 209, 1957), concluded that rates were not without their faults, but were more practical and equitable than any other option and could be made acceptable by changes to the grant system and a reduction in industrial derating. Similarly, the uproar after the 1963 revaluation resulted in yet another investigation and yet another White Paper (Cmnd. 2923, 1966). It concluded once again, that for a whole host of practical reasons, the rating system was 'here to stay' and could be made acceptable by the introduction of a reformed grant system, domestic relief and 100 per cent rebates.

This was the situation which existed as of 1970 when the Heath Government came to office. Developments thereafter are detailed in Chapter Three, and then both the specific demise of domestic rates and the advent of the Poll Tax are detailed in Chapters Four, Five, Six and Seven.

Bibliography

The undernoted newspapers and journals have been consulted in the course of research for the present work. Specific articles utilised are detailed after this listing, along with specific references for all other materials used in some way (i.e. books, government publications etc.). It should be noted, however, that references for specific 'news' articles in newspapers have been identified only at the appropriate location(s) in the main text.

British Farmer, British Journal of Political Science, Business and Finance in Scotland, Business Scotland, Capital and Class, CBI News, Conservative Newsline, Contemporary Record, CPAG Newsletter, Critical Social Policy, Crofter, Daily Record, Daily Telegraph, Director, Economic History Review, Economist, Economy and Society, Edinburgh and Leith Chamber of Commerce Quarterly, Evening Times, Financial Times, Glasgow Herald, Government and Opposition, Guardian, House Magazine, Insider Bulletin, Independent, Journal of Glasgow Chamber of Commerce, Journal of Public Policy, Journal of Theoretical Politics, Labour and Trade Union Review, Labour Party News, Lloyds Bank Review, Local Economy, Local Government Chronicle, Local Government Studies, London Chamber of Commerce Newsletter, Municipal Journal, Municipal Review, New Left Review, National Westminster Bank Quarterly Review, Observer, Parliamentary Affairs, Policy and Politics, Political Quarterly, Political Studies, Politics, Politics Today, Public

Administration, Public Administration Review, Public Finance and Accountancy, Public Interest, Quarterly Economic Commentary (Fraser of Allander Institute), Radical Scotland, Radical Wales, Rating and Valuation Report, Scottish Business Insider, Scottish Economic and Social History, Scottish Farmer, Scottish Gazette, Scottish Journal of Political Economy, Scottish Industrial and Commercial Property Review, Scottish Labour Activist, Scottish Trade Union Review, Scotsman, Small Business Bulletin, Sunday Times, Times, Voice of the Unions.

Aaronovitch, S. et al. (1981), *The Political Economy of British Capitalism*, McGraw-Hill: London.

Abolition of Domestic Rates Etc. (Scotland) Act, (1987), HMSO: London.

Adams, D. (1986), 'Unfairness of Poll Tax', *Local Government Chronicle*, 30 May 1986, p. 593.

Adonis, A. (1990), *Parliament Today*, Manchester University Press: Manchester.

Alderman, R.K. and Carter, N. (1991) 'The Ousting of Mrs Thatcher', *Parliamentary Affairs*, Vol. 44, no. 2, pp. 125-39.

Althusser, L. (1979), *For Marx*, Verso: London, 2nd edition.

Ancram, M. (1986), 'Rates Reform and You', *Business Scotland*, December, p. 8.

Ancram, M, (Scottish Office Minister for Home Affairs, 1983-87), (1991), Interview with Author.

Anderson, J.E. (1976a), *Cases in Public Policy-making*, Holt, Rinehart and Winston: New York, 2nd edition.

Anderson, P. (1976b), 'The Antinomies of Antonio Gramsci', *New Left Review*, No. 100, pp. 5-78.

Anderson, A. and Cochrane, J. (1989), *Politics in Transition*, Sage: London.

Artis, A. (1989), *Prest and Coppock's The UK Economy*, Weidenfeld and Nicholson: London, 12th edition.

Association of District Councils (1986), *Towards Accountability: Association of District Councils' Response to the Green Paper "Paying for Local Government"*, Association of District Councils: London.

Bachrach, P. and Baratz, M.S. (1970), *Power and Poverty: Theory and Practice*, Oxford University Press: Oxford.

Baker, K. (1993), *The Turbulent Years: My Life in Politics*, Faber and Faber: London.

Bailey, S.J. (1986), 'Rates Reform - Lessons From the Scottish Experience', *Local Government Studies*, Vol. 12, No. 3, May-June, pp. 21-36.

Bailey, S.J. (1987), 'A Poll Tax for Scotland?', *Critical Social Policy*, No. 20, Autumn, pp. 57-65.

Bailey, S.J. (1988), 'The Uniform Business Rate: A Policy of Despair', *Local Economy*, Vol. 3, no. 1, May, pp. 3-10.

Bailey, S.J. and Paddison, R. (eds.), (1988), *The Reform of Local Government Finance in Britain*, Routledge: London.

Bailey, S.J. (1990), 'The Poll Tax in Scotland - The First Year', *Local Government Studies*, September-October, pp. 57-80.

Balchin, P.N. and Bull, G.H. (1987), *Regional and Urban Economics*, Harper and Row: London.

Banham, J.M.M. (1986), 'Paying for Local Government', *Lloyds Bank Review*, No. 161, July, pp. 1-18.

Barber, J. et al. (1989), *Barriers to Growth in Small Firms*, Routledge: London.

Batley, R. (1987), 'Reviving Local Government in the Face of Centralisation', *Local Government Studies*, Vol. 13, no. 6, November-December, pp. 1-5.

Bauer, R.A. and Gergen, K.J. (eds.), (1968), *The Study of Policy Formation*, Free Press; New York.

Bealey, F. (1988), *Democracy in the Contemporary State*, Clarendon Press: Oxford.

Begg, H. and McDowall, S. (1986), 'Regional Industrial Policy', in McCrone, D. (ed.), *The Scottish Government Yearbook 1986*, Unit for the Study of Government in Scotland: Edinburgh.

Benn, T. (1982), *Parliament Power and People*, Verso and NLB: London.

Bennett, R.J. (1988), 'Non-Domestic Rates and Local Taxation of Business', in Bailey, S.J. and Paddison, R. (eds.), *The Reform of Local Government Finance in Britain*, Routledge: London.

Bentham, J. (1970), *The Principles of Morals and Legislation*, Hafner: Connecticut.

Berridge, J. (1988), 'The Politicisation of Local Government', in Bailey, S.J. and Paddison, R. (eds.), *The Reform of Local Government Finance in Britain*, Routledge: London.

Birdseye, P. and Webb, T. (1984), 'Why the Rate Burden on Business is a Cause for Concern', *National Westminster Bank Quarterly Review*, February, pp. 2-15.

Blackburn, R. (ed.) (1979), *Ideology in Social Science*, Fontana/Collins: London.

Blair, P. (1988), 'The Implication of a National Non-Domestic Rate and Revaluation', *Local Government Studies*, Vol. 14, no. 2, March-April, pp. 1-10.

Bochel, J.M. and Denver, D. (1983), 'The 1983 General Election' in McCrone, D. (ed.), *Scottish Government Yearbook 1984*, Unit for the Study of Government in Scotland: Edinburgh.

Bochel, J. and Denver, D. (1984), 'The District Elections of 1984', in McCrone, D. (ed.), *Scottish Government Yearbook 1985*, Unit for the Study of Government in Scotland: Edinburgh.

Bochel, J. and Denver, D. (1987), 'Labour Predominance Reasserted: The Regional Elections of 1986', in McCrone, D. (ed), *Scottish Government Yearbook 1987*, Unit for the Study of Government in Scotland: Edinburgh.

Bosanquet, N. (1983), 'Social Policy' in Drucker, H. et al. (eds.), *Developments in British Politics*, MacMillan: London.

Bottomore, T. (ed.), (1983), *A Dictionary of Marxist Thought*, Basil Blackwell: Oxford.

Boyle, S. et al. (1989), *Scotland's Economy: Claiming the Future*, Verso in Association with the STUC: London, 2nd edition.

Brand, J. (1992), *British Parliamentary Parties*, Clarendon Press: Oxford.

Braybrooke, D. and Lindblom, C.E. (1970), *A Strategy of Decision*, Free Press: New York.

Brereton, M. (1986), 'Reform Must Meet Weight of Local Reservations', *Local Government Chronicle*, 21 February, p. 215.

British Petroleum (1986), *BP Group Comments on the Green Paper "Paying for Local Government"*, British Petroleum Company plc: Edinburgh.

Brown, G. (ed.), (1975), *The Red Paper on Scotland*, EUSPB: Edinburgh.

Bruce-Gardyne, J. (1984), *Mrs Thatcher's First Administration*, MacMillan: London.

Buchanan, J.M. and Tullock, G. (1962), *The Calculus of Consent*, University of Michigan Press: Michigan.

Burden, T. and Campbell, M. (1985), *Capitalism and Public Policy in the UK*, Croom Helm: London.

Butcher, H. et al. (1990), *Local Government and Thatcherism*, Routledge: London.

Butler, D. and Kavanagh, D. (1985), *The British General Election of 1983*, MacMillan: London.

Butler, D. (1989), *British General Elections Since 1945*, Basil Blackwell: Oxford.

Butler, E. and Pirie, M. (eds.), (1981), *Economy and Local Government*, Adam Smith Institute: London.

Byrne, T. (1990), *Local Government in Britain*, Penguin: London, 5th edition.

Cameron, G. (1985), 'Alternative Ways Out of the Rating Saga of Woe', *Glasgow Herald*, 2 April, p. 10.

Cannan, E. (1927), *The History of Local Rates in England*, P.S. King and Son: Westminster, 2nd edition.

Carley, M. (1980), *Rational Techniques in Policy Analysis*, Heinemann: London.

Carnoy, M. (1984), *The State and Political Theory*, Princeton University: New Jersey.

Carvel, J. (1985), 'Mrs Thatcher's Ever Increasing Rate of Knots', *Guardian*, 1 April, p. 19.

Cassell, M. (1986), 'Battle to Remove Scottish Rates Will Resound in Westminster', *Financial Times*, 28 November, p. 16.

CBI (1985a), 'Jenkin Told: Act Now on Rates', *CBI News*, 3 May, p. 3.

CBI (1985b), 'Rates Cash Conflict as Baker Says No To Ceiling: On Uneasy Terms', *CBI News*, 16 May, p. 1.

CBI (1986a), Supplement to *CBI News* on CBI National Conference at Harrogate 17-19 November 1985, 7 February.

CBI (1986b), 'Business Rates - First Reaction', *CBI News*, 7 March, p. 5.

CBI (1986c), 'On Uneasy Terms', *CBI News*, 16 May, p. 1.

CBI (1986d), 'Rates Reform Proposals - The Business View', *CBI News*, 24 October, p. 5.

CBI Scotland (1986), *Paying for Local Government: Response by CBI Scotland to Cmnd. 9714*, CBI Scotland: Glasgow.

Central Statistical Office, (Various Editions 1974-87), *Monthly Digest of Statistics*, HMSO: London.

Channon, D. (1978), *The Service Industries*, MacMillan: London.

CIPFA Scottish Branch (1984), *Rating Review: Estimates of Income and Expenditure 1984-85*, CIPFA Scottish Branch: Edinburgh.

CIPFA Scottish Branch (1985a), *Rating Review: Estimates of Income and Expenditure 1985-86*, CIPFA Scottish Branch: Edinburgh.

CIPFA Scottish Branch (1985b), *Rating Review: Actual Income and Expenditure 1984-85: Summary Volume*, CIPFA Scottish Branch: Edinburgh.

CIPFA Scottish Branch (1986a), *The Community Charge - Operational Issues: Comments of the Scottish CIPFA Branch*, CIPFA Scottish Branch: Edinburgh.

CIPFA (1986b), *Paying for Local Government: Beyond the Green Paper - A Detailed Analysis*, CIPFA: London.

CIPFA (1987), *Paying for Local Government: Impact of a Uniform Business Rate and a Revaluation on Non-Domestic Rates*, CIPFA: London.

CIPFA (1988), *Local Government Trends 1988*, CIPFA: London.

Clarke, S. (1977), 'Marxism, Sociology and Poulantzas' Theory of the State', *Capital and Class*, No. 2, pp. 1-31.

Clayton, H. (1984), 'Rates: How to Cap the Cappers', *Times*, 11 October, p. 10.

Cmnd. 209 (1957), *Local Government Finance (England and Wales)*, HMSO: London.

Cmnd. 2582 (1965), *Committee of Inquiry into the Impact of Rates on Households, Report (Allen Report)*, HMSO: London.

Cmnd. 2923 (1966), *Local Government Finance (England and Wales)*, HMSO: London.

Cmnd. 4584 (1971), *Local Government in England: Government Proposals for Reorganisation*, HMSO: London.

Cmnd. 4741, (1971), *The Future Shape of Local Government Finance*, HMSO: London.

Cmnd. 4811 (1971), *Report of the Committee of Inquiry on Small Firms (Bolton Report)*, HMSO: London.

Cmnd. 6453 (1976), *Local Government Finance: Report of the Committee of Enquiry (Layfield Report)*, HMSO: London.

Cmnd. 6813 (1977), *Local Government Finance*, HMSO: London.

Cmnd. 8449 (1981), *Alternatives to Domestic Rates*, HMSO: London.

Cmnd. 9008 (1983), *Rates*, HMSO: London.

Cmnd. 9018 (1983), *Valuation and Rating in Scotland: Proposals for Reform*, HMSO: Edinburgh.

Cmnd. 9691 (1985), *Reform of Social Security*, HMSO: London.

Cmnd. 9714 (1986), *Paying for Local Government*, HMSO: London.

Coates, D. (1980), *Labour in Power*, Longman: London.

Cochrane, A. (1993), *Whatever Happened to Local Government?*, Open University Press: Buckingham.

Cockburn, C. (1977), *The Local State*, Pluto Press: London.

Cole, G.D.H. and Postgate, R. (1976), *The Common People 1746-1946*, Methuen: London, 4th Edition.

Conservative Party (1979), *The Conservative Manifesto 1979*, Conservative Central Office: London.

Conservative Research Department (1987), 'Reform of Local Government Finance: Questions and Answers', *Politics Today*, No. 11, August, pp. 178-88.

Cornforth, M. (1987), *Materialism and the Dialectical Method*, Lawrence and Wishart: London, 5th Edition.

COSLA (1984), *Rate Support Grant and Housing Support Grant Scotland 1985-86*, COSLA: Edinburgh.

COSLA (1985a), Letter 18 March from Albert Tait (Depute Finance Secretary) to all Chief Executives on the Subject of Revaluation and Rate Support Grant 1985-86, COSLA: Edinburgh.

COSLA (1985b), Letter 30 May from Albert Tait (Depute Finance Secretary) to All Representatives on the Rating and Valuation Committee and the Working Party on Local Government Finance, COSLA: Edinburgh.

COSLA (1986a), *Paying for Local Government: The Convention's Response*, COSLA: Edinburgh.

COSLA (1986b), Letter 8 December from Ken Fagan (President) to All Scottish Members of Parliament, COSLA: Edinburgh.

COSLA et al. (1987), *Queen's Speech June '87 - Paying for Local Government: A Joint Briefing Prepared by the Local Authority Associations*, COSLA et al: Edinburgh and London.

Costello, N. et al. (1989), *Beyond the Casino Economy*, Verso: London.

Cotterell, A. (1984), *Social Classes in Marxist Theory*, Routledge and Kegan Paul: London.

Coxall, B. and Robins, L. (1989), *Contemporary British Politics: An Introduction*, MacMillan: London.

Craig, F.W.S. (1975), *British General Election Manifestos 1900-1974*, MacMillan: London.

Craig, F.W.S (ed.), (1989), *British Electoral Facts 1832-1987*, Gower: Aldershot, 5th edition.

Crenson, M.A. (1971), *The Unpolitics of Air Pollution*, John Hopkins Press: Baltimore.

Crick, M. and Van Klaveren, A. (1991), 'Mrs Thatcher's Greatest Blunder', *Contemporary Record*, Vol. 5, no. 3, Winter, pp. 397-416.

Crossman, R. (1979), *The Crossman Diaries (Condensed Version)*, Methuen: London.

Curran, J. (1986), *Bolton Fifteen Years On: A Review and Analysis of Small Business Research in Britain 1971-1986*, Small Business Research Trust: London.

Dahl, R. (1961), *Who Governs?*, Yale University Press: New Haven and London.

Dahl, R.A. (1971), *Polyarchy*, Yale University Press: New Haven and London.

Dahl, R. (1982), *Dilemmas of a Pluralist Democracy*, Yale University Press: New Haven and London.

Dahl, R. (1985), *A Preface to Economic Democracy*, Polity Press: Cambridge.

Dahl, R.A. *Democracy and its Critics*, Yale University Press: New Haven and London.

Davis-Coleman, C. (1985a), 'Time to Pay the Local Authority His Due', *Municipal Journal*, 29 March, pp. 492-3.

Davis-Coleman, C. (1985b), 'Poll Tax is a "Cruel Deceit"', *Municipal Journal*, 5 April, p. 526.

Davis-Coleman, C. (1986c), 'Government Action Pledge on Rates Reform by End of Year Younger Tells Angry Scots', *Municipal Journal*, 17 May, p. 796.

Davis-Coleman, C. (1985d), 'Councils Must Have a Rolling Element for Budget Planning', *Municipal Journal*, 4 October, pp. 1622-3.

Davis-Coleman, C. (1986a), 'Rates Reform "Dawn" Has Some Dark Clouds', *Municipal Journal*, 28 March, pp. 490-1.

Davis-Coleman, C. (1986b), 'Owen's Reform Plans', *Municipal Journal*, 10 October, p. 1752.

Derbyshire, J.D. and Derbyshire, I. (1990), *Politics in Britain: From Callaghan to Thatcher*, Chambers: Edinburgh.

Derrick, P. (1986), 'What kind of Tax Reform', *Voice of the Unions*, March, p. 3.

de Smith, S.A. (1974), *Constitutional and Administrative Law*, Penguin: Middlesex, 2nd edition.

Devine, T.M. and Mitchison, R. (eds.), (1988), *People and Society in Scotland: Volume 1: 1760-1830*, John Donald: Edinburgh.

Dicey, A.V. (1965), *Introduction to the Study of the Law of the Constitution*, MacMillan: London, 10th edition.

Dickson, T. (ed.), (1981), *Scottish Capitalism*, Lawrence and Wishart: London.

Dillon, G.M. (1976), 'Policy and Dramaturgy: A Critique of Current Conceptions of Policy-Making', *Policy and Politics*, Vol. 5, no. 1, September, pp. 47-62.

Dobb, M. (1947), *Studies in the Development of Capitalism*, George Routledge: London.

DoE (1986), *Paying for Local Government: Summary of Responses to the Green Paper in England*, DoE: London.

DoE, (1991), *Local Government Review: The Structure of Local Government in England: A Consultation Paper*, DoE, London.

DoE (1991), *Scottish and Welsh Office, A New Tax for Local Government*, HMSO: London.

Donaldson, P. and Farquhar, J. (1988), *Understanding the British Economy*, Penguin: London.

Douglas, J. (1989), 'Review Article: The Changing Tide - Some Recent Studies of Thatcherism', *British Journal of Political Science*, Vol. 19, no. 3, July, pp. 399-424.

Dowell, S.D. (1965), *A History of Taxation and Taxes in England*, Vols. 1-4, Frank Cass: London, 3rd editions.

Dowle, M, (1986), 'The Year at Westminster: Younger's Unhappy Centenary', in McCrone, D. (ed.), *Scottish Government Yearbook 1986*, Unit for the Study of Government in Scotland: Edinburgh.

Dowle, M, (1987), 'The Year at Westminster' in McCrone, D. (ed.), *Scottish Government Yearbook 1987*, Unit for the Study of Government in Scotland: Edinburgh.

Dowle, M. (1988), 'The Year at Westminster: All Change', in McCrone, D. and Brown, A. (eds.), *Scottish Government Yearbook 1988*, Unit for the Study of Government in Scotland: Edinburgh.

Downs, A. (1957), *An Economic Theory of Democracy*, Harper and Row: New York.

Downs, A. (1972), 'Up and Down With Ecology - The "Issue Attention" Cycle', *Public Interest*, No. 28, Summer, pp. 38-50.

Dror, Y. (1983), *Public Policymaking Re-examined*, Transaction: New Brunswick, 2nd edition.

Duncan, S and Goodwin, M. (1988), *The Local State and Uneven Development*, Polity Press: Cambridge.

Dunleavy, P, 'Voting and the Electorate', in Drucker, H. et al. (eds.), *Developments in British Politics*, MacMillan: London.

Dunleavy, P and O'Leary, B. (1987), *Theories of the State*, MacMillan: London.

Dunleavy, P. (1990), 'Reinterpreting the Westland Affair: Theories of the State and Core Executive Decision Making', *Public Administration*, Vol. 68, Spring, pp. 29-60.

Dunleavy, P. (1991), *Democracy, Bureaucracy and Public Choice*, Harvester Wheatsheaf: London.

Dunn, D. (1990), *Poll Tax: The Fiscal Fake*, Chatto and Windus: London.

Dye, T.R. (1976), *Policy Analysis*, University of Alabama Press: Alabama.

Easton, D. (1965), *A Systems Analysis of Political Life*, John Wiley and Sons: London.

Eccleshall, R. (1984), *Political Ideologies: An Introduction*, Hutchinson: London.

Economist (1985), 'Local Government: How the Tories Muffed Reform', *Economist*, 16 March, pp. 38-40.

Economist (1986a), 'Baker is no Local Hero', *Economist*, 25 January, pp. 21-2.

Economist (1986b), 'Thatcher Impaired', *Economist*, 1 February, pp. 12-3.

Economist (1986c), 'Local Government Finance: Impractical, Improbable', *Economist*, 1 February, pp. 20-2.

Economist (1986d), 'The Rates: A Better Madhouse', *Economist*, 26 July pp. 25-6.

Economist (1987a), 'The Economy Says a Summer Election', *Economist*, 3 January, pp. 21-2.

Economist (1987b), 'Local Rates: Up Up and Away', *Economist*, 7 March, pp. 34-5.

Economist (1987c), 'Scotland's Dreams of Self-Government', *Economist*, 25 April, pp. 29-30.

Economist (1987d), 'Poll Tax: A Loser at the Polls', *Economist*, 25 April, pp. 30-1.

Economist (1987e), 'Local Taxes: Ouch', *Economist*, 9 May, pp. 21-2.

Edinburgh and Leith Chamber of Commerce (1987), 'Battle of the Rates', *Edinburgh and Leith Chamber of Commerce Quarterly*, March, p. 8.

Edwards, K. (1986), 'Business Rates Reform', *CBI News*, 30 August, p. 3.

Elcock, H. (1982), *Local Government: Politicians, Professionals and the Public in Local Authorities*, Methuen: London.

Elder, M. (Scottish Secretary of the Labour Party, 1988-92), (1989), Interview with Author.

Engels, F. (1972), *The Origin of the Family, Private Property and the State*, Lawrence and Wishart: London.

Engels, F. (1978), *Anti-Duhring*, Progress: Moscow.

Englander, D. (1983), *Landlord and Tenant in Urban Britain 1938-1918*, Clarendon Press: Oxford.

Enston, M. (1990), 'Implementing the Unthinkable. The First Community Charges', in Brown, A. and Parry, R. (eds.), *Scottish Government Yearbook 1990*, Unit for the Study of Government in Scotland: Edinburgh.

Fairburn, J.A. and Kay, J.A. *Mergers and Merger Policy*, Oxford University Press: Oxford.

Fairley, A. 'The Community Charge and Local Government Finance in Scotland', in McCrone, D. and Brown, A. (eds.), *Scottish Government Yearbook 1988*, Unit for the Study of Government in Scotland: Edinburgh.

Faux, R. (1985), 'Rates: Where the Tories are Really Trembling', *Times*, 1 April, p. 12.

Fine, B. and Harris, L. (1985), *The Peculiarities of the British Economy*, Lawrence and Wishart: London.

Firn, J.R. (1975), 'External Control and Regional Development: The Case for Scotland', *Urban and Regional Studies*, Discussion Paper No. 16, University of Glasgow: Glasgow.

Forsyth, M. (1982), *Down With the Rates*, Conservative Political Centre: London.

Forsyth, M. (1985a), 'Poll Tax is the Only Fair Alternative', *Scotsman*, 19 March, p. 9.

Forsyth, M.B. (1985b), *The Case for a Poll Tax*, Conservative Political Centre: London,

Foster, C.D. (1977), *Central Government's Response to the Layfield Report*, Centre for Environment Studies: London.

Foster, C.D. et al. (1980), *Local Government Finance in a Unitary State*, George Allen and Unwin: London.

Foster, J. and Woolfson, C. (1986), *The Politics of the UCS Work-In*, Lawrence and Wishart: London.

Foster, J. (1989), 'Nationality, Social Change and Class: Transformations of National Identity in Scotland', in McCrone, D. et al. (eds.), *The Making of Scotland: Nation, Culture and Social Change*, Edinburgh University Press: Edinburgh.

Fowle, T.W. (1898), *The Poor Law*, MacMillan: London.

Fowler, N. (1991), *Ministers Decide: A Memoir of the Thatcher Years*, Chapmans: London.

Frame, R. (1990), *The Political Development of the British Isles*, Oxford University Press: Oxford.

Franklin, M.N. (1985), *The Decline of Class Voting in Britain: Changes in the Basis of Electoral Choice 1964-1983*, Clarendon Press: Oxford.

Fraser of Allander Institute (Years 1980-88), *Quarterly Economic Commentary*, Fraser of Allander Institute: Glasgow, University of Strathclyde.

Fry, M. (1988), 'Lord Goold: Thatcher's Scottish Devotee', *Observer Scotland Sunday*, 11 December, p. 7.

FSR (1984), Factsheet, FSR: Edinburgh.

FSR (1985a), Letter 27 March from Mary Whitehouse (Chairwoman) to the Secretary of State for Scotland, FSR: Edinburgh.

FSR (1985b), Factsheet, FSR: Edinburgh.

FSR, (1985c), Letter 12 November from Mary Whitehouse (Chairwoman) to the Secretary of State for Scotland, FSR: Edinburgh.

FSR (1986), Letter 31 July from Mary Whitehouse (Chairwoman) to the Secretary of State for Scotland in Formal response to the Green Paper Paying for Local Government (Cmnd. 9714), FSR: Edinburgh.

Fyfe, M. (1987), 'On the Scottish Case at Westminster', *Scottish Trade Union Review*, No. 35, Summer, pp. 8-9.

Gallup (1985-87), *Gallup Political Index*, Social Surveys (Gallup Poll) Ltd: London.

Gamble, A. (1990), 'Theories of British Politics', *Political Studies*, Vol. XXXVIII, pp. 404-20.

Gann, L.H. and Duignan, P. (eds.), (1969), *Colonialism in Africa 1870-1960: Vol. 1: The History and Politics of Colonialism 1870-1914*, Cambridge University Press: Cambridge.

Gardner, N. (1987), *Decade of Discontent: The Changing British Economy Since 1973*, Basil Blackwell: Oxford.

Garrett, J. (1992), *Westminster: Does Parliament Work?*, Victor Gollancz: London.

Gaventa, J. (1980), *Power and Powerlessness*, Clarendon Press: Oxford.

Gibson, J.G. (1987), 'The Reform of British Local Government Finance: The Limits to Local Accountability', *Policy and Politics*, Vol. 15, no. 3. pp. 167-74.

Gibson, J. (1989), 'The Presentation of the Poll Tax', *Political Quarterly*, Vol. 60, no. 3, July-September, pp. 332-48.

Goldberg, P.J.P. (1990), 'Urban Identity and the Poll Taxes of 1377, 1379 and 1381', *Economic History Review*, Vol. XLIII, no. 2, pp. 194-216.

Goodin, R.E. (1982), *Political Theory and Public Policy*, University of Chicago Press: Chicago.

Goold, J. (1991), (Scottish Conservative Party Chairman, 1983-1989), Interview with Author.

Government Statistical Service (1986), *Regional Trends*, No. 21, HMSO: London.

Gramsci, A. (1978), *Selections from Prison Notebooks*, Lawrence and Wishart: London.

Grant, W. (1987), *Business and Politics*, MacMillan: London.

Green, F. (1989), *The Restructuring of the UK Economy*, Harvester Wheatsheaf: Hemel Hempstead.

Greene, C. (1985), 'Should Socialists Defend Rates', *Radical Scotland*, No. 15, June-July, p. 14.

Gregory, R. (1989), 'Political Rationality or Incrementalism? Charles E. Lindblom's Enduring Contribution to Policy Making Theory', *Policy and Politics*, Vol. 17, No. 2, pp. 139-53.

Gyford, J. (1985), *The Politics of Local Socialism*, George Allen and Unwin: London.

Hailsham, L. (1978), *The Dilemma of Democracy*, Collins: London.

Hale, R. (1985a), *Poll Tax: Some Initial Analyses*, CIPFA: London.

Hale, R. (1985b), *Non-Domestic Rates: Some Options*, CIPFA: London.

Hall, S. and Jacques, M. (eds.), (1983), *The Politics of Thatcherism*, Lawrence and Wishart: London.

Ham, C. and Hill, M. (1984), *The Policy Process in the Modern Capitalist State*, Wheatsheaf: Brighton.

Harcourt, T.V. (1982), *UK Companies Performance Analysis: Including a Study on the Effects of the Recession*, Monks Publications: Essex.

Harper, J.R. (1985), *Rates Revaluation: The Great Myth*, The Society of Scottish Conservative Lawyers: Glasgow.

HC (1986-87), *Abolition of Domestic Rates Etc. (Scotland) Bill*, Nos. 9, 82 and 152, HMSO: London.

HC Debates (1981-82 to 1990-91), ('Hansard'), Various Volumes, HMSO: London.

HC Debates (1985-86), *Paying for Local Government*, Vol. IX, Scottish Grand Committee, HMSO: London.

HC Debates (1985-86), *Scottish Estimates*, Vol. IX, Scottish Grand Committee, HMSO: London.

HC Debates (1986-87), *Abolition of Domestic Rates Etc. (Scotland) Bill, 1st Scottish Standing Committee*, Vol. IV, HMSO: London.

HC 217 I, II & III (1981-82), *Enquiry into Methods of Financing Local Government in the Context of the Government's Green Paper (Cmnd. 8449)*, Second Report from the Environment Committee, HMSO: London.

HC 219 (1986-87), *First Scottish Standing Committee: Minutes of Proceedings on the Abolition of Domestic Rates Etc. (Scotland) Bill*, HMSO: London.

HC 328-i and ii (1984-85), *Scottish Aspects of the Government's Public Expenditure Plans 1985-86 to 1987-88*, Scottish Affairs Committee, HMSO: London.

Heald, D. et al. (1981), 'Breaking Mr Younger's Runaway Train: The Conflict Between the Scottish Office and Local Authorities Over Local Government Expenditure', in Drucker, H.M. and Drucker N.L. (eds.), *Scottish Government Yearbook 1982*, Paul Harris Publishing: Edinburgh.

Heald, G. and Wybrow, R.J. *The Gallup Survey of Britain*, Croom Helm: London.

Healey, P. (1990), 'Policy Process in Planning', *Policy and Politics*, Vol. 18, No. 1, pp. 91-103.

Heclo, H. and Wildavsky, A. (1981), *The Private Government of Public Money*, MacMillan: London, 2nd edition.

Hedley, C. (1985), 'Business Tax - The Uniform Approach', *Municipal Journal*, 6 September, pp. 1468-9.

Hegel, G.W.F. (1977), *Phenomenology of Spirit*, Oxford University Press: Oxford.

Held, D. (1989), *Political Theory and the Modern State*, Polity Press: Cambridge.

Hennessy, P. (1988), *Cabinet*, Basil Blackwell: Oxford.

Henry, J. (Deputy General Secretary of the STUC, 1978-1988), (1989), Interview with Author.

Hepworth, N. (1986), 'Reform of Local Government Finance', *Public Finance and Accountancy*, 10 January, pp. 9 and 12-16.

Heseltine, M. (1990), 'The Poll Tax: Let the People Choose', *Times*, 10 May, p. 14.

Hill, C. (1969), *Reformation to Industrial Revolution*, Penguin: Middlesex.

Hilton, R, (ed.), (1976), *The Transition from Feudalism to Capitalism*, NLB: London.

Hilton, R. (1982), *Bond Men Made Free*, London: Methuen.

Hilton, R. (1990), 'Unjust Taxation and Popular Resistance', *New Left Review*, No. 180, March-April, pp. 177-84.

Himsworth, C.M.G. and Walker, N.C. (1989), *The Scottish Community Charge*, W. Green and Son: Edinburgh.

HL (1986-87), *Abolition of Domestic Rates Etc. (Scotland) Bill*, Nos. 88, 120, 133, HMSO: London.

HL Debates (1986-87) ('Hansard'), Various Volumes, HMSO: London.

HL Sessional Papers, (1986-87), Vol. 1, HMSO: London.

Hobsbawm, E.J. (1968), *Labouring Men*, Weidenfeld and Nicholson: London.

Hoggett, P. and Burns, D. 'The Revenge of the Poor: The Anti-Poll Tax Campaign in Britain', *Critical Social Policy*, No. 33, Winter, pp. 95-110.

Hogwood, B.W. and Gunn, L.A. (1984), *Policy Analysis for the Real World*, Oxford University Press: Oxford.

Hogwood, B.W. (1986), 'If Consultation is Everything, Then Maybe It's Nothing', *Strathclyde Papers on Government and Politics*, No. 44, University of Strathclyde: Glasgow.

Hogwood, B.W. (1987), *From Crisis to Complacency*, Oxford University Press: Oxford.

Hood, N. and Young, S. (1982), *Multinationals in Retreat: The Scottish Experience*, Edinburgh University Press: Edinburgh.

Horsborough, F. (1985a), 'Rates: Can the Tories Really Risk Alienating Their Good Boys?', *Glasgow Herald*, 7 March, p. 11.

Horsborough, F. (1985b), 'Bridging Gulf Between Councils and Westminster', *Glasgow Herald*, 12 November, p. 11.

House of Lords Information Office (1989), *Composition of the House (Breakdown by Party)*, House of Lords Information: London.

Howard, D. (1972), *The Development of the Marxian Dialectic*, Southern Illinois Press: Carbondale.

Hughes, S. (1986), 'How London Will Fare Under Rates Reform Plan', *Municipal Journal*, 7 February, pp. 182-3.

Huxley, A. (1940), *Ends and Means*, Chatto and Windus: London.

Industry Department Scotland (1990), *Overseas Ownership in Scottish Manufacturing Industry 1950-1989*, Statistical Bulletin No. A3.3, Industry Department Scotland: Edinburgh.

Ingham, G. (1984), *Capitalism Divided?: The City and Industry in British Social Development*, MacMillan: London.

Ingham, K. and Love, J. (eds.), (1983), *Understanding the Scottish Economy*, Martin Robertson: Oxford.

Jackman, R. (1986a), 'Paying for Local Government', *Local Government Studies*, Vol. 12, no. 4, July-August, pp. 51-7.

Jackman, R. (1986b), 'A Reply', *Local Government Studies*, Vol. 12, No. 4, July-August, pp. 63-4.

Jackman,R. (1988), 'Local Government Finance and Macroeconomic Policy', in Bailey, S.J. and Paddison, R. (eds.), *The Reform of Local Government Finance in Britain*, Routledge: London.

Jackson, P.M. (1982), *The Political Economy of Bureaucracy*, Philip Allan: Oxford.

Jenkins, W.I. (1978), *Policy Analysis*, Saint Martins Press: New York.

Jessop, B. (1982), *The Capitalist State*, Martin Robertson: Oxford.

Jessop, B. et al. (1988), *Thatcherism: A Tale of Two Nations*, Polity Press: London.

Johnson, C. (1988a), *Measuring the Economy: A Guide to Understanding Official Statistics*, Penguin: Middlesex.

Johnson, R.J. (1988b), *The Electoral Map of Great Britain 1979-1987: A Nation Dividing?*, Longman: London.

Johnson, T. (1929), *A History of the Working Classes in Scotland*, Forward Publishing: Glasgow, 2nd edition.

Jones, G. and Stewart, J. (1985), *The Case for Local Government*, George Allen and Unwin: London, 2nd edition.

Jones, G. et al. (1986), 'A Rejoinder to Jackman', *Local Government Studies*, Vol. 12, no. 4, July-August, pp. 59-63.

Jones, M. (1986), 'Coming Next: The Rates Row', *Sunday Times*, p. 19 January, p. 15.

Jones, R. (1987), *Wages and Employment Policy 1936-1985*, Allen and Unwin: London.

Jordan, A.G. (1981), 'Iron Triangles, Woolly Corporatism and Elastic Nets: Images of the Policy Process', *Journal of Public Policy*, Vol. 1, no. 1, pp. 95-123.

Jordan, G. and Richardson, J. (1982), 'The British Policy Style or the Logic of Negotiation', in Richardson, J. (ed.), *Policy Styles in Western Europe*, George Allen and Unwin: London.

Jordan, A.G. and Richardson, J.J. (1987), *British Politics and the Policy Process: An Arena Approach*, Allen and Unwin: London.

Jordan, G. (1990a), 'Policy Community Realism', *Political Studies*, Vol. XXXVIII, pp. 470-84.

Jordan, G. (1990b), 'Sub Government, Policy Communities and Networks: Refilling the Old Bottles', *Journal of Theoretical Politics*, Vol. 2, no. 3, pp. 319-38.

Judge, D. (1981a), 'Specialists and Generalists in British Central Government: A Political Debate', *Public Administration*, Vol. 59, Spring, pp. 1-14.

Judge, D. (1981b), *Backbench Specialisation in the House of Commons*, Heinmann: London.

Judge, D (ed.), (1983), *The Politics of Parliamentary Reform*, Heinmann: London.

Judge, D. (1990a), 'Parliament and Interest Representation', in Rush, M. (ed.), *Parliament and Pressure Groups*, Manchester University Press: Manchester.

Judge, D. (1990b), *Parliament and Industry*, Dartmouth Publishing: Aldershot.

Judge, D. (1993), *The Parliamentary State*, Sage: London.

Kautsky, K. (1983), *Karl Kautsky: Selected Political Writings*, MacMillan: London.

Kavanagh, D. (1989), *Thatcherism and British Politics: The End of Consensus*, Oxford University Press: Oxford.

Kavanagh, D. (1986), *Margaret Thatcher: A Study in Prime Ministerial Style*, Centre for the Study of Public Policy: Glasgow, University of Strathclyde.

Kay, C. (1990), 'The House of Lords', in Rodgers, W. (ed.) *Government and Industry: A Business Guide to Westminster and Whitehall*, Longman: London.

Kay, J. et al. (1986), *Privatisation and Regulation - The UK Experience*, Clarendon Press: Oxford.

Keating, M. (1984), 'Confrontation Looms as Scots Councils Become United in Defiance', *Municipal Journal*, 14 December, p. 1968.

Keating, M. (1985a), 'Triple Blow to Ratepayers Sparks Off Political Row', *Municipal Journal*, 22 March, pp. 458-9.

Keating, M. (1985b), 'Rates Reform Pledge May Limit Damage But Government Will Learn There is no Painless Form of Taxation', *Municipal Journal*, 24 May, pp. 842-3.

Keating, M. (1985c), 'Local Government Spending and Central Control', *Quarterly Economic Commentary*, Vol. 10, May, Fraser of Allander Institute: Glasgow, pp. 69-73.

Keating, M. (1986), 'Will a "Poll Tax" Prove a Pole-Axe for the Conservatives North of the Border?', *Municipal Journal*, 28 February, pp. 308-9.

Keith-Lucas, B. and Richards, P.G. (1978), *A History of Local Government in the Twentieth Century*, George Allen and Unwin: London.

Kellas, J.G. (1989), *The Scottish Political System*, Cambridge University Press: Cambridge, 4th edition.

Kenneth Ryden and Partners (1985), 'Rates', *Scottish Industrial and Commercial Property Review*, April, pp. 2 and 4.

King, A. (ed.), (1988), *The British Prime Minister*, MacMillan: London, 2nd edition.

King, R. (ed.), (1983), *Capital and Politics*, Routledge and Kegan Paul: London.

Kingdon, J. (1984), *Agendas, Alternatives and Public Policies*, Little, Brown and Company: Boston and Toronto.

Labour Party Scottish Council (1985), *Report of the Executive for the 70th Annual Conference 1985*, Labour Party Scottish Council: Glasgow.

Labour Party Scottish Council (1986), *Report of the Executive for the 71st Annual Conference 1986*, Labour Party Scottish Council: Glasgow.

Labour Party Scottish Council (1987), *Report of the Executive for the 72nd Annual Conference 1987*, Labour Party Scottish Council: Glasgow.

Labour Party Scottish Council (1988), *Report of the Executive for the 73rd Annual Conference 1988*, Labour Party Scottish Council: Glasgow.

Labour Research (1985), *Breaking the Nation: A Guide to Thatcher's Britain*, Pluto: London.

Laski, H.J. (1938), *Parliamentary Government in England*, George Allen and Unwin: London.

Lavalette, M. and Mooney, G. (1989), 'Undermining the "North-South" Divide? Fighting the Poll Tax in Scotland, England and Wales', *Critical Social Policy*, Autumn, No.29, pp. 100-19.

Lawson, I. (1989), (Chairman - Campaign for the Communication of Conservative Policies, 1987), Interview with Author.

Lawson, N. (1992), *The View From No. 11: Memoirs of a Tory Radical*, Transworld: London.

Leathers, C.G. (1989), 'Scotland's New Poll Taxes as Hayekian Policy', *Scottish Journal of Political Economy*, Vol. 36, no. 2, May, pp. 194-201.

Lenin, V.I. (1961), 'Conspectus of Hegel's Book The Science of Logic', *Collected Works*, Vol. 38, Lawrence and Wishart: London.

Lenin, V.I. (1962a), 'On the Question of Dialectics', *Collected Works*, Vol. 14, Progress: Moscow.

Lenin, V.I. (1962b), 'Materialism and Empirio-Criticism', *Collected Works*, Vol. 14, Progress: Moscow.

Lenin, V.I. (1965), 'Democracy and Dictatorship', *Collected Works*, Vol. 28, Lawrence and Wishart: London.

Lenin, V.I. (1976), *The State and Revolution*, Foreign Languages Press: Peking.

Leys, C. (1985), 'Thatcherism and British Manufacturing: A Question of Hegemony', *New Left Review*, May-June, pp. 5-25.

Leys, C. (1990), 'Still a Question of Hegemony', *New Left Review*, No. 181, pp. 119-28.

Liddell, H. (1991), (Scottish Secretary of the Labour Party, 1977-88), Interview with Author.

Lindblom, C.E. (1959), 'The Science of "Muddling Through"', *Public Administration Review*, Vol. XIX, no. 2, Spring, pp. 79-88.

Lindblom, C.E. (1965), *The Intelligence of Democracy*, Free Press: New York.

Lindblom, C.E. (1977), *Politics and Markets*, Basic Books: New York.

Lindblom, C.E. (1979), 'Still Muddling, Not Yet Through', *Public Administration Review*, No. 39, November-December, pp. 517-26

Local Government Chronicle, (1986), 'Rates Why the Change?', Local Government Chronicle, 31 January, p. 111.

Locke, J. (1990), *Two Treatises of Government*, Cambridge University Press: Cambridge, 2nd edition.

Lord, R. (1985), 'A Real Alternative to Rates', *Local Government Chronicle*, 12 July, pp. 792-3.

Luckás, G. (1971), *History and Class Consciousness*, Merlin: London.

Lukes, S. (1974), *Power: A Radical View*, MacMillan: London.

Lythe, S.G.E and Butt, J. (1975), *An Economic History of Scotland 1100-1939*, Blackie: Glasgow and London.

Lythe, C. and Majmudar, M. (1982), *The Renaissance of the Scottish Economy*, George Allen and Unwin: London.

Mair, D. (1986), 'Industrial Derating: Panacea or Palliative?', *Scottish Journal of Political Economy*, Vol. 33, no. 2, pp. 159-70.

Marsh, D. and Rhodes, R.A.W. (1990), *Policy Communities, Policy Networks and Issue-Networks: Beyond a New Typology*, University of Essex and University of York: Essex and York.

Martlew, C. (1986), 'Consulting Non-Domestic Ratepayers in Scotland', *Local Government Studies*, Vol. 12, no. 1, January-February, pp. 57-66.

Marx, K. (1975a), *Selected Writings in Sociology and Social Philosophy*, Bottomore, T.B. and Rubel, M. (eds.), Penguin: Middlesex, 2nd Edition.

Marx, K. (1975b), 'Critical Marginal Notes on the Article "The King of Prussia and Social Reform. By a Prussian"', *Collected Works*, Vol. 3, Lawrence and Wishart: London.

Marx, K. and Engels, F. (1975c), 'The Holy Family', *Collected Works*, Vol. 4, Lawrence and Wishart: London.

Marx, K. and Engels, F. (1975d), *Manifesto of the Communist Party*, Foreign Languages Press: Peking.

Marx, K. (1975e), 'Economic and Philosophical Manuscripts', in *Karl Marx: Early Writings*, Penguin: Middlesex.

Marx, K. (1975f), 'Critique of Hegel's Dialectic and General Philosophy', in *Karl Marx: Early Writings*, Penguin: Middlesex.

Marx, K. (1976), *Capital*, Volume 1, Penguin: Middlesex.

Marx, K. (1978), 'The German Ideology', in Tucker, R.C. (ed.), *The Marx-Engels Reader*, Norton: New York, 2nd edition.

Marx, K. (1981), *Capital*, Volume 3, Penguin: Middlesex.

Mason, D. (1985), *Revising the Rating System*, Adam Smith Institute: London.

Mason, D. (1989), (Domestic Policy Adviser, Adam Smith Institute, 1984-), Interview with Author.

Mathias, P, (1984), *The First Industrial Revolution*, Methuen: London, 2nd edition.

May, T. (1984), 'The Businessman's Burden: Rates and the CBI', *Politics*, Vol. 4, No. 1, April, pp. 34-8.

Meek, B, (1986), 'Conservatives Alienate the Young Ones', *Scotsman*, 14 May, p. 11.

Mepham, J. and Ruben, D.H. (1979), *Issues in Marxist Philosophy Volume 1: Dialectics and Method*, Harvester: Sussex.

Midwinter, A. et al. (1983), '"Excessive and Unreasonable": The Politics of the Scottish Hit List', *Political Studies*, Vol. XXXI, pp. 394-417.

Midwinter, A. (1984), *The Politics of Local Spending*, Mainstream: Edinburgh.

Midwinter, A. (1985a), 'Government Problems Mount Over Rates Revaluation', *Local Government Chronicle*, 3 May, p. 512.

Midwinter, A. (1985b), 'Tory Backlash Fails to Damage Case for Retaining Rates', *Scotsman*, 9 May, p. 11.

Midwinter, A. and Mair, C. (1986), 'Rhetoric and Reason', *Scotsman*, 9 December, p. 11.

Midwinter, A. and Mair, C. (1987a), *Rates Reform*, Mainstream: Edinburgh.

Midwinter, A. et al. (1987b), 'Rating Reform Revisited', in McCrone, D. (ed.), *Scottish Government Yearbook 1987*, Unit for the Study of Government in Scotland: Edinburgh.

Midwinter, A. (1989), 'Economic Theory, the Poll Tax and Local Spending', *Politics*, Vol. 9, no. 2, October, pp. 9-15.

Midwinter, A. (1990), 'A Return to Ratepayer Democracy?: The Reform of Local Government Finance in a Historical Perspective', *Scottish Economic and Social History*, Vol. 10, pp. 61-9.

Midwinter, A. (1991). 'Tories Pass the Poll Tax Test', *Scotland on Sunday*, 28 April, p. 4.

Miliband, R. (1973), *The State in Capitalist Society*, Quartet: London.

Miliband, R. (1982), *Capitalist Democracy in Britain*, Oxford University Press: Oxford.

Mill, J.S. (1984), *On Liberty*, Penguin: Middlesex.

Miller, D. 'We Must Get Rid of the Rates!', *Conservative Newsline*, May p. 10.

Miller, K. (1985), 'Scots Evaluate Rates Alternatives', *Local Government Chronicle*, 29 March, p. 364.

Miller, K. (1986), 'Scotland's Two Views on Rates', *Local Government Chronicle*, 27 March, pp. 339-40.

Mitchell, J. (1986), 'Tories Gamble Their Future on Poll Tax', *Scotsman*, 18 November, p. 11.

Mitchell, J. (1990), *Conservatives and the Union*, Edinburgh University Press: Edinburgh.

Mockler, C. (1987), *Reforming Local Government Finance: Alternatives to the Community Charge*, Tory Reform Group: London.

Mohan, J. (1989), *The Political Geography of Contemporary Britain*, MacMillan: London.

Morton, A.L. *A People's History of England*, Lawrence and Wishart: London, 2nd edition.

Mueller, D.C. (1979), *Public Choice*, Cambridge University Press: Cambridge.

MacAskill, E. (1987), 'Rates Reform Comes Bottom of Bill', *Scotsman*, 11 February p.11.

MacAlman, J. (1985), 'Raising the Roof Over New Rates', *Glasgow Herald*, 8 March, 1985.

McConnell, A. (1990), 'The Birth of the Poll Tax', *Critical Social Policy*, No. 28, Summer, pp. 67-78.

McConnell, A. (1991), *The Poll Tax: Public Consultation and the Green Paper 'Paying for Local Government'*, Occasional Paper No. 2, Paisley College, Department of Applied Social Studies: Paisley.

McConnell, A. (1993), 'Parliamentarism, Policy Networks and the Poll Tax', *Strathclyde Papers on Government and Politics*, University of Strathclyde: Glasgow.

McConnell, A. and Pyper, R. (1994), 'The Revived Select Committee on Scottish Affairs: A Case Study of Parliamentary Contradictions', *Strathclyde Papers on Government and Politics*, University of Strathclyde: Glasgow.

MacGregor, S. (1988), *The Poll Tax and the Enterprise Culture*, CLES: Manchester.

MacKay, D. (1985), 'What's So Good About the Poll Tax?', *Scotsman*, 13 May, p. 12.

McLean, B. (1985), 'Experts Agree - Rating is Still the Best Local Taxation System', *Municipal Journal*, 3 May, pp. 700-1.

McLean, B. (1986), 'Ancram Faces Anger on Rates Reform and Revaluation', *Municipal Journal*, 25 April, pp. 652-3.

McManus, J.J. et al. (1987), *Paying for Local Government: The Community Charge: A Report to the Convention of Scottish Local Authorities and the Scottish Consumer Council*, Dundee University: Dundee.

MacPherson, C.B. (1978), *The Real World of Democracy*, Oxford University Press: Oxford.

McCrone, D. (1986), 'A Commentary', in McCrone, D (ed.) *Scottish Government Yearbook 1986*, Unit for the Study of Government in Scotland: Edinburgh.

McCrone, D. (1987), 'A Commentary', in McCrone, D (ed.) *Scottish Government Yearbook 1987*, Unit for the Study of Government in Scotland: Edinburgh.

National Liberal Club (1846), *Local Taxes of the United Kingdom*, Charles Knight: London.

Newton, K. and Karran, T.J. (1985), *The Politics of Local Expenditure*, MacMillan: London.

Niskanen, W.A. (1971), *Bureaucracy and Representative Government*, Sage: Beverley Hills.

Norman, R. and Sayers, S. (1980), *Hegel, Marx and Dialectic*, Harvester Press: Sussex.

Norton, P. (1975), *Dissension in the House of Commons 1954-74*, MacMillan: London.

Norton, P. (1980), *Dissension in the House of Commons 1974-1979*, Clarendon Press: Oxford.

Norton, P. (1984), *The Constitution in Flux*, Basil Blackwell: Oxford, 2nd edition.

Norton, P. (1993), *Does Parliament Matter?*, Harvester Wheatsheaf: London.

Oakley, R. (1986a), 'Government Launches its "Rates Revolution" After 13-year Struggle', *Times*, 27 November p. 5.

Oakley, R. (1986b), 'Trouble Ahead for Reform of Rates', *Times*, 28 November, p. 7.

OECD (1983), *Economic Surveys 1982-1983: United Kingdom*, OECD: Paris.

Offe, C. (1975), 'The Theory of the Capitalist State and the Problem of Policy Formation', in Lindberg, L.N. et al. (eds.), *Stress and Contradiction in Modern Capitalism*, Lexington: Massachusetts.

Offe, C. (1984), *Contradictions of the Welfare State*, Hutchinson: London.

Offer, A. (1981), *Property and Politics 1870-1914*, Cambridge University Press: Cambridge.

Oppenheim, C. (1987), 'A Tax on All the People', *CPAG Newsletter*, 7 December, p. 7.

Overbeek, H. (1980), 'Finance, Capital and the Crisis in Britain', *Capital and Class*, No. 11, pp. 99-120.

Parkhouse, G. (1985), 'Is Isolation Symbolic of Thatcher's Intransigence?', *Glasgow Herald*, 25 March, p. 12.

Paul, W. (1986), 'Alternative to Rates Rejected - 30 Years Ago', *Scotsman*, 3 January, p. 9.

Parliamentary Correspondent (1985), 'Few Hints for Tories of Kenneth Baker's New Rating Formula', *Municipal Journal*, 18 October, pp. 1702-3.

Parsons, W. (1988), *The Political Economy of British Regional Policy*, Routledge: London.

Paterson, K. (1984), 'Scottish Authorities Learn of Switch in Domestic-Industrial Rating Balance', *Municipal Journal*, 21 December, pp. 2002-3.

Penniman, H.R. (ed.), (1981), *Britain at the Polls, 1979: A Study of the General Election*, American Enterprise Institute for Public Policy Research: Washington D.C. and London.

Pierson, C. (1986), *Marxist Theory and Democratic Politics*, Polity Press: Cambridge.

Pilgrim, M. (1984), 'Report Sets the Ball Rolling - Now It's in the Government's Court', *Municipal Journal*, 31 August, pp. 1354-5.

Pilgrim, M. (1986), 'True Cost of a Pledge', *Municipal Journal*, pp. 316-7.

Pollard, S. (1983), *The Development of the British Economy 1914-1980*, Edward Arnold: London, 3rd edition.

Poulantzas, N. (1973), *Political Power and Social Classes*, NLB and Sheed and Ward: London.

Pross, A.P. (1986), *Group Politics and Public Policy*, Oxford University Press: Toronto.

Quirk, B. (1986), 'Paying for Local Government: Beyond the Financial Issues', *Local Government Studies*, Vol. 12, no. 5, September-October, pp. 3-11.

Race, R. (1987), 'Why the Tory Poll Tax is a Snooper's Charter', *Voice of the Unions*, June, p. 3.

Radical Scotland (1985), 'Editorial', *Radical Scotland*, No. 15, June-July, p. 3.

Radical Scotland (1986), 'Cold Climate Settles Over Scotland's Tories', *Radical Scotland*, No. 18, December-January, pp. 6-7.

RAGE (1985), *Lothian Rager*, April, RAGE: Edinburgh.

Rench, R. (1986), Letter published in *Municipal Journal*, 24 October, p. 1840.

Rhodes, R.A.W. (1979), *Public Administration and Policy Analysis*, Saxon House: Farnborough.

Rhodes, R.A.W. *Control and Power in Central-Local Government Relations*, Gower: Aldershot.

Rhodes, R.A.W. (1986), *The National World of Local Government*, Allen and Unwin: London.

Rhodes, R.A.W. (1988), *Beyond Westminster and Whitehall*, Unwin Hyman: London.

Rhodes, R.A.W. (1990), 'Policy Networks: A British Perspective', *Journal of Theoretical Politics*, Vol. 2, no. 3, pp. 293-317.

Richards, P.G. (1988), 'The Recent History of Local Fiscal Reform', in Bailey, S.J. and Paddison, R. (eds.), *The Reform of Local Government Finance in Britain*, Routledge: London.

Richardson, J.J. and Jordan, A.G. (1979), *Governing Under Pressure*, Martin Robertson: Oxford.

Richardson, J. (ed.), (1982), *Policy Styles in Western Europe*, George Allen and Unwin: London.

Riddell, P. (1983), *The Thatcher Government*, Basil Blackwell: Oxford.

Rifkind, M. (1986), 'Why Local Income Tax Would Not Succeed', *Glasgow Herald*, 26 March, p. 9.

Rose, A. (1964), *The Negro in America*, Harper and Row: New York.

Rose, R. (1976), 'Models of Change', in Rose, R. (ed.), *The Dynamics of Public Policy: A Comparative Analysis*, Sage: London.

Rose, R. (1982), *British MPs: A Bite as Well as a Bark?*, Centre for the Study of Public Policy: University of Strathclyde, Glasgow.

Runciman, P. (1986), 'President's Address: Paying for Local Government', *Journal of Glasgow Chamber of Commerce*, March, p. 63.

Rush, M. (1981), *Parliamentary Government in England*, Pitman: London.

Salmond, A. and Walker, J. (1986), 'The Oil Price Collapse: Some Effects on the Scottish Economy', *Quarterly Economic Commentary*, Fraser of Allander Institute: Glasgow, Vol. 12, no. 2, November, pp. 63-9.

Sandilands, R. (1986), 'The Green Paper on Local Government Finance', *Quarterly Economic Commentary*, Glasgow: Fraser of Allander Institute, Vol. 11, no. 3, February, pp. 53-60.

Savage, S.P. and Robins, L. (eds.), (1990), *Public Policy Under Thatcher*, MacMillan: London.

Saville, R. (ed.), (1980), *The Economic Development of Modern Scotland 1950-1980*, John Donald: Edinburgh.

Scott, D. (1985a), 'Ancram Stands by Fairness of Rating Revaluations', *Scotsman*, 5 March, p.9.

Scott, D. (1985b), 'Tories Struggle to Escape Rates Morass', *Scotsman*, 18 March, p. 9.

Scott, D. (1985c), 'Councils Decide Price of Silence is Too High', *Scotsman*, 27 March, p. 9.

Scott, D. (1985d), 'Call for Tory Unity on Rates Reform', *Local Government Chronicle*, 24 April, p. 600.

Scott, D. (1985e), 'Strict Legislation Could Raise Problems', *Local Government Chronicle*, 28 June, p. 744.

Scott, D. (1985f), 'The Countdown to Scotland's Revaluation Crisis', *Local Government Chronicle (Supplement)*, 27 September, p. 15.

Scott, D. (1985g), 'Younger Determined to Pioneer Rates Revolution in Teeth of Cabinet Opposition', *Scotsman*, 11 October, p. 15.

Scott, D. (1985h), 'Maxton Enters Local Arena', *Scotsman*, 9 November, p. 7.

Scott, D, (1986a), 'Labour Looks to Local Income Tax', *Scotsman*, 30 January, p. 11.

Scott, D. (1986b), 'The Future of Local Taxation in Scotland', *Local Government Chronicle*, 14 February, p. 192.

Scott, D. (1986c), 'Low Rates Rises Not Good Enough for Ministers', *Scotsman*, 13 March, p. 13.

Scott, D (1986d), 'Ministers Stick To Rates Reform Plan', *Scotsman*, 10 June, p. 9.

Scott, D. (1986e), 'SOLACE Attacks Rates Plans', *Local Government Chronicle*, 20 June, p. 676.

Scott, D. (1986f), 'Tory Rates Reforms: Odds 3-1 Against Rifkind', *Scotsman*, 22 August p. 13.

Scott, D. (1986g), 'Changes Are "Unwelcome and Unacceptable"', *Local Government Chronicle*, 5 September, p. 1001.

Scott, D, (1986h), 'Pole Position for Community Charge Plans', *Scotsman*, 27 November, p. 10.

Scott, D. (1986i), 'Local v Central Government: The Spending Conflict', in McCrone, D. (ed.), *Scottish Government Yearbook 1986*, Unit for the Study of Government in Scotland: Edinburgh.

Scott, D. (1987), 'Consequences of Ignoring Rifkind Pleas', *Scotsman*, 11 March, p. 4.

Scottish Consumer Council (1986), *SCC's Submission to the Government's Proposals*, Scottish Consumer Council: Glasgow.

Scottish Development Department, (1988), *Housing Trends in Scotland*, HSU No. 2, Scottish Development Department: Edinburgh.

Scottish Labour Activist (1985), 'Looking After Their Own', *Scottish Labour Activist*, No. 14, June, p. 3.

Scottish Local Government Information Unit (1987), *Scottish Opinion Poll on Community Charge/Poll Tax*, Scottish Local Government Information Unit: Glasgow.

Scottish Office (1982), *Scottish Economic Bulletin*, No. 25, Summer, Scottish Office: Edinburgh.

Scottish Office (1986a), *Paying for Local Government - The Scottish Approach*, S86/255, Scottish Office, Edinburgh.

Scottish Office (1986b), *Scottish Economic Bulletin*, No. 33, June, Scottish Office: Edinburgh.

Scottish Office (1989), *Scottish Economic Bulletin*, No. 39, June, Scottish Office: Edinburgh.

Scottish Office, (1991), *The Structure of Local Government in Scotland: The Case for Change: Principles of the New System*, Scottish Office: Edinburgh.

Scottish Trades Union Congress (1985), *88th Annual Report*, Scottish Trades Union Congress: Glasgow.

Scottish Trades Union Congress (1986a), *89th Annual Report*, Scottish Trades Union Congress: Glasgow.

Scottish Trades Union Congress (1986b), *STUC Response to Green Paper: "Paying for Local Government"*, Scottish Trades Union Congress: Glasgow,

Scottish Trades Union Congress (1987), *90th Annual Report*, Scottish Trades Union Congress: Glasgow.

Scottish Trades Union Congress (1988), *91st Annual Report*, Scottish Trades Union Congress: Glasgow.

Self, P. (1979), *Administrative Theories and Politics*, George Allen and Unwin: London, 2nd edition.

Self, P. (1985), *Political Theories of Modern Government: Its Role and Reform*, George Allen and Unwin: London.

Shell (UK) Ltd., (1986), Letter 4 June to Scottish Office in Response to the Green Paper "Paying for Local Government", Shell (UK) Ltd.: London.

Simon, H.A. *Administrative Behavior*, MacMillan: London, 2nd edition.

Skidelsky, R (ed.), (1988), *Thatcherism*, Chatto and Windus: London.

Smith, A. (1976), *An Inquiry into the Nature and Causes of the Wealth of Nations*, Clarendon Press: Oxford.

Smith, S. and Squire, D. (1986), *Who Will Be Paying for Local Government?*, Institute for Fiscal Studies: London.

SNP (1985a), *End Rates Farce Pleas by SNP*, News Release 5 March, SNP: Edinburgh.

SNP (1985b), *Rates - The Way Ahead: A Discussion Paper*, April, SNP: Edinburgh.

SNP (1985c), *SNP Demand "Action, Not Words" on Rates*, News Release 29 April, SNP: Edinburgh.

SNP (1986), *Rates Reform Green Paper*, News Release 28 January, SNP: Edinburgh.

Special Correspondent (1985), 'The Lessons That Can Be Learned From Ratings Scottish Experience', *Municipal Journal*, 27 September, pp. 1592 and 1594.

Spungen, M. (1985), 'The State of the Rate', *Local Government Chronicle*, 15 February, p. 187.

Stallworthy, M. (1989), 'Central Government and Local Government: The Uses and Abuses of Constitutional Hegemony', *Political Quarterly*, Vol. 60, no. 1, January, pp. 22-37.

Stanworth, J. et al. (1982), *Perspectives on a Decade of Small Business, Research: Bolton Ten Years On*, Gower: Aldershot.

Steele, D. (1985), 'How Scotland is Reacting to Rates Rise', *Glasgow Herald*, 27 March, p. 9.

Stewart, J.D. (1977), 'The Green Paper on Local Government Finance: A Viewpoint', *Local Government Studies*, October, pp. 9-15.

Stoker, G. (1988), *The Politics of Local Government*, MacMillan: London.

Strathclyde Regional Council Policy and Resources Committee (1986), *Paying for Local Government: Report by the Chief Executive in Conjunction with the Director of Finance and the Assessor and Electoral Registration Officer*, Strathclyde Regional Council: Glasgow.

Stringer, J.K. and Richardson, J.J. (1980), 'Managing the Political Agenda: Problem Definition and Policy Making in Britain', *Parliamentary Affairs*, Vol. 23, pp. 23-9.

System Three (1988), *Summary of Opinion Polls on Voting Intentions in Scotland 1985-1988*, System Three: Edinburgh.

Tait, A. (COSLA Depute Finance Secretary 1982-), (1989), Interview with Author.

Taylor, T. (1985a), 'Could "Big Bertha" Be the Answer to Rates', *Business and Finance in Scotland*, Vol. 11, no. 10, April, p. 4.

Taylor, T. (1985b), 'Premier Faces A "No More Changes for Now" Problem', *Business and Finance in Scotland*, Vol. 11, no. 11, May, p. 4.

Taylor, T. (1985c), 'Agriculture's to Go?', *Business and Finance in Scotland*, Vol. 11, no. 11, May, p. 4

Taylor, T (1985d), 'Rating Reform is Proving a Real Hot Potato', *Business and Finance in Scotland*, Vol. 12, no. 1, July, p. 5.

Taylor (1985e), 'Rating Reform Pledge is Still Tories' Achilles Heel', *Business and Finance in Scotland*, Vol. 12, no. 3, September, p. 4.

Taylor, T. (1985f), 'Reshuffle: No Luck for Patrick Jenkin', *Business and Finance in Scotland*, Vol. 12, no. 5, November pp. 4-5.

Taylor, T. (1985g), 'Despite Those Fears, Rates Reform Will Go Ahead', *Business and Finance in Scotland*, Vol. 12, no. 6, December, p. 4.

Taylor, T. (1986), 'England May Not Follow Scotland On Rates Changes', *Business and Finance in Scotland*, Vol. 12, no. 10, April, p. 4.

Thatcher, M. (1977), *Let Our Children Grow Tall*, Centre for Policy Studies: London.

Thatcher, M. (1993), *The Downing Street Years*, Harper Collins: London.

Thompson, E.P. (1980), *The Making of the English Working Class*, Penguin: Middlesex.

Thompson, G. (1977), 'The Relationship Between the Financial and Industrial Sector in the United Kingdom Economy', *Economy and Society*, Vol. 16, pp. 235-83.

Thornhill, W. (ed.), (1971), *The Growth and Reform of English Local Government*, Weidenfeld and Nicholson: London.

Travers, T. (1986a), 'Tackling the Crucial Issue of Accountability', *Municipal Journal*, 7 March, pp. 376-7.

Travers, T. (1986b), *The Politics of Local Government Finance*, Allen and Unwin: London.

Truman, D.B. (1951), *The Governmental Process*, Alfred A. Knopf: New York.

Turner, S.H. (1908), *The History of Local Taxation in Scotland*, William Blackwood and Sons: Edinburgh and London.

Waine, P. (1985), 'Cap the Business Rate', *Municipal Journal*, 9 August, pp. 1322-3.

Waldergrave, W. (1985), 'Finding the Best Financial Regime for a Healthy Local Democracy', *Municipal Journal*, 28 June, pp. 1076-7.

Walker, D. (1985), 'In Search of Life After Rate-Capping', *Times*, 7 March, p. 10.

Walker, P. (1991), *Staying Power*, Bloomsbury: London.

Ward, I. (1986), 'Two Areas Where the Green Paper is Lacking Information', *Municipal Journal*, 21 February, pp. 266-7.

Ward, I. and Williams, P. (1986), 'The Government and Local Accountability Since Layfield', *Local Government Studies*, Vol. 12, no. 1, January-February, pp. 21-32.

Watson, R. (1986), 'Scottish Tories Struggle to Keep Lid on Revolt', *Scotsman*, 25 January, p. 11.

Webb, S. and Webb, B. (1963a), *English Local Government Volume 1: The Parish and the County*, Frank Cass: London.

Webb, S. and Webb, B. (1963b), *English Local Government Volume 2: The Manor and the Borough*, Frank Cass: London.

Webb, S. and Webb, B. (1963c), *English Local Government Volume 3: The Manor and the Borough*, Frank Cass: London.

Webb, S. and Webb, B. (1963d), *English Local Government Volume 4: Statutory Authorities for Special Purposes*, Frank Cass: London.

Weber, M. (1971), 'Legitimate Authority and Bureaucracy' in Pugh, D.S. (ed.), *Organisation Theory*, Penguin: Middlesex.

Weber, M. (1984), *The Protestant Ethic and the Spirit of Capitalism*, George Allen and Unwin: London, 2nd edition.

Welsh Office (1986), *Cmnd. 9714 Paying for Local Government: Responses to Consultation in Wales*, Welsh Office: Cardiff.

Welsh Office, (1991), *The Structure of Local Government in Wales: A Consultation Paper*, Welsh Office, Cardiff.

Whitehouse, M. (Chairwoman of the Federation of Scottish Ratepayers, 1982-87), (1990), Interview with Author.

Whitelaw, W. (1989), *The Whitelaw Memoirs*, Aurum Press: London.

Widdicombe, D. et al. (1968), *Ryde on Rating*, Butterworth and Shaw: London, 12th edition.

Williamson, P.J. (1989), *Corporatism in Perspective*, Sage: London.

Wolmar, C. (1990), 'Thatcher Toppled by Poll Tax', *Independent*, 23 November, p. 6.

Woolfson, C. and Foster, J. (1988), *Track Record: The Story of the Caterpillar Occupation*, Verso: London.

Wright, M. (1988), 'Policy Community, Policy Network and Comparative Industrial Policies', *Political Studies*, No. 4, December, pp. 593-612.

Yorke, J. (1984), 'Scots Bearing the Brunt of Rates Burden?', *Glasgow Herald*, 27 November, p. 17.

Young, J. (1985), Letter published in *Glasgow Herald*, 6 March, p. 8.

Young, J.D. (1990), Letter published in *Glasgow Herald*, 17 September p. 8.

Young, K. (1988), 'Local Government in Britain: Rationale, Structure and Finance', in Bailey, S.J. and Paddison, R. (eds.), *The Reform of Local Government Finance in Britain*, Routledge: London.

Younger, G. (Secretary of State for Scotland, 1979-1986), (1990), Interview with Author.

Younis, T. and Davidson, I. (1989), 'The Introduction of the Community Charge in Scotland - A Policy Analysis and Urban Policy Perspective', *Local Government Studies*, January-February, pp. 25-37.

Index

Abolition of Domestic Rates
    Etc. Scotland Bill
    background to passage
    through House of Commons,
    162-5, 178-9
    background to passage
    through House of Lords,
    172-3
    Government criticism of
    opposition amendments,
    168-9, 171-2, 176, 178, 179
    House of Commons
    discussion of Lords'
    amendments, 178-9
    media criticism of Labour's
    opposition to, 169
    opposition amendments
    tabled on, 168, 171, 175,
    177, 178, 182n
    origins of title, 161
    policy formation and, 180-1,
    194-5
    report stage in House of

Commons, 170-2
    second reading in House of
    Commons, 165-6
    standing committee stage in
    Commons, 166-70
    third reading in House of
    Commons, 170, 171, 172
ACC *see* Association of County
    Councils
ADC *see* Association of District
    Councils
Adam Smith Institute, 113, 114
    -15, 129-30n, 140, 190
Age Concern (Scotland), 165,
    173, 174
ALA *see* Association of London
    Authorities
Allen Report, 54, 203
AMA *see* Association of
    Metropolitan Authorities
Ancram, M., 91, 106n, 112,
    144, 152, 165, 166, 167,
    168, 172, 179, 191, 195

Douglas-Hamilton, J., 87, 120
Downs, A., 3, 9-10, 29, 33, 38, 40, 183

Easton, D., 7
Edwards, N., 128
Elder, M., 150
Engels, F., 17, 18, 34

Federated Association of Owner-Occupiers of Glasgow, 116, 148
Federation of Scottish Ratepayers, 90-2, 113, 115, 116, 126-7, 140, 144, 156, 165, 173, 174, 182n, 190, 192
Forsyth, M., 83, 87, 92, 115, 118, 119, 120, 130n, 172
Forum of Private Business, 94, 111, 149, 165, 173, 188
Foster, C., 112
Fowler, N., 152
FSR *see* Federation of Scottish Ratepayers

Gamble, A., 30
GLC, 69
Goold J., 91, 100, 101, 102, 104, 115, 118, 119, 122, 131n, 189
Gould, B., 3
Greater London Council *see* GLC
green paper 'Paying for Local Government'
criticisms of, 140-3, 144, 145-50, 153-5, 158
formal responses to consultation exercise, 152-6, 160n
Government's attitude to, 2, 139-40, 150-2, 156, 157,

158, 192-4
Government's use as a basis for introducing legislation, 139-40, 150-1, 156, 157, 180, 192-4
long-term reaction to, 144-52
proposals contained in, 136-40
short-term reaction to, 140-3
green papers on local government finance, 2, 38, 54-5, 67-8, 69, 71, 108, 128 132-60 *passim*

Harper, R., 118, 119, 130
Heathcoat-Amory, D., 120
Heath Government 1970-74
general politics and policies, 49-50
local government finance and, 53-5
Heclo, H. and Wildavsky, A., 12, 16
Heiser, T., 112
Hennessy, P., 42
Heseltine, M., 64-5, 123, 128
Highgate, J., 100, 126
Hirst, M., 87, 102, 120, 170
Hodson, D., 112
Hoffman, L., 112
Hogwood, B. and Gunn, L., 7-8, 38
House of Commons, *see* Parliament
House of Lords
general independence of, 173
passage of Abolition of Domestic Rates Etc. (Scotland) Bill through, 172-8, 195
political composition of, 173